THE MARLBOROUGH MOUND

THE MARLBOROUGH MOUND

Prehistoric Mound, Medieval Castle, Georgian Garden

Edited by Richard Barber

THE BOYDELL PRESS

First published 2022
The Boydell Press, Woodbridge

ISBN 978 1 78327 186 3

The Boydell Press is an imprint of Boydell & Brewer Ltd
PO Box 9, Woodbridge, Suffolk, IP12 3DF, UK
and of Boydell & Brewer Inc.
668 Mount Hope Avenue, Rochester, NY 14620–2731, USA
website: www.boydellandbrewer.com

The publisher has no responsibility for the continued existence or accuracy of
URLs for external or third-party internet websites referred to in this book, and
does not guarantee that any content on such websites is, or will remain, accurate or
appropriate

A CIP catalogue record for this book is available from the British Library

Contents

List of Figures

Illustrations marked * are reproduced with kind permission of Marlborough College Archives

List of Figures

The editor, contributors and publisher are grateful to all the institutions and persons listed for permission to reproduce the materials in which they hold copyright. Every effort has been made to trace the copyright holders; apologies are offered for any omission, and the publisher will be pleased to add any necessary acknowledgement in subsequent editions.

Acknowledgements

The editor is very grateful for a variety of help and support during the researching and compilation of this book. At Marlborough College, Matt Blossom has answered all kinds of questions, including a search, sadly abortive for the buttress of the keep said to be extant in the 1930s. He has also been a vital link to the personnel of the College. Gráinne Lenehan, the College archivist, has supplied copies from the *Report of the Marlborough Natural History Society* and much other material, besides investigating a number of items which have disappeared over the years, notably the finds of early excavations recorded in 1922.

In terms of the medieval history of the castle, Jonathan Mackman has done invaluable work in the National Archives, finding and analysing some six hundred records in the medieval royal accounts relating to Marlborough. All the essays in this book are based on annual lectures given under the auspices of the Mound Trust. Jeremy Ashbee kindly allowed the use of his lecture in 2015, to which the idea of recreating the appearance of the medieval castle by looking at contemporary fortresses is indebted.

The GPR surveys of the lower bailey and the excavations exploring the foundations of the castle wall since 2015 have been guided by Tony Roberts of Archeoscan, and his help with Appendix D, and particularly the map showing the result of the GPR investigation, is much appreciated.

This book could not have appeared without the generous encouragement of the Marlborough Mound Trust, which has made the research and publication possible.

Preface

When, in 2000, Eric Elstob set up and endowed the Marlborough Mound Trust, he was intent on focussing much-needed attention on the remarkable, but neglected, monument that nestled, largely obscured by trees and bushes, in a corner of the grounds of Marlborough College. Though the Mound played a part in the lives of college pupils, including Eric, serving as a place of escape for adventure and contemplation, and was occasionally referred to in the academic literature, it had little presence in the public imagination, nor did it feature large in current archaeological debate. The Trust changed all that. Working closely with the College over the last two decades, it has given the Mound a new visibility, in all senses of the word, and has worked to stabilize its fragile fabric for future generations to continue to enjoy.

The Marlborough Mound is a 'special place' – a location that, for four thousand years, has been of continuing significance to successive genera-tions. As a place where springs break out of the ground and flow into the River Kennet, it clearly had meaning to the Late Neolithic population who, for reasons which we will never know, decided to mark the spot with a great mound sixteen metres high and nearly eighty metres in diameter. It echoed the even larger mound of Silbury Hill, eight kilometres up river, both being elements in a complex ritual landscape which we are only now beginning to untangle. In this way the monumentalizing of the landscape began, and this mound, built at the end of the third millennium BC, has dominated human actions ever since. Roman engineers used it as a siting point for laying out a road, Normans found it to be a convenient base for a castle, which flour-ished as a royal residence and regional stronghold throughout the twelfth and thirteenth centuries, and from the seventeenth century it became the visual focus of a formal garden belonging to the Seymour family. Thus it has an unusual and distinguished history and one well worthy of considered attention.

The first task of the Trust was to ensure the stability of the Mound by removing most of the trees and bushes and other encumbrances, restoring the spiral path constructed when the Mound became a garden feature, and stabi-lizing the slopes with an appropriate vegetation cover. In parallel with this, archaeological investigations and new historical research have been under-taken to create a firm chronology for the monument, including confirming its Neolithic origins. And to give the Mound greater public visibility a series of annual lectures have been organised to present the most up to date research.

The present volume is based on the lecture series and is offered as celebration of what has so far been achieved. It is a tribute to the vision of Eric Elstob and to the continued, wholehearted, support of the College.

Barry Cunliffe
March 2022

Fig. 1.1 Marlborough Mound, 2021, aerial view from drone.

Fig. 1.2 Silbury Hill.

1

'One remarkable earthen-work': The Neolithic Origins of the Marlborough Mound

Jim Leary and Joshua Pollard

One remarkable earthen-work however, must not be passed over in silence. I allude to the mount within the gardens of the Castle Inn, a huge pile of earth, and inferior in proportion only to Silbury Hill near Abury. Each are situated on the river Kennet; the one near its source, the other near its margin; and I have no doubt but that in ancient times each had some corresponding connection with the other.

These words were written by the well-known antiquarian Richard 'Colt' Hoare in 1821.[1] Hoare is unlikely to be the first to comment on the similarity between the Marlborough Mound and the nearby mound of Silbury Hill, but he seems to have been the first to record his comments. Silbury Hill, an enormous 31m-high mound lying a little more than 8km further upstream of the River Kennet, was known to be pre-Roman in date since the antiquarian William Stukeley commented on it in the eighteenth century. Although only a little over half its height, the Marlborough Mound is certainly of similar form to Silbury Hill, and in a comparable topographic location, being next to the River Kennet, at a confluence (with the now canalized brook that formerly rose in Barton Dene to the north), and with springs at its base. Hoare's suggestion of a 'corresponding connection' between the Marlborough Mound and its prehistoric neighbour meant that it subsequently entered the literature as an enigma, with some authors feeling that there is no hard evidence that the mound is of that date,[2] while others have been more accepting.[3]

An enigmatic mound

Brentnall, a schoolmaster at Marlborough College, outlined the history and archaeological evidence for Marlborough Castle[4] and fuelled the case for prehistoric origins on discovery of some antlers found embedded in chalk on the slopes of the mound. These were recovered during work for a boiler-house chimney that included cutting a channel for the flue up the north-western side of the mound in 1912. The antlers, which were recovered halfway up and several feet into the mound, comprised six fragments from red deer lying together: 'three of these fragments consist of the burr and broken brow-tine, and two others seem to be consecutive portions of the beam of the antler to which one of the brow tines belonged. The largest fragment measured 246 millimetres (about 9½ inches) in circumference just above the burr.'[5] Brentnall suggested that it is 'unlikely that the fragments, which were thoroughly impregnated with chalk, could have been buried in that position at any date subsequent to the erection of the mound, and it is thought that their discovery may possibly throw some light on the question of the date of that work'.[6] While cautious, he argued persuasively that they were pre-Norman and potentially of Neolithic date. Before this, in the 1890s, a single antler was found on the opposite side of the mound,[7] and again in the 1930s an antler tine was found 'on the slope of the chalk 40yds to the north'.[8]

Brentnall also recorded the old ground surface during the 1912 investigation, which he noted gently sloped from the north to the south and appeared alluvial. At the base, the Mound was excavated into by some 14ft (4.2m), allowing Brentnall to see a thin layer of charcoal overlying the old ground surface. This in turn was covered by half an inch of 'reddish clay, containing a few broken flints, showing surface exposure, and some tertiary flint gravel pebbles'.[9] These layers deepened towards the interior of the Mound, and above this was the mound material. However, in 1955, excavations on the western side of the Mound found medieval refuse, including Norman pottery, overlying the old ground surface. In 1956, a second trench cut 2.1m into the side of the Mound confirmed this stratigraphy and produced further Norman pottery.[10]

Best[11] reviewed the evidence for a prehistoric date for the Mound and concluded that, although large, it does fit within the size range for medieval mottes, while Field *et al.*[12] pointed to the topographical comparisons with Silbury Hill, particularly of the adjacent springs, but, considering the presence of the Norman pottery and the lack of prehistoric material, concluded that 'in the absence of data to the contrary, the available archaeological and documentary evidence indicates that the mound is essentially a medieval construction'.[13] The 2001 Archaeological Research Agenda for the Avebury World Heritage Site summed up the situation as: 'It would appear, however, sensible to reserve judgement until the date of antlers associated with the mound are known.'[14]

The alignment of the Roman road between Marlborough and Silbury Hill has often been used to support an early date for the Mound in that, like Silbury, Roman surveyors may have used it as a marker.[15] However, the exact location of the Roman road at this point is unknown[16] and it may have taken a more northerly alignment as an early medieval route appears to have done,[17] or indeed one to the south. Certainly, there was a Roman presence in the area. Stukeley believed that the Mound lay on the site of a Roman fort and noted

'Roman coins have been found in shaping the mount' in the seventeenth century,[18] indicating at least some pre-Norman activity.

Two Roman coins and a possible pair of shears have been recovered from trenches cut into a nearby cricket field in 1892,[19] while Brentnall[20] also described the discovery of Roman coins.

The Mound was clearly used as the motte for a medieval tower, first of timber and then re-built in stone.[21] The castle was ruinous by 1541 when Leland visited Marlborough,[22] and Sir Francis Seymour had constructed a house in the grounds by 1621.[23] The Mound featured in hostilities during the English Civil War, used by both sides as the fortunes of war changed, and is likely to have been fortified during this time. By 1654, it was being used as a garden mount by the Seymours, who had landscaped it and cut or re-cut the spiral path terraced into the sides and leading to the summit.[24] The ditch surrounding the Mound is likely to have been re-cut at this stage. Celia Fiennes, passing through at the beginning of the eighteenth century, described the Mound surrounded by a canal that emptied into a fishpond. This is a feature depicted by Stukeley, who stayed at Marlborough House on a number of occasions and drew the house and gardens, showing the Mound as an integral part of the garden layout (Fig. 1.3). Clearly, the northern part of the ditch surrounding the Mound had become incorporated into a formal geometric water feature by the eighteenth century and presumably this part

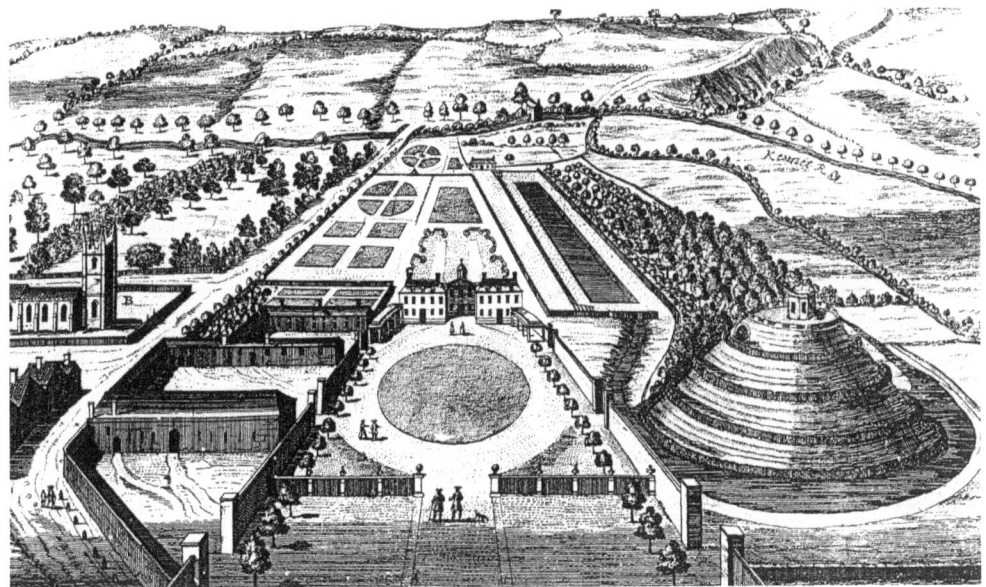

Fig. 1.3 Marlborough Mound as drawn by William Stukeley, from his *Itinerarium Curiosum* published in 1724.

3

had been scoured out for this purpose. The ditch was filled in sometime before 1850, and during observations of the digging of foundations over the ditch for the Victorian Physical Laboratory in the late nineteenth century, a horseshoe and a portion of a glazed tile were recovered.[25] Brentnall recovered two Roman coins from the 'castle ditch',[26] probably residual although perhaps suggesting that not all of the ditch was re-cut, while in 1956, footings for new physics laboratories encountered a section of dressed sarsen stone under ten metres from the edge of the Mound and interpreted as dating to the seventeenth century.[27] A new cart-shed was constructed in 1892 over the surrounding ditch and concrete was laid as the ground was described as 'spongy earth and mud'.[28] This also cut slightly into the northern side of the Mound, revealing that beneath the chalk at the base of the Mound was a deposit of 'stiff creamy clay'.

Core values

Following a collapse on the top of Silbury Hill in 2000 – the result of numerous earlier investigations into the mound – a multi-million-pound project to investigate and conserve the mound began. This involved re-opening old tunnels into the mound, recording and sampling the archaeology, and then backfilling them to ensure the long-term integrity of the monument. With fieldwork at Silbury Hill completed in 2008 and the post-excavation underway,[29] attention turned to the Marlborough Mound as a possible comparative site.[30] With the antler and charcoal from previous excavations lost, and in the absence of any other dateable material from the Mound, a project was developed to recover new material for dating and to investigate the structure of the monument. There was no intention to start a whole new project along the lines of the Silbury tunnel, which would have been far too destructive and costly (the former investigation was in direct response to conservation needs and not solely for research). But a way of accessing material deep within Marlborough Mound without any major intrusive excavations was needed. The answer was to drill a small diameter core (10cm across) running from the top of the motte right the way down through the mound make-up until it had reached – and gone through – the underlying old ground surface.

This work, organised and paid for by the Marlborough Mound Trust, saw a specialist geotechnical engineering company drill two boreholes from the summit to the base of the Mound, as well as a sequence of three boreholes on the north side of the presumed ditch, during the school half-term in October 2010. The cores through the Mound were drilled to a depth of around twenty-two metres, well into the natural chalk bedrock, while the ditch cores were drilled from the modern ground level to four or five metres below (Fig. 1.4). All cores were removed in plastic sleeves and in manageable lengths (generally 1.5m), clearly labelled with start and finish depths for each

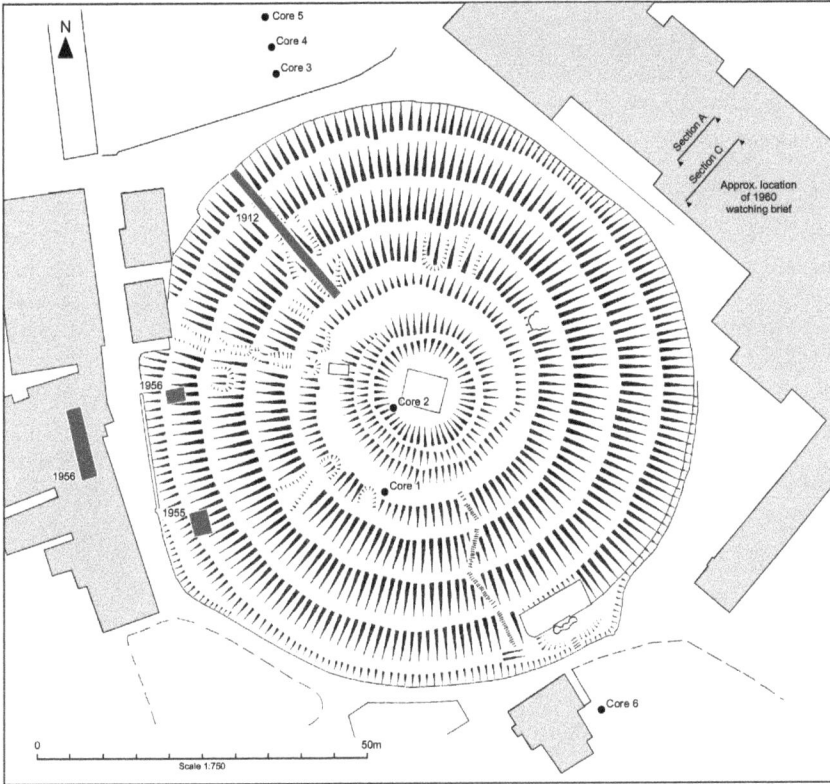

Fig. 1.4 Map of position of cores taken at Marlborough Mound in 2010.

segment so that the complete core could be reconstructed. It was then taken to the Historic England laboratories at Fort Cumberland, Portsmouth. Here the core sleeves were sliced open and the material described and analysed. Each segment was then photographed before sampling for assessment of palaeoenvironmental remains was carried out. The material within the cores was left largely intact throughout the work and has subsequently been repatriated with the Mound.

New dates for an old mound

Small specialist samples were taken from various points within these cores where charcoal fragments were observed or where organic-rich deposits with the potential to contain macroscopic plant remains were encountered. The main purpose of these samples was to obtain material suitable

5

for radiocarbon dating and recover any biological or cultural remains. Samples were gently wet-sieved over a 250-micron mesh and this resulted in the recovery of six charcoal fragments. These were then submitted to the Scottish Universities Environmental Research Centre (SUERC) and Oxford Radiocarbon Accelerator Unit (ORAU) for radiocarbon dating. The results were striking: they clearly showed that the main body of the Mound was contemporary with Silbury, dating to the second half of the third millennium BC. Hoare's hunch had proven correct: the Marlborough Mound was connected to Silbury Hill. It was another Neolithic monument, only this time it was hiding from us in plain sight; a prehistoric mound that had been re-appropriated as a motte in the Norman period, just as it had been re-used as a garden mount later on.

The four radiocarbon measurements from the Mound itself are statistically significantly different, so represent a range of different actual ages. Given the difficulty of understanding the taphonomic relationships between these fragments of charcoal and the construction of the Mound, it is probably safest to take the latest of these dates as a *terminus post quem* (the earliest possible date) for completion. This is 2300–2040 cal BC (95 per cent confidence; SUERC-34082), or 2280–2140 cal BC (68 per cent confidence). Since all the dates fall in the second half of the third millennium cal BC, it seems plausible that this date is not substantively earlier than the actual completion of this monument.

The dating of the Marlborough Mound to the second half of the third millennium cal BC means that we can now place it within the context of major monumental building practices taking place at Stonehenge and Durrington Walls, at Marden henge in the Vale of Pewsey, as well as at Silbury Hill and Avebury, and Mount Pleasant in Dorchester. The completion of the mound at Marlborough, if one accepts the *terminus post quem* cited above as being close to this event, would have occurred in the generations after the combined sarsen and bluestone monument was built at Stonehenge,[31] and likely the outer circle and avenues at Avebury.[32]

Corresponding connections

Although considerably smaller than Silbury Hill, the 18m-high Marlborough Mound now ranks as the second largest Neolithic mound in Britain and possibly in Europe, and together Silbury Hill and the Marlborough Mound represent an astonishing pair. And in fact, to these two we can add a third mound: the Hatfield Barrow located within Marden henge in the Vale of Pewsey.

Also originally investigated by Richard Hoare, the Hatfield Barrow was said to have been as much as 15m high, although it is now demolished. Recent excavations over its footprint have, however, revealed that a thin remnant of the mound has survived, providing some insight into its construction, as well

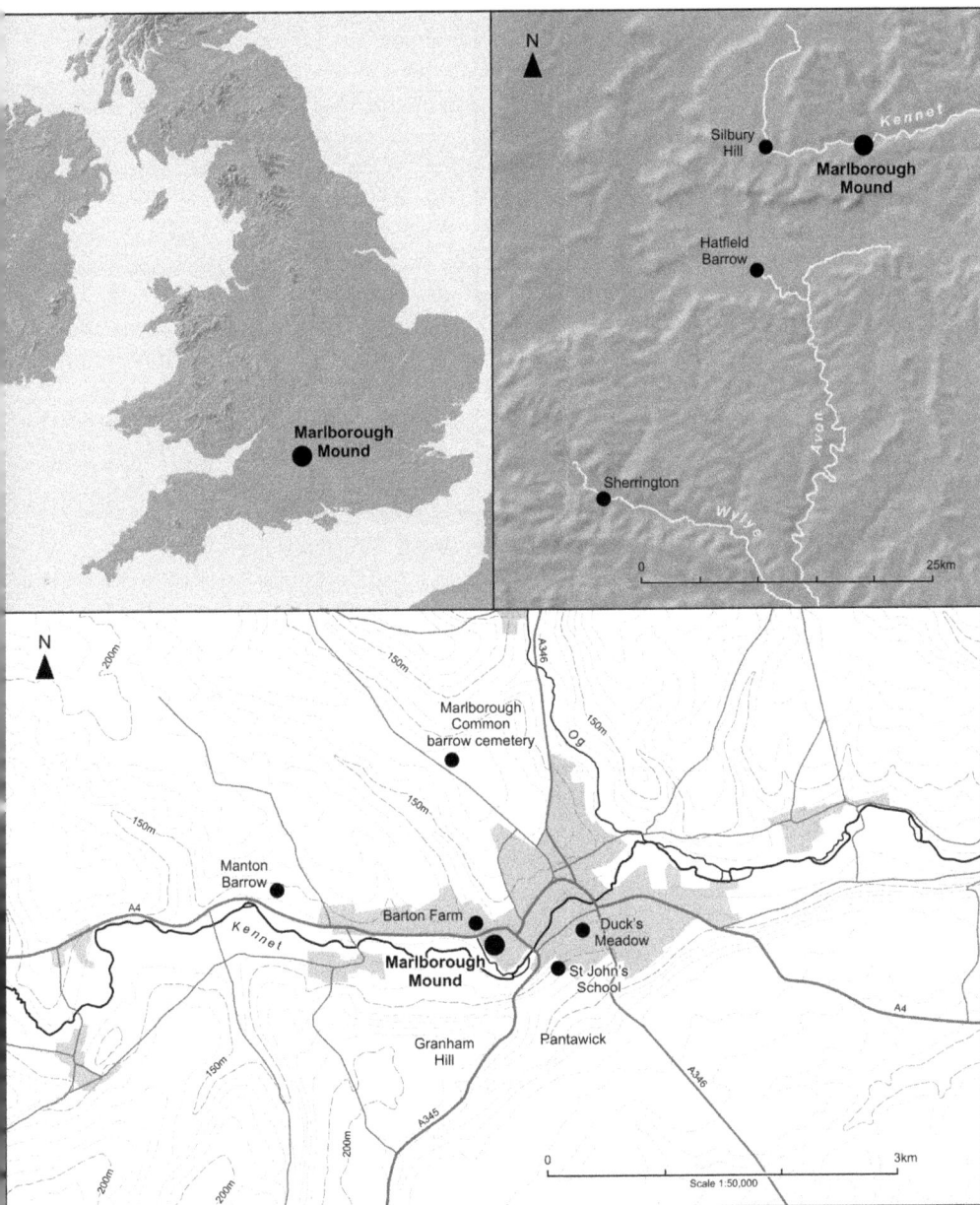

Fig. 1.5 Location map showing the Marlborough Mound relative to Silbury Hill, Hatfield Barrow, Sherrington mound sites and rivers around it.

as material suitable for radiocarbon dating, showing that it too dates to the Late Neolithic period.[33]

The dating of the Marlborough Mound finally confirms that its origins are broadly contemporary with both Silbury Hill and the Hatfield Barrow. The, albeit imprecise, estimate for the date of the Marlborough Mound when compared to Silbury Hill[34] and the Hatfield Barrow[35] does suggest that these three mounds are broadly contemporary, and indicates that large-scale mound building, at least in this part of Wiltshire, has a late third millennium cal BC currency. However, in order to evaluate the chronological relationship of these three mounds and further explore the exact timings of their building and the tempo of this activity, at least some small-scale excavation of the Marlborough Mound will be required – as, in order to fully exploit the potential of chronological modelling for producing robust date estimates, a thorough understanding of both the taphonomy and stratigraphic relationship between samples is required. Clearly, though, the area and period witnessed mound building (as well as the construction of other monument types) on a scale unknown before or after, at least until the Norman Conquest.

The investigations at Silbury showed that its construction sequence was far more complex than previously imagined, with numerous phases – the mound seemingly growing through many small events, rather than a few grand constructions.[36] To briefly summarise the Silbury sequence, the first clear evidence for construction activity is a low, fairly unimpressive, gravel mound. Subsequently, a series of layers of topsoil, subsoil and turf, perhaps representing basket loads of material, probably derived from the immediate locality, were dumped over the gravel mound, forming a larger mound (just over a metre high, and over sixteen metres in diameter). A sequence of stakes demarcated the edge of this mound, while a series of pits were dug into the top of it. Further, smaller mounds were also constructed around this area. These early mounds were sealed under a series of interleaved layers of different material, comprising a mix of topsoil and subsoil chiefly from soils that had developed over chalk, as well as basket loads of chalk, clay, gravel and turf. Together these layers formed a mound perhaps as high as 5 or 6m with an estimated diameter of 35m. It is clear, therefore, that the earliest phases of Silbury Hill do not simply consist of one mound – but a number of mounds, becoming consolidated into a single monument only later. This larger mound was then surrounded by at least five chalk banks that presumably formed rings around it, each new ring expanding the monument outward by a few more metres. And surrounding it all was a large ditch with an internal bank. Activity at the site continued, although we did not see these later phases, until the final mound was eventually formed. What is clear is that the mound we now call Silbury Hill was not simply one single, homogenous phase, but a series of complex phases, the mound growing in size incrementally.[37] We can see the mound developing from initial ground preparation to a small gravel mound, to organic mounds to chalk mounds; from pits to banks to

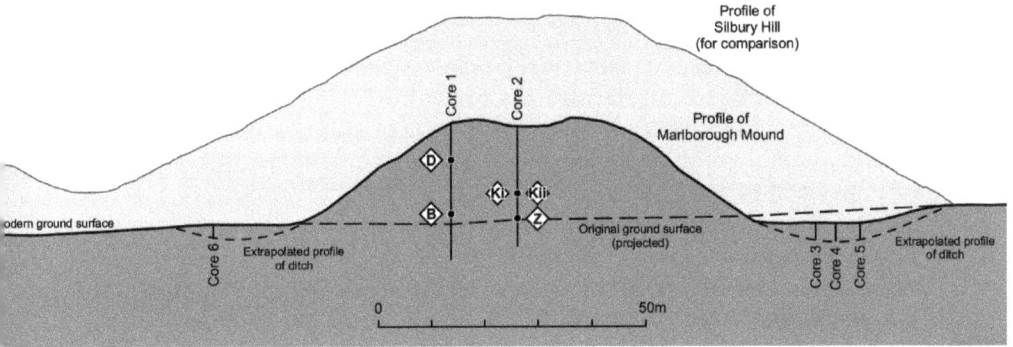

Fig. 1.6 Comparative diagram contrasting Silbury Hill and Marlborough Mound profiles.

an enclosure. The monument grew additionally; developing, mutating and evolving. The site was not a single construction project but the focus for an array of activities – activities that may well have been quite different, and, as the monument changed, so too might perceptions of it.[38]

The Silbury tunnel allowed a wonderful view through the construction sequence of the mound. The cores through the Marlborough Mound, of course, do not provide a comparable view, but there are hints from them that the stratigraphy in the Marlborough Mound was similarly complex. The sequence showed that over the chalk bedrock was a layer of compressed topsoil, which produced a range of preserved remains, including fragments of charcoal, insect remains and animal bone, as well as a few tiny flakes of flint; probably the result of flint knapping. This was overlain with a series of interleaved layers of silt, clay, chalk and flints representing episodes of construction of the Mound, eventually bringing it up to a height of 16.26m. Interestingly, the cores record that early on in the construction of the Mound there were two flood events, possibly local flash floods, but they must have obscured the earlier phases of the Mound. Finally, the top two metres of the Mound contain brick and tile and are therefore likely to be related to the construction of the medieval tower. The interleaved layers of the Neolithic portion provide tentative hints that the Mound was constructed over a number of phases rather than a single construction project, again emphasising the significance of the process over that of the final form. Unfortunately, due to the demolition of the Hatfield Barrow in the nineteenth century, we do not have comparable data for its completion; but the remaining thin layer does hint at a complex sequence as well: a posthole cutting the remnant mound material and then sealed over by further mound material suggests that this mound was to some degree also multi-phased.[39]

Given the medieval and post-medieval landscaping and modification, the Marlborough Mound's original form can only be guessed at. The radiocarbon dates indicate the presence of Neolithic deposits to a height of 11.54m and, accepting the nature of the succeeding material, it is suggested it may have reached 16.26m. This is a substantial height and given the likelihood of deep medieval disturbance for foundations of the tower, and perhaps truncation of the original prehistoric summit, it may have been higher. The diameter of the Mound is currently 83m, but the excavations in 1955 and 1956 indicate that medieval deposits were present at ground level for at least two metres into the Mound; assuming that this continues around the base of the Mound, it may represent a bracing or revetment. Certainly, there is documentary evidence of a *cingulum* or 'girth' being placed around the motte,[40] presumably to arrest silting. Assuming that this was placed equally around the Mound, subtracting these two metres from each side of the base, the diameter can be guessed at something less than 79m; slightly larger than the Hatfield Barrow, which has recently been shown to have measured around 70m in diameter.[41]

It is interesting to speculate on the spiral access and the extent to which it was really the result of post-medieval landscaping or whether this re-cut a Norman or perhaps even earlier feature. At Silbury Hill, the spiral was dated to the eleventh century, although Atkinson suggested that this was a re-cut of a Neolithic feature.[42] Despite their difference in size, both Silbury Hill and the Marlborough Mound are of similar diameter at the top (around 36m and 31m respectively), and this may support an argument that the summit at both mounds had been truncated to form similarly sized areas that were subsequently built on.

Rivers and springs

As noted by Hoare, the similarities between Silbury and Marlborough can also be extended to their locations. They are both situated on or near the valley floor, at a confluence and near springs, suggesting a focus upon water and the river. Stukeley noted that springs rise in the Marlborough Mound's ditch,[43] while a spring rises to the north at Barton Farm. Indeed, springs rising near the Mound once provided the domestic water supply for the house,[44] and springs seem to occur alongside the Kennet itself. G. K. Maurice[45] observed springs alongside the Treacle Bolly (the riverside path just to the south of the Mound), describing how 'the water welled up from underground, always in turmoil, ceaselessly carrying grit and tiny bits of gravel to the surface and letting them sink again'. It would appear that the whole area was interlaced by springs and the course of the Kennet at this point was probably influenced by them. As seems to be the case at Silbury Hill,[46] and also the Hatfield Barrow,[47] this juxtaposition with rivers and springs seems to have been of significance to the Neolithic builders. The economic impact of water is, of course, implicit, and its life-giving properties must undoubtedly have had enormous importance. But the special qualities of water may also have had cosmological significance. Water represents a potent metaphor – a metaphor for movement and journeying, as well as carrying notions of purity, while rivers, streams and lakes create physical boundaries, and divide the world. The rivers perhaps marked major routeways and the mounds emphasised rights and belonging to communities along the river valley, while also encompassing metaphysical and religious concerns.

In this light, it is interesting to note that the Marlborough Mound cores tentatively suggest that there were two significant flood events early on in the building process of the Mound that must have entirely inundated the Mound, and yet the building continued, and one wonders how such events were viewed, perhaps driving activity further. The springs noted above that rise close to the Marlborough Mound were said by Stukeley to rise from the ditch itself and may have made for some turbulence locally, and these flood events may have been related.

A Neolithic landscape for Marlborough

It is unlikely that the Mound stood isolated in this landscape, and it is tempting to think that, as at Silbury Hill and the Hatfield Barrow, other Late Neolithic monuments existed near it. The valley floor here is little more than 300m wide and was unfortunately set to constructed water meadows in the seventeenth century,[48] which will have obscured the earlier topography. It is likely that sarsen stones were formerly common in the local area, and Maurice[49] noted how the Kennet at this point was lined with sarsens to revet the banks. Any above ground traces of monuments contemporary with the Mound will have been levelled or obscured by later works, including the construction of the medieval castle and the western end of the town. Potential exists for their recognition, if present, during groundworks associated with development. In this regard, a curved section of very substantial ditch revealed on a spur of higher ground *c.* 180m north of the Mound during construction of a swimming pool in 1999 is intriguing.[50] The upper fills of the four-metre deep, V-shaped ditch contained twelfth- to fourteenth-century pottery, but finds from the lower fills, which could have dated its digging, were absent. Seemingly curving to define a large, enclosed space to the north, there is a possibility this may be part of a prehistoric earthwork, albeit the V-shaped profile makes it more likely this is of Iron Age date than Neolithic.

In the wider landscape, Mesolithic activity is attested in Marlborough and beyond,[51] while a possible Early Neolithic long barrow occupies Granham Hill to the south of the Marlborough Mound. In addition, a fragment from a Neolithic stone axe was found at Barton Farm, immediately north of the Mound (given to Wiltshire Museum in 1943 by Lt Col. Cunnington).[52] J. W. Brooke, a local collector with a private museum based in Marlborough,[53] and the famous archaeologist J. G. D. Clark,[54] then a schoolboy at Marlborough

College, both collected numerous flint implements from Granham Hill, 1.5km to the south-west, and from around the Pantawick area, a kilometre to the south-east, pointing to a certain amount of prehistoric activity in this part of Marlborough. Brooke[55] described accumulating 2,964 pieces from the area in a single year, the greater part of which came from Pantawick. The finds available for inspection[1] appear to be of mixed date, but the greater part is the typically crude material that is often associated with the clay-with-flints.[56] As Clark mentions,[57] the assemblage is scraper-dominated, but includes a leaf-shaped arrowhead and an adze as well as some Palaeolithic hand axes.[58]

In addition to the evidence provided by finds of lithics, two recent excavations undertaken in advance of development within Marlborough have revealed traces of Late Neolithic occupation, in the form of pits containing pottery and worked flint. Both highlight the significance of the area to the south of this part of the river. The first was located *c.* 600m to the east of the Mound in the area of St Mary's Primary School.[59] A series of pits or tree-throw holes uncovered in separate phases of work during 1997 and 2017 were found to contain over 470 sherds of Grooved Ware pottery from about twenty different vessels and over a thousand pieces of worked flint. The latter included four oblique arrowheads, along with scrapers, knives and other small tools; all consistent with settlement activity. Off Salisbury Road, 350m to the south-east, a further two Late Neolithic pits and another of probable Early Neolithic date were found during excavations in 2012 and 2017.[60] There were sherds from four or five vessels and a small range of worked flint, again including scrapers and a knife. At both sites the sherds are from Durrington Walls-style Grooved Ware vessels, and include pots decorated with rows of twisted cord, a technique that may show Beaker influence. The pottery finds parallels in the assemblages from Durrington Walls itself, and from the West Kennet palisade enclosures, set in the shadow of Silbury Hill.[61] Radiocarbon dates associated with the Grooved Ware activity at the palisades overlap with those from the Marlborough Mound and Silbury Hill,[62] raising the intriguing possibility of this being settlement activity linked to the building of the Mound or currently unknown associated monuments.

Combined with Clark and Brooke's flint assemblages, it would appear that the area to the south of the Mound, on the opposite bank of the Kennet, extending to Granham Hill in the west, may have been a focus for activity, and perhaps activity at scale, during the Late Neolithic period, and future research should focus there. Its position on the opposite side of the Kennet, to the south and east of the Mound, recalls that of the West Kennet palisades in relation to Silbury Hill. The present town masks much of this area, and only recently has there been archaeological monitoring prior to building and other kinds of development. Many small and relatively ephemeral pits of the

---

[1]   Only a fraction of the numbers quoted are now in the Wiltshire Museum at Devizes.

kind found at St Mary's and off Salisbury Road would previously have gone undetected. Early Bronze Age activity continued in the area generally, as evidenced by the Marlborough Common barrow group, 1.5km to the north at Barton Dene, and the rich Manton barrow two kilometres to the west.

Interpreting Neolithic round mounds

The monumental proportions of Silbury Hill, the Marlborough Mound and the Hatfield Barrow place them in an especial league, but they are not without parallel. Other monumental round mounds, of lesser proportions, but still significantly more substantial than Early Bronze Age round barrows, attend major henge sites and palisade enclosure sites in Wessex and beyond. Closely linked in time, setting and association to Marlborough and Silbury are the mounds of the Conquer Barrow, Mount Pleasant, Dorchester, and the Great Barrow at Knowlton, Cranborne Chase.[63] Recent modelling of radiocarbon dates from the Mount Pleasant henge complex places the construction of the Conquer Barrow in the decades around 2500 cal BC, slightly earlier than the Marlborough Mound and Silbury Hill.[64] Much further afield, Droughduil, the mound adjacent to the Late Neolithic palisaded enclosure complex at Dunragit in Dumfries and Galloway, Scotland, was formerly considered to be a motte, but its size (fifty metres in diameter and ten metres in height), coupled with the results of recent excavations that encountered a Bronze Age cairn on the summit, as well as OSL dates, has encouraged comparisons with Silbury Hill.[65] Castle Hill, Catterick, is a further motte site, in this case within sight of the palisaded enclosure at Marne Barracks that has been suggested as potentially Neolithic.[66] Coring work of this mound as part of the Round Mounds Project (see the Afterword below, p. 19) has, however, shown Castle Hill to be formed of natural ground and therefore contains nothing that could be datable.

The examples given above show a close association between large mounds, artificial and perhaps occasionally natural, and other major corporate constructions such as henge enclosures and palisades. Their distribution extends from Scotland to the south coast of England, with a notable concentration in the Wessex region (Wiltshire and Dorset). Current dating shows their creation falling within a relatively short period centred on the third quarter of the third millennium BC. Their construction can be considered an inter-linked phenomenon, but how do we understand them? What was their role? What was the inspiration for their creation? Certainly, the idea of creating round mounds was one with some tradition and ancestry in Neolithic societies in Britain, Ireland and beyond, and inspiration might be sought among earlier round mound building practices. Early and Middle Neolithic earthen round barrows covering single burials and collective mortuary deposits are known from lowland Britain,[67] though their distribution is heavily regionalised, with notable concentrations in areas such as East Yorkshire and the Thames Valley. They are rare in Wessex, examples local to Marlborough including the first phase of West Overton G19,[68] Westbury 7[69] and the Compton Barrow.[70] All of these barrows are rather modest in scale, with diameters rarely exceeding 20m; and this, combined with funerary function, sets them apart from the monumental mound tradition.

Closer comparisons of form and scale take us further afield.[71] Inspiration for the creation of giant mounds such as that at Marlborough could have been drawn from mid-late fourth millennium BC passage-graves found in Ireland and Orkney. Dating to the period *c.* 3200–3000 cal BC, the massive passage-graves of Newgrange and Knowth in the Boyne Valley in the east of Ireland were built on a scale that shares a degree of equivalence with the later Wessex mounds;[72] and these were also elements within emergent monument complexes. Continental late fifth to early third millennium BC monuments such as the Montelirio passage-grave, near Sevilla, south-west Spain, with a mound 75m in diameter,[73] and the Carnac mounds in Brittany,[74] offer other models that may have been a source of emulation. A degree of power and potency, and perhaps with it time-sanctioned authority, could have attached to reference to distant and already ancient monuments such as these,[75] each no doubt wrapped in stories of heroic achievement and deep connection to notable ancestors and sacred realms.

A process of emulation is useful to speculate on, but does not in itself explain the historical, political and belief-centred conditions within which constructions like the Marlborough Mound were created. There is another issue, too, which cannot be easily side-stepped. Both the Marlborough Mound and Silbury Hill, as described above, show evidence of construction across a number of distinct phases, with Silbury undergoing a considerable metamorphosis from a small gravel mound to organic mounds, to an enclosure, and to an ever-expanding and encasing chalk mound. A 'monument in motion',[76] it is highly unlikely its final massive mounded form was conceived from the outset. What is required is not analogy of form, but analogy of process, and it is through this that we can begin to gain insight into the logic of mound building during the Late Neolithic and Chalcolithic. Placing a lens on the processes of mound building rather than final form highlights a recurrent set of practices which saw the deliberate burial of both monuments and settlement traces under round mounds of varied scale. Behind these acts lies a logic of wrapping, containment, closure and marking that has resonance with the 'technologies of enclosure' seen with contemporary henges and timber and stone circles.[77]

The sites of Dyffryn Lane, Bulford and Duggleby Howe provide excellent examples of these mound building processes. Dyffryn Lane is located in the Severn Valley, Powys.[78] It survives as a circular mound *c.* 40m in diameter, much reduced by ploughing, and enclosed within a henge earthwork *c.* 85m across. Antiquarian investigation and systematic excavation by Alex Gibson in 2006 showed a brief phase of Middle Neolithic occupation followed by the construction of a stone circle *c.* 11m in diameter sometime before *c.* 2900–2500 cal BC.[79] The circle became ruinous and was subsequently enclosed within the henge earthwork at some point during the third or fourth quarter of the third millennium BC (broadly Late Neolithic or Chalcolithic). Following on from this, or possibly contemporary with the henge, was the wholesale burial of the stone circle under a round mound of turf and mixed material, effectively concealing its presence. There is no evidence of funerary activity linked to the mound, so we cannot see this as a simple development from a stone circle to a barrow. A similar, but perhaps more time-compressed, sequence is seen at Bulford, 25km to the south of Marlborough.[80] On the edge of a terrace overlooking the Nine Mile River close to its confluence with the Avon, two 'paired' hengiform monuments were constructed in the twenty-sixth to twenty-fifth centuries BC. At a point in the Early Bronze Age, around the twentieth century BC, both were encircled by conjoining ring-ditches and covered by mounds. Once again, there was no trace of funerary activity associated with these, and the implication is that the creation of the mounds was explicitly intended to bury the earlier hengiform monuments, bringing about a radical transformation of space and access in the process. Comparable sequences of construction are seen with Henges 1 and 2 at Forteviot, Perth and Kinross, Scotland: initially comprising free-standing post rings (associated with cremation burials), followed by henge earthworks, followed by mound construction.[81] Such monumental metamorphosis is also played out with Early Bronze Age Clava Cairns and stone circles in central and north-east Scotland;[82] and later still with the remarkable, massive, circular Late Iron Age timber building at Navan in Northern Ireland, which was deliberately burnt then buried under a 40m-diameter mound marked out with radial divisions.[83] In each instance the creation of a mound marks the final point in the sequence.

At Dyffryn Lane, Bulford and Forteviot, formerly open monuments were closed and sealed by the creation of mounds. At Duggleby Howe, in the Great Wold Valley, Yorkshire, the effect was different, in that an existing round barrow containing a remarkable and nationally-important series of burials was transformed into a monumental mound encircled by a penan-nular interrupted ditched enclosure *c.* 350m in diameter.[84] At nearly 40m in diameter and originally perhaps nine metres high, Duggleby Howe invites close comparison to the monumental mounds of Wessex and Droughduil, and should perhaps be thought of as intimately related – a Yorkshire cousin. The sequence here is long, the first inhumation burials on the site taking place in the mid-fourth millennium BC, with subsequent burial occurring intermit-tently over a period of several hundred years.[85] Sealing these burials, the first mound dates to the twenty-ninth century BC, and in scale and form is compa-rable with many other Neolithic round barrows.[86] Into this were inserted numerous cremations, perhaps in the early third millennium BC. The final part of the sequence sees a radical transformation. The ditched enclosure was dug around the mound and chalk from this seemingly used in the building of a massive chalk capping to the primary mound.[87] These events occurred in the third quarter of the third millennium BC, so broadly coincident with the construction of the Marlborough Mound and Silbury Hill.[88] It seems likely knowledge of all these constructions was common among their respective communities, not least because of evidence from the West Kennet palisade enclosures of contact with East Yorkshire through material exchange or even direct movement.[89]

It was not just monuments that found themselves transformed into mounds during the Late Neolithic, Chalcolithic and Early Bronze Age. At Upper Ninepence in Powys,[90] Ringlemere in Kent,[91] and Tye Field in Essex,[92] round mounds without direct evidence of funerary function were created over areas of dense settlement debris and structural features dating to the later Neolithic. In each instance the mounds are sited over the core of former settlement areas, strongly suggesting a direct connection and purposeful intent to seal and/or memorialise those traces, even though the interval between settlement abandonment and mound building could be one of several centuries. They could be seen as purposeful acts of memory work,[93] or of intentional forgetting. Perhaps there was something qualitatively different about these places and former settlement events, linked to remembered events (even traumatic ones), or individuals or communities of renown? Alternatively, were these traces of former habitation unintentionally brought back to the fore through disturbance – tillage, for example – that required respectful burial?

In the far north of the British Isles, on the Orkney archipelago, and here within a firm Late Neolithic context, mounding was also employed to mark and seal former traces of settlement. Clay platforms and layers of midden were purposefully spread over truncated structural remains at a number of Orcadian sites.[94] This could be slow, incremental and a component of routine settlement maintenance, resulting from the dumping and gradual accumulation of midden material over structures and activity areas that had fallen out of use. In other instances, the practices were more dramatic and deliberately transformatory. We see this most clearly with events surrounding the abandonment and 'decommissioning' of Structure 10 – a communal hall? – within the remarkable monumental settlement of the Ness of Brodgar, located on a narrow peninsular of land between the Lochs of Harray and Stenness.[95] Following a final phase of use around 2500 BC, deposits of Grooved Ware and cattle bone were placed in the area of the central hearth, and the building partially dismantled. The interior was then infilled with rubble and midden, creating 'a cairn-like mound over the building, turning it, effectively, into a different kind of monument'.[96] A century or so later this hall-cum-cairn was the focus for the deposition of the remains of over four hundred cattle.[97]

A much larger mound occupied the tip of the isthmus dividing the Lochs of Stenness and Harray at the south-east end of the Ness settlement. Partially levelled in the nineteenth century, recent excavations show this to comprise deposits of midden material and refuse from the settlement which overlie at least one building. These deposits are prodigious in scale, surviving as a mass 70m in diameter and up to six metres deep, yet originally they were far more substantial, offering a striking landmark in their final manifestation.[98] It might be tempting to view this mound as an oversized rubbish heap, and, indeed, it did form incrementally through the routinised and protracted disposal of waste generated within the settlement. However, there was surely intent in the process of working material accumulation to produce the final mounded form, and with time it likely came to symbolise something of the longevity, subsistence success, identity and community of those living on the Ness. In this sense, it was as much a monument as the Marlborough Mound.

Conclusions

Showing that the construction of the Marlborough Mound dates to the Neolithic period was one of the great archaeological discoveries in Wiltshire (a landscape not unused to great discoveries) of the first decade of the twenty-first century. It has kickstarted a large-scale project dating mottes up and down the country (see the Afterword below) as well as reinvigorated research on the prehistoric origins of Marlborough town. The Marlborough Mound, to quote Hoare once again, 'must not be passed over in silence'. Knowledge of the Mound's Neolithic date, and increased awareness of contemporary activity along the adjacent southern bank of the Kennet, highlights the need for further archaeological investigation within the town and grounds of the College. There remains a strong likelihood that the Mound is one element in a larger monument complex, much of which may have been levelled or heavily modified during the construction of the castle and the later formal grounds of the seventeenth-century house. There is scope for detailed geophysical survey, targeted excavation, and – in the settlement zone to the south of the river, especially – perhaps even 'back garden' test-pitting as a community project.

Coring of the Mound has shown potential complexity in its construction: it is far from a large heap of chalk. As we have shown, analogy with the sequence at Silbury Hill, and awareness of mound building as a process during the Late Neolithic and in the centuries following, raises the distinct possibility that the Mound was both created in stages and that there could be considerable metamorphosis within the unfolding of such a sequence. It may well not have started as a mound. If the diverse examples of mound building offered above illustrate anything, it is of process over form, and an awareness of the sometimes fluid and contingent character of monumental construction during the currency of the Mound.

There has been a natural tendency to seek function in Late Neolithic monumental mounds, often as providing raised platforms or surfaces upon which a select few might observe otherwise concealed activities within adjacent monuments.[99] However, if their form was not necessarily prescribed or envisaged from the outset, but much more emergent, such recourse to formal function appears misplaced. The significance to mounding may well lie in closure, in bringing sequences of events and their material traces to an end.

Afterword: The Round Mounds Project

Jim Leary, Elaine Jamieson and Phil Stastney

The obvious question that arises from the dating work at the Marlborough Mound is: how many other 'Norman' mottes up and down the country were also constructed in the prehistoric period? Their supposed medieval date is actually largely speculation – an idea put forward in the early twentieth century by castle scholars like Ella Armitage – when in fact no-one has ever attempted to date castle mounds archaeologically; they are too large to excavate and too expensive to tunnel into, not to mention the damage work like this would cause to the sites themselves. Seen in this light, could other large prehistoric monumental mounds exist, fossilised as later medieval mottes? Can we at least put rough dates on these huge and much-loved monuments?

In order to answer these questions a project, known as the Round Mounds Project and funded by the Leverhulme Trust, was set up. This was a two-and-a-half-year initiative with one simple central aim: to identify mottes in England with prehistoric potential and, through a programme of targeted, minimally intrusive investigation, determine their date of construction, how they developed, and the environmental context in which they were built.

Funding to investigate twenty mottes across England was provided, so careful research and a detailed review of existing information related to castle mottes, examining national data sets, published works, grey-literature reports and topographic data, was undertaken first. Key search criteria were developed using information from Silbury Hill, the Hatfield Barrow and the Marlborough Mound, and included each monument's scale, topographic setting, relationship to known monuments and other archaeological evidence. From nearly nine hundred mottes or motte-and-bailey castles recorded on the Historic England NRHE (National Record of the Historic Environment), a database of 154 mounds with prehistoric potential was created and, from these, forty-six were shortlisted for field reconnaissance.

This second phase involved visiting each shortlisted site to assess the mound in its landscape context. The prehistoric potential of each mound was evaluated, as well as the fieldwork strategy and site logistics that would be involved in investigating it further, along with compiling photographs, details of any previous archaeological investigations and local geological data. This provided huge amounts of new information to add to the project and, based on these details, twenty were selected. The landowners of each mound were then contacted (not always an easy task!), and applications for Scheduled Monument Consent were submitted to the relevant Historic England Inspector of Ancient Monuments.

Environmental evidence

The coring was carried out in two tranches over the autumn of 2015 and the autumn of 2016. As at the Marlborough Mound, cores were drilled down from the summit of the mottes, through the mound make-up into the underlying old ground surface, with the deepest – at Wallingford castle, Oxfordshire – going down 15m. Over the course of the project, the twenty sites yielded a total of 263 metre-long plastic-lined sediment cores and more than 150 samples of bulk sediment, each containing a wealth of information.

Each length of core was catalogued before being placed into cold storage until they were ready to be opened and photographed. The samples were then assessed using standard sedimentological tests to measure the moisture, organic carbon and carbonate content within the cores, as well as targeted examination of some layers for their particle size (using laser granulometry) and to determine whether there was any pollen present. Finally, small bulk samples were wet-sieved to recover any small artefacts or preserved plant or animal remains – valuable insights into the mounds' environmental context – and selected materials like seeds and charred plant remains were sent to SUERC for radiocarbon dating.

The sites were revisited during the winter months to see them when local vegetation was at its lowest and the leaves were off the trees, allowing the details of the earthworks to be recorded precisely, providing us with a topographic model of each mound. This work was often the first detailed survey some of the mottes had ever undergone and, through meticulous examination of the earthwork remains, successive phases of monument construction and alteration were unpicked at several of the sites, as well as relationships between the mounds and the wider archaeological and natural landscape. Combined with the core samples, this body of evidence proved illuminating and subtle external markers (such as regular breaks-of-slope and ledges carried around all or most of the circumference of the mound) were assessed as true indicators of chronological depth – that is, whether the earthworks reflected what lay within.

A motley crew of mounds

Radiocarbon dating revealed that 70 per cent of our sample mounds were indeed constructed in the medieval period; more specifically, in the decades around the late eleventh or early twelfth centuries, placing their probable construction in the years following the Norman Conquest. For example, the motte at Wallingford castle returned a minimum age (*terminus post quem*) at 95 per cent confidence of AD 1026–1151. Northamptonshire's Fotheringhay castle, the birthplace of Richard III, returned a minimum date of AD 1033–1176, while Pilsbury castle in Derbyshire yielded a minimum age of AD 1056–1215.

This means that the majority of the mounds studied appeared to be exactly what they had always been suspected to be: Norman castle mottes. But the coring work also produced hosts of new information on the material make-up of such monuments, granting new insights into the siting and construction of motte-and-bailey castles. Assessment of the cores from Clifford Hill motte castle (located towards the eastern fringe of the county town of Northampton), for example, revealed clear layering of deposits from the time that the motte was raised. However, radiocarbon dates from three samples taken from different locations within the mound were statistically indistinguishable, suggesting the motte had in fact been constructed in a relatively short period of time. Over at Tickhill castle in South Yorkshire, coring revealed that this motte was constructed almost entirely of sand, its medieval builders sculpting and enhancing a natural sandstone outcrop to create an impressive mound standing over 17m high.

The earthwork surveys have also produced huge amounts of new information on not only the mounds but the castles themselves. Investigations at Fotheringhay, for example, revealed the layout of the buildings within the inner bailey, including the likely location of the castle's great hall where Mary Queen of Scots was executed in 1587. At Castle Hill, Bishopton, work was also able to determine that the bailey had been accessed from the north by way of a raised causeway – a feature which was clearly secondary to the initial castle construction, providing an insight into how these sites could change through time. Finally, the work has also identified echoes of how many of these sites were re-used long after the castle itself was abandoned: at Bramber castle in West Sussex, for example, where the site was turned into a visitor attraction in the early twentieth century – with the castle's curtain wall enclosing a tea garden and fairground – the remnants of the tearoom can still be seen as slight earthwork remains.

Some unusual outliers

Although the majority of the mounds were found to date to the Norman period, there were some interesting exceptions. The Mount in Lewes was shown to date to the late fifteenth century or later, and is therefore not a castle motte at all, but is likely to have originated as a post-medieval ornamental garden feature known as a prospect mound. Similarly, Forbury Mound in Reading was probably constructed as a Civil War gun emplacement. One of the mottes at Hamstead Marshall (Castle 3) also appears to be somewhat later than the Norman period; it dates to the latter half of the twelfth or early thirteenth century, which places it after the Anarchy period and within the lifetime of the remarkable individual William Marshall (after whom the settlement is in part named) – often described as 'the greatest knight', he was one of the key architects of Magna Carta.

While these sites were later than expected, others were earlier. Montem Mound in Slough, for example, returned a number of consistent dates suggesting that the mound was built during the early Saxon period – rather than a castle motte, it is likely to be a Saxon burial mound, similar to that at nearby Taplow, Berkshire. The date of another early site proved extremely interesting: initial dating from Skipsea castle mound, East Yorkshire, returned a consistent series of radiocarbon dates clustering in the Early to Middle Iron Age (800–400 BC), indicating possible prehistoric origins. Additional dating material was obtained from the cores, and this second phase of radiocarbon analysis yielded a distinct cluster of Iron Age dates obtained from the buried soil horizon beneath the mound – almost certainly indicating some form of activity or occupation of the site during this period. Both Iron Age and medieval dates were obtained from the make-up of the mound itself, although the latter were only found in the uppermost sediment layers, indicating that the body of the mound was constructed during the Iron Age.

Rounding off the mounds project

The work at the Marlborough Mound directly created the Round Mounds Project. The project may not have found many other lost prehistoric mounds disguised as mottes, but it has been successful in all other ways. The first thing to note is that it successfully returned dates on all but three of the mounds selected for investigation, showing that the coring methodology does work for this type of earthwork dating project. It could, therefore, be usefully employed in other circumstances, perhaps to investigate Bronze Age mounds, or the banks and ditches of hillforts or henges.

The project has also been able to scientifically confirm for the first time that mottes are, on the whole, Norman features. Furthermore, more than half of the sites dated represent rural castles for which very little archaeological or historical information was previously known – a situation replicated for rural castles nationally. The sites that were investigated, therefore, now represent some of the best dated medieval settlement sites in England. But the project has also shown that some 30 per cent of the sites are of other periods and, if the sample is representative, this means that a considerable number of mottes require further work to establish their date.

The coring work has allowed us to characterise the material make-up of castle mounds, revealing new information on their physical form, while the earthwork surveys have not only produced new details about the mounds, but on castle sites more broadly, with 50 per cent of the selected castles surveyed in their entirety. The data collected as part of the project can therefore not only help to define dates for the origin and development of England's medieval mottes more tightly, but also has the potential to contribute significantly to our understanding of the medieval period more broadly. The last point to note is that the three Wiltshire giants – Silbury Hill, the Marlborough Mound and the Hatfield Barrow, remain, for now at least, unique monuments within England.

2

Castles and the Landscape of Norman Wessex, *c.* 1066–1154

Oliver H. Creighton

Writing in the late twelfth century, the chronicler William of Newburgh famously described England's royal castles as forming 'the bones of the kingdom',[1] reflecting their strategic and symbolic roles as the scaffold around which royal authority was constructed. If castles were the bones of Norman England, then Wessex was its heart. This chapter considers the structures, distribution and landscape contexts of castles in Wessex generally, and the region around Marlborough more specifically, in order to illuminate something of the wider pattern of castle-building in the eleventh and twelfth centuries within which Marlborough castle can most appropriately be understood. From the start, however, it is important to emphasise that, in terms of the historical and archaeological study of fortification, Wessex is a region far more closely associated with Anglo-Saxon defence, in the form of *burhs* (or fortified centres) like Cricklade, Oxford, Wallingford and Wareham, than Norman fortresses. We often think, talk and write about 'Norman castles' – like *burhs* – as if they were a single species of fortification when this is far from the truth. Just as modern archaeological scholarship is revealing the variety of *burhs* and other types of fortification that dotted the landscape of Anglo-Saxon Wessex, including private thegnly (or aristocratic) *burhs*, tower-naves and civil defence infrastructure such as beacons and military roads,[2] then so too are we now much more aware of the greater number and variety of Norman castles than previously recognised, and also the myriad functions that these sites served beyond their military roles.

Frequently bracketed together and explained away as the means by which an incoming alien elite conquered and dominated a hostile population, the Norman castles of Wessex have been characterised by historians and archaeologists alike as essentially military features of the landscape.[3] In the *Archaeological Research Framework for South-West England*, published in 2007, for example, castles are subsumed under the sub-heading 'Defence and Warfare',[4] underlining our continuing obsession with viewing these sites through the lens of military history and architecture. This chapter takes a rather different approach and stresses that we should pay equal, if not greater, attention to the day-to-day roles of Norman castles as high-status residences and estate centres and to their symbolic importance as emblems of authority and lordship.[5]

For many people the term 'Norman castle' – and indeed the word 'castle' itself – is synonymous with major stone monuments; the quintessential Norman castles of Wessex are sites such as Corfe (Dorset), Old Sarum (Wiltshire), Sherborne (Dorset) and Winchester (Hampshire), comprising major masonry fortifications – and modern-day heritage sites – with impressive features of military architecture such as gatehouses, curtain walls and keeps.[6] Nevertheless, these sorts of places represent only the tip of the iceberg in terms of the total number of Norman castle sites. As this chapter makes clear, Norman castles were built at a variety of scales and forms, and using varied technologies, by different members of the social elite, ranging from the king and his barons and bishops with national and even international power bases to lords of the manor whose interests were purely local. A distribution map of known and suspected castles of the late eleventh and twelfth centuries in the region of north Wessex within which Marlborough lies (Fig. 2.1) immediately highlights the large number and wide distribution of

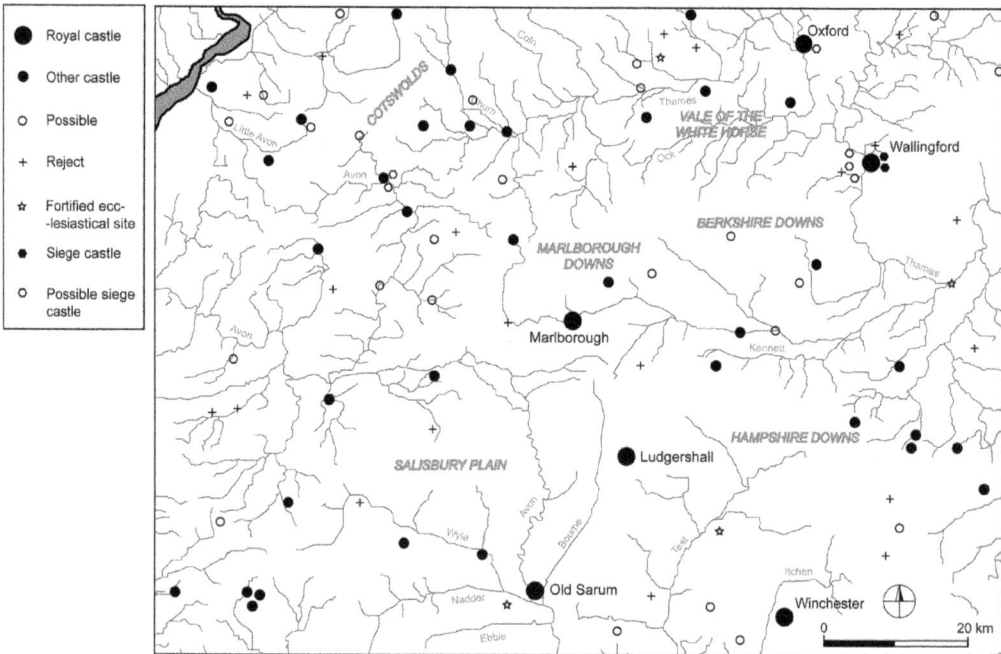

Fig. 2.1 Map of early castles in north Wessex.

castles, but also the considerable number of places where it remains uncertain whether or not a castle actually existed in a particular location. Many former stone fortresses have left little or nothing in terms of above-ground masonry remains, but a great number of castles were fortified with earth and timber and survive in the form of earthworks, often of vestigial form and sometimes undocumented, which leave considerable potential for confusion. Other types of Norman fortification stretch the definition of 'castle', including siege castles (or 'counter castles', built to blockade an enemy castle or town) and fortified ecclesiastical sites, all of which are represented on the distribution map. While sometimes side-lined in the scholarship on the subject, these sorts of sites all have an important place in the archaeology and history of Norman castles.

Against this background, this chapter reviews the evidence for Norman castles in the landscape of Wessex between the Norman Conquest of 1066 and the mid-twelfth century. Exploring the evidence at a variety of scales – from castle distribution, through to the architecture, landscape settings, below-ground archaeology and history of the sites themselves – the chapter also assesses our current state of knowledge and highlights some areas where new discoveries and research directions are casting different shades of light on the subject. It examines both the castles of the Norman Conquest itself and the place of the castle within the following phases of consolidation and colonisation, before considering castle-building in the region during the civil war of the reign of King Stephen (1135–54), and then making some brief conclusions.

Wessex and the Norman Conquest

The Norman castles of Wessex have an important place in the history of Norman England more generally, as we are concerned with fortification in a region that was central to English kingship and governance. At the time of the Norman Conquest, Wessex was one of the wealthiest regions of England, and as the heart of the great Earldom of Wessex – which in 1066 was held by Harold Godwin (King Harold II) and stretched from Kent to Cornwall – an area of prime political importance with high-status associations and ancestry. In the immediate post-Conquest years, the proximity to Normandy of the region's coast and ports leant it additional geostrategic value. It is important to underline, however, that the political cohesion that Wessex had retained to 1066 was utterly shattered by the Conquest and the wholesale redistribution of lands to a new incoming Norman aristocracy, as recorded in Domesday Book (1086). The Earldom of Wessex was bestowed on William FitzOsbern, William the Conqueror's steward and trusted favourite, soon after the victory at Hastings, but after his death in 1071, the earldom lost its power and jurisdiction, so by Domesday Book the pattern of landholding across the region was a complex mosaic of different interests – royal, ecclesiastical and aristocratic. That said, it was probably the case that Wessex was already losing some of its political identity and pre-eminence in the first half of the eleventh century, given the circumstances of the turbulence around the end of Æthelred the Unready's reign and the accession of Cnut, when several leading West Saxon families disappeared and London became an increasingly important royal centre at the expense of Winchester.[7]

The explosion of Norman castle-building, led by the king, his bishops, major magnates and aristocratic lords, shows how new and different structures of power cut across the old order. Domesday Book records castles only incidentally and mainly for financial reasons, and as discussed below (p. 38) there is considerable uncertainty about the number built in the late eleventh century and the chronology of their construction. In Wessex, the key castle sites documented in Domesday Book are Dunster (Somerset), Carisbrooke (Isle of Wight), Corfe (as 'Wareham castle') (Dorset), Montacute (Somerset), Okehampton (Devon), and Wallingford and Windsor (Berkshire).[8] At Wallingford, Domesday Book records that eight houses were destroyed in the town to make way for the castle, while at other boroughs extensive damage to property is recorded but castle-building is not explicitly identified as the cause.[9] A number of other castles documented before 1086 are not mentioned in Domesday Book, however, including Exeter (Devon), Old Sarum (Wiltshire) and Oxford, and many more castles suspected to have been built in the late eleventh century have no documentation whatsoever.

The architecture and ownership histories of castles highlight how Wessex was brought into the European sphere as many higher-ranking castle-builders, including major magnates and bishops, held properties not just more widely within England, but also on both sides of the English Channel.[10] However, alongside this fracture with the past, so too do we see some fundamental continuities either side of the Norman Conquest. Despite the wholesale replacement of one aristocracy with another and the presence of castles, along with new cathedrals and monastic houses, as most prominent manifestations of the new Norman presence, there are good reasons to question whether 1066 heralded a major horizon in the development of the English countryside. Wessex was spared the worst excesses of Norman ravaging, which affected south-east England during the Hastings campaign of 1066, and areas of the midlands and, especially, Yorkshire and the north in 1069–70.[11] Anglo-Saxon revolts centred on Montacute and Exeter (1068) were quickly put down, and the campaigns involved castle-building (such as Exeter castle, founded in 1068), but the damage to the economy recorded in Domesday Book is modest compared to the north and south-east of England. Archaeological approaches to the Norman Conquest, meanwhile, are stressing how material culture evidence suggests underlying continuity despite the coming of a new regime: in terms of burial practices, pottery and vernacular architecture, for example, very little changed tangibly and immediately. Likewise, the fabric of the countryside remained essentially unaltered. An interesting reflection on this issue is the very small number of new Norman-French place-names in the English landscape. In Wessex, as elsewhere, new Norman place-names were associated with elite sites, as with Devizes (Wiltshire) (derived from the Norman-French for 'the divisions', and reflecting the imposition of the new castle and town at the junction of two existing hundreds) and Montacute (Somerset) ('pointed hill').[12] This was an elite takeover rather than a folk movement involving large-scale immigration into the English countryside. Even the 'Norman yoke' caricature of the post-Conquest countryside as a place where rapacious castle-building Norman aristocrats were able to demand services from repressed peasants as never before can be seen as the ratcheting up of a process of intensifying lordly control that was already well in train in the Late Saxon period.[13]

Royal Castle-Building

The Wessex region remained a favoured locale for kings and their courts throughout the Norman period. Royal itineraries and charters demonstrate that Norman kings visited the area frequently and held court and councils within royal castles, as well as other properties and locations. By mapping the distribution of place-dated Norman royal charters, the historian Thomas Keefe highlighted the particular importance to the monarchy of the area of the Thames Valley and central Wessex that he characterised as a 'royal enclave' – an administrative core which the royal court frequented and around which great swathes of land were granted to curial magnates.[14] The area in question was defined by a line drawn from London south-west to Portchester on the south coast, then north-west up to Salisbury, Gloucester and Worcester, then eastwards across to Northampton and down again to London.

Situated right at the heart of this region, Marlborough castle (Fig. 2.2) was a royal fortification, in common with other well-known sites built for Norman kings, such as Ludgershall, Old Sarum, Oxford and Wallingford. Despite the label 'royal castles', these sites were strikingly varied in their size, status and functions, and not all were in the hands of the monarchy throughout their entire histories. Several royal castles were major administrative foci that played significant roles in national and international events. For example, the royal castle at Old Sarum was the place where Domesday Book was ceremonially handed to William the Conqueror in a great open-air ceremony when his council was held there in August 1086, with all the great landholders of the realm in attendance and paying homage to the king. Other royal castles were much more low-key, secluded installations favoured by the royal court because of their proximity to hunting resources. Indeed the concentration of royal forests and parks in the Wessex region is a key reason why kings maintained such a large number of residences here.

Ludgershall castle (Fig. 2.3) is a good example: a location in south-east Wiltshire without any obvious strategic purpose, it nestled on the edge of the

Fig. 2.2 Aerial view of the motte of Marlborough castle, Wiltshire.

Fig. 2.3 Aerial view of Ludgershall castle, Wiltshire.

royal forest of Chute with its attendant community and probably originated as a late Anglo-Saxon hunting estate.[15] Besides this network of royal castles, the Norman kings maintained an extensive network of non-defended houses, palaces and hunting lodges across the region. Often situated within or on the fringes of forests and parks, these sites accommodated hunting parties and hosted royal officials and sometimes also prisons for the incarceration of forest offenders.[16] The distinction between these non-defended royal properties and castles is actually rather arbitrary; for royal officials and accountants detailing the costs of construction, upkeep and refurbishment these sites all constituted 'the king's houses', regardless of whether they possessed defences.[17]

The king's visitations to even the most favoured royal castles were sporadic and on a day-to-day basis their running was entrusted to officials, such as constables/custodians and sheriffs.[18] Many royal castles in urban settings, such as Oxford, were the official bases of new Norman sheriffs, whose primary responsibilities were for shires rather than the boroughs that these castles lay within.[19] If there is a clear strategy in the pattern of early Norman castle-building, then it is manifested in this early group of royal urban castles superimposed within Anglo-Saxon *burhs* and other fortified centres. The key urban castles in Wessex were Bristol, Christchurch, Exeter, Old Sarum, Oxford, Southampton, Wallingford, Wareham and Winchester, all of which were built between 1066 and the late 1080s. They were the product of a Norman policy whereby towns, as key fortified strategic places and centres of administration and shire government, were brought quickly and firmly under royal control. This is not to say that all towns in Wessex were dominated by newly built castles soon after the Conquest, however. Indeed Wiltshire and Somerset both present anomalies, as the only major urban castle of the late eleventh century in Wiltshire was at Old Sarum, while the larger settlement of nearby Wilton was ignored, and Somerset had no early urban castle at all in the immediate post-Conquest period, as Taunton castle was built in the twelfth century.[20]

For those urban centres that were the focus of castle-building, Norman policy saw the face of authority utterly transformed. While it is firmly established that the incoming Norman regime positioned urban castles strategically to take advantage of pre-existing town defences (Fig. 2.4),[21] what is considerably less clear is the extent to which these new fortifications also perpetuated the sites of elite Anglo-Saxon complexes.

Winchester, the ancient capital of Wessex, continued to function as in effect England's capital city in the immediate aftermath of the Conquest and beyond, and its townscape was one of the first to bear the footprint of royal castle-building. Still girdled within the ancient circuit of its Roman walls, suitably refurbished by the Kings of Wessex, the Norman city featured a great royal castle, founded in 1067 and planned around a motte and bailey superimposed into the south-west corner of the circuit (in doing so sealing part of the Anglo-Saxon street grid), and also a separate royal palace, of

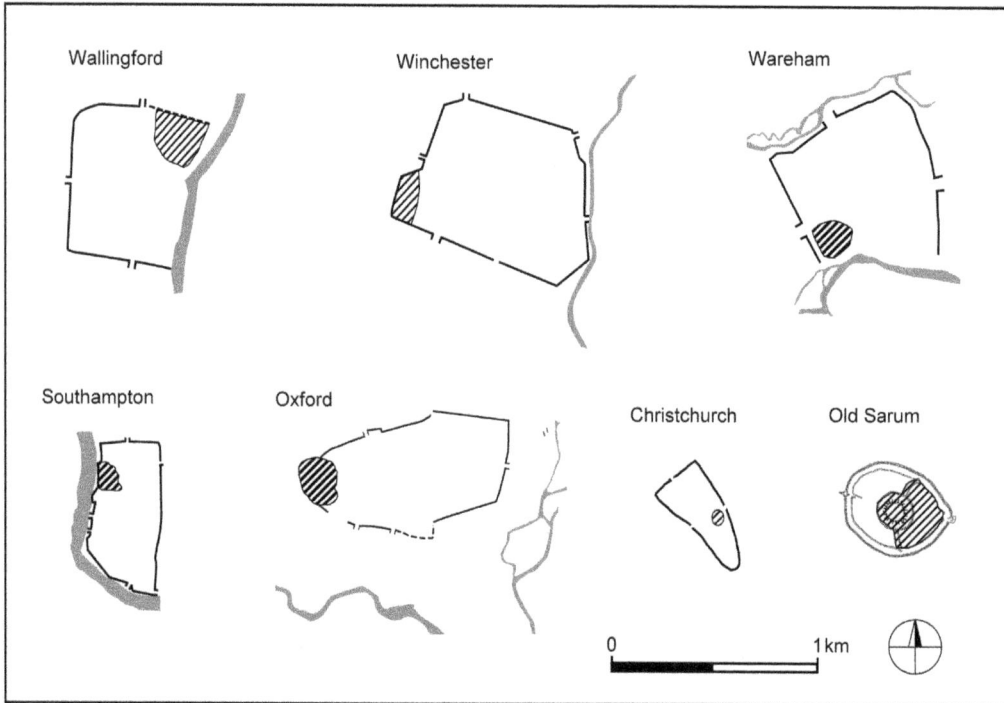

Fig. 2.4 Comparative plans of Norman urban castles, showing the relationship between town defences and castles of the immediate post-Conquest period.

Anglo-Saxon origin but enlarged by William the Conqueror, near the centre of the re-planned city.[22] It was the castle that housed the royal treasury. The treasury was viewed by William Rufus, who saw gems and purple cloths as well as gold and silver, and upon his death was immediately seized by Henry I.[23] It was not until part-way through the troubled reign of King Stephen (1135–54) that the gravitational centre of Norman government shifted to London, situated firmly in the royalist region of south-east England.[24]

The town of Wallingford (Oxfordshire, but in the Norman period the shire town of Berkshire) has been the focus of a major programme of modern archaeological investigation which, combined with re-analysis of earlier excavations, provides an illuminating case study of the impact of Norman castle-building on a late-Saxon townscape (Fig. 2.5).[25] The motte-and-bailey castle was again early, being established in 1066 when Duke William's forces made an encircling approach on London, and typically for an urban castle was built in the corner of the extant urban defences, nestled in the north-east corner of the *burh*. The weight of circumstantial historical evidence suggests that it overlies an Anglo-Saxon royal site, although there is no direct

a Phase 1: *c*.1080

Castle Street

castle precincts

gatehouse ?

college

meadows

0   150m

b Phase 2: *c*.1150

middle bailey

c

? Earthworks
∴ Scheduled area
⊕ Church — extant
+ Church — site of

C L A P C O T

CASTLE MEADOWS

North Gate

King's Meadow

BULLCROFT

CASTLE GARDENS

Queen's Arbour

Borough Boundary

Site of priory

Bear Lane

West Gate

High Street

High Street

East Gate

Wallingford Bridge

CROWMARSH CASTLE

KINECROFT

Market Place

RIVERSIDE MEADOWS

Borough Boundary

Portway (line of)

River Thames

C R O W M A R S H

South Gate

0   200m

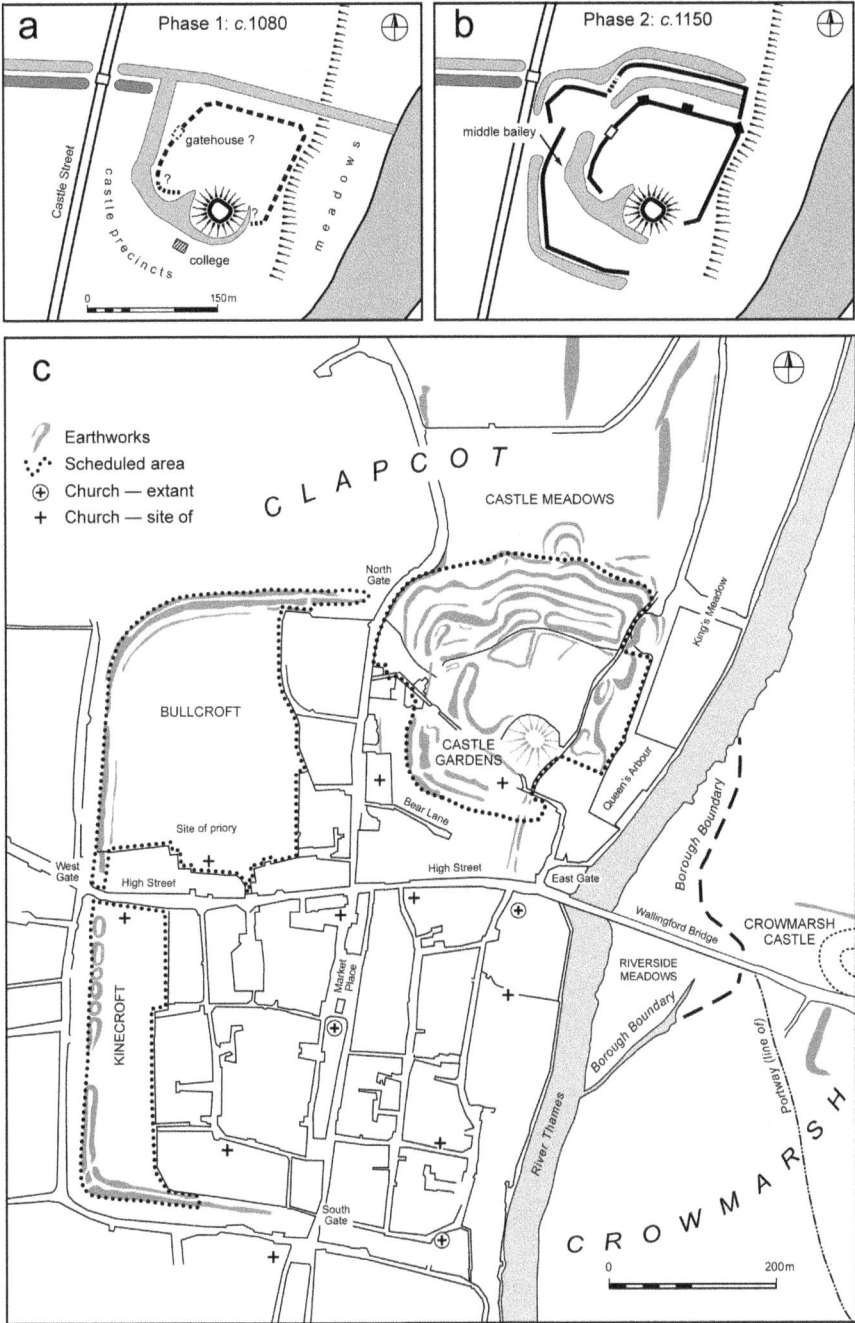

Fig. 2.5 The town and castle of Wallingford, Oxfordshire: (top) development of the castle c. 1066–1150; (bottom) topography of the town showing key sites.

archaeological evidence for this.[26] The new castle was soon 'twinned' with a Benedictine priory, thereby transforming the northern third of the town into an elite enclave, while there are hints that a small immigrant French community was present soon after the Conquest.[27]

Founded in 1071, the motte-and-bailey castle at Oxford (Fig. 2.6) was similarly positioned on the edge of the town, its bailey defences incorporating part of the rampart of the late-Saxon *burh*. Despite its royal origins and status this was never a castle of the first rank, however, and royal visitations were infrequent. It was rarely used as a lodging by the king, who instead preferred the non-defended residences at Beaumont Palace, on the edge of the city, or Woodstock, in the countryside beyond. It is the site's day-to-day function for much of its post-Conquest history as a centre of justice and punishment (especially as the county gaol from the twelfth century), rather than its sometime status as an elite residence and military installation, that stands out most prominently from the archaeological and historical record.[28]

Fig. 2.6 The motte of Oxford castle.

Form and Appearance

Very little castle fabric from the late eleventh and early twelfth centuries survives in Wessex. The earliest examples of stone-built castle architecture consist of the simple rectangular gatehouses at Exeter (Devon) (*c.* 1068) and Sherborne (Dorset) (*c.* 1130s). Also of great importance is the surviving herringbone masonry in the lower walls of the 'Old Hall' at Corfe castle (Dorset), as it could conceivably represent a pre-castle building, especially given that the site perpetuates a royal estate, or else the use of Saxon craftsmen by Norman overlords. The remains of the hall at Christchurch castle (Hampshire) are a little later, dating to *c.* 1155–80 and probably equating to a high-status chamber block rather than a great hall *per se.* Surviving donjons (or keeps) in the region are few. The key example is the rectangular late eleventh-century Great Tower at Old Sarum (Fig. 2.7), which stands on the defences of the inner bailey and was probably the first stone-built element of the site, perhaps alongside the East Gate. Other important early masonry survives in the form of shell keeps at Wareham and Windsor and Portchester's rectangular donjon, all of the twelfth century, and the

Fig. 2.7 The Great Tower, Old Sarum.

remnants of Ludgershall's small 'great tower', of the late twelfth or early thirteenth century.

For the most part, however, Norman stonework has been robbed and lost, replaced by later re-building, or can else only be recovered through archaeological excavation. An illuminating case in point is Devizes castle, which the chronicler Henry of Huntington memorably styled as the most splendid in the whole of Europe, but about which precious little is known given that its site is covered by a Victorian-era folly-castle.[29] Recent excavations on the perimeter of the site in advance of building work in 2017, however, revealed a tower or bridge abutment, of twelfth- or thirteenth-century date, with walls over 3m thick, cut into the remains of an outer rampart (Fig. 2.8).[30] Built by Bishop Roger of Salisbury in the first half of the eleventh century, the site's splendour was doubtless magnified by the planned town at its foot and the great deer park that surrounded the fortress (see below, p. 41). Indeed, Wessex has something of a concentration of ambitious episcopal building projects

Fig. 2.8 Archaeological excavation of part of the outer defences of Devizes castle in 2017.

of the early to mid-twelfth century, including those of Henry of Blois at Wolvesey Palace, Winchester, and Bishop Roger's other works at Malmesbury (Wiltshire) and Sherborne (Dorset).[31] At Sherborne, archaeological evidence highlights the considerable sophistication of Bishop Roger's fortress-palace, built between *c.* 1122 and 1135 and comprising a precisely planned courtyard complex with a great tower, set within a walled ward, with a deer park and water features completing a grand setting.[32] Ecclesiastical magnates did not simply buy into the world of fortification in order to emulate their secular counterparts; in some cases, bishops' castles were at the very cutting edge of military architecture and set standards of domestic sophistication.

While the focus of this chapter so far has primarily been on masonry fortresses, the majority of Norman castles were neither built nor ever reconstructed in stone. Rather, most were timber castles, comprising earthworks topped with and enclosing timber structures, that were mainly built in one of two forms: mottes (artificial mounds, topped with towers) with or without baileys (defended enclosures) and ringworks (ditched and embanked enclosures, also with and without baileys). The earthworks of these timber castles are often unimpressive. Eroded, disturbed and obscured by vegetation, their plans can be difficult to appreciate on the ground and their sites are often not readily amenable to serious archaeological investigation. That said, Robert Higham and Philip Barker's important 1992 book *Timber Castles* buried forever the notion of the earth and timber castle as necessarily inferior to the castle of stone and established that these sites could be impressive and defensible edifices of lordship.[33] Key questions in the study of timber castles remain, however. There is considerable uncertainty around how many were built and the chronology of their construction, given that so many are undocumented and so few have seen serious archaeological study. Only rarely has the excavation of mottes in Wessex cast genuinely new light on how they were built, although the large-scale excavations in advance of the redevelopment of Oxford castle following the closure of the prison on the site in 1996 present a rare example. These showed the enormous (*c.* 15m high, 60m wide) Norman mound to have been built in ziggurat-like form with a series of steps cut into its flanks in order to stabilise it.[34] Construction of motte-and-bailey castles entailed gargantuan earth-moving operations: even modest examples could take a workforce of a hundred men at least four to six months, and larger examples took longer still.[35] Moreover, such calculations do not take into account the manpower and resources required to create the timber palisades, gateways, buildings and motte superstructures.

Other excavations of Norman castles pose major challenges of interpretation. In the case of Ludgershall (Wiltshire), for example, ambitious large-scale excavations of the royal castle and hunting lodge carried out between 1964 and 1972 in order to make the site more intelligible to the public were published in full only in 2000.[36] This publication details the site's complex chronology, relates the documentation to the physical remains and presents a rich assemblage of finds of exceptional significance for our understanding of everyday life in the castle. But the report had a 'long and difficult genesis',[37] so that by the time of publication topographic work carried out in the 1990s had proposed radically different interpretations of the site's pre-castle phases and later landscaping which were totally at odds with original findings. For example, the castle is suggested to have been superimposed on a prehistoric hillfort, while the site's outer bank, conventionally understood as a rampart, was re-interpreted as a viewing platform and walkway from which the surrounding parkland could be admired.[38] The case of Ludgershall castle highlights how castle studies had moved on between the original excavation and the late 1990s and twenty-first century, which saw new research horizons open up for the subject.

The total distribution map of Norman castles in Wessex (Fig. 2.1) includes a large number of disputed sites. Attempts to estimate the total number of sites are bedevilled by the very large number of 'possible', 'probable' and 'alleged' castles where it is impossible to judge for sure whether a surviving field monument is, in fact, an undocumented castle.[39] Several different landscape features of alternative origin can be mistaken for early castles (especially mottes), including prehistoric and Anglo-Saxon burial mounds, medieval windmill mounds, post-medieval prospect (or viewing) mounds and natural features. Ringworks, meanwhile, can be confused with prehistoric enclosures. Equally, however, there are also many proven examples of sites where Norman castle-builders re-used earlier features, of which Marlborough's castle mound is an exemplar.[40] We also have to consider 'vanished' castle sites, where their construction or existence is attested in documentary sources but where no physical evidence survives.

An illustrative case of mistaken identity is the mound at Bradenstoke, near Lyneham, Wiltshire, known as Clack Mount, which has often been identified as a motte and is recognised as such in its Scheduled Ancient Monument listing. But the feature is quite unlike a motte: standing only 1.8m high without a surrounding ditch, and set centrally within the supposed 'bailey', which would be very unusual, it is much more likely to be a late- or post-medieval garden feature, especially as it lies within the grounds of Bradenstoke Priory, although the possibility that it is a re-used barrow cannot be ruled out.[41] The issue is that once sites were identified by early field archaeologists as early castles, then the label has tended to stick, despite the fact that we now have a far greater awareness of these alternative forms of monument so easily mistaken for mottes.

The total distribution map of Norman castles highlights that mottes and ringworks were located in a wide variety of places. Decisions of castle siting balanced multiple considerations, which naturally included the defensibility of a location, but also its visibility, prominence and accessibility with regard to communications routes and hunting resources. The image of the hilltop castle is deeply engrained in our thinking about the subject and exemplified

Fig. 2.9 Aerial view of Bincknoll castle, Wiltshire.
Note the rectangular earthwork of a building within the bailey.

by sites such as Corfe castle and Old Sarum. However, much more typical of the landscape of Norman Wessex was the castle set in exactly the same sort of position as earlier and later manor houses – often forming a recognisable core within the settlement pattern, yet slightly removed from the peasantry, and closely associated with a church or chapel and other appurtenances of lordship. The motte at Sherrington (Wiltshire) is a good example. Some 5m high and almost 50m across, the motte has no surviving superstructure and no recorded history whatsoever. Its landscape context, nestled in the core of the settlement in a low-lying position next to the River Wyle (which fed its wet moat) and adjacent to the mill and parish church, speaks of its status as an estate centre rather than an installation situated for military potential.[42]

The little-known and completely undocumented site of Bincknoll castle, located in an isolated position high on a chalk escarpment in north Wiltshire (Fig. 2.9), is a good example of how analysis of an undocumented castle's landscape context can shed new light on its character and development. In the area immediately below (and to the north of) the hilltop castle, archaeological excavations in 2014–15 revealed a previously unknown chapel dated to the late eleventh/early twelfth century that is likely to have been contemporary with the castle and has been tentatively identified as the chapel of the castle lord.[43] In Domesday Book, Bincknoll was one of five apparently contiguous manors held in chief by Gilbert of Breteuil and comprising the core of his Wiltshire holdings. In contrast, most of Gilbert's other Wiltshire manors were subinfeudated (i.e. held by sub-tenants). The likelihood is, therefore, that Bincknoll castle was built as a defended estate centre at the heart of the most valuable and important block of Gilbert of Breteuil's holdings. The castle's plan was dictated by its dramatic topographical setting atop a narrow chalk spur: a small motte, *c.* 3m in elevation, was raised at the apex of the tongue of land, isolated from a trapezoidal bailey containing the earthworks of buildings and defined by earthwork defences cut transversely across the promontory. Another, larger (outer) bailey lay to the south, which might be a good candidate for an enclosed accompanying medieval settlement or a stock enclosure. It is also important to reflect that it is only through the presence of a motte that the site can be identified as a medieval castle at all, as the morphology of the enclosure earthworks would otherwise suggest a late prehistoric promontory fort, and the possibility of re-use seems strong.

It has long been recognised that the heartland of Wessex contains a high ratio of ringworks to mottes compared to other areas: in 1969, King and Alcock produced a map that identified Wiltshire, Hampshire and Dorset as a hotspot of ringwork construction.[44] This pattern is not easy to explain. It is not determined by any single geological factor; instead, it probably reflects a process of local and regional emulation, while the fact that Wessex contains quite a large number of siege-works, which often tended to be built as ringworks (see below, p. 49), is another factor. Like mottes, many ringworks are found in 'manorial' contexts rather than highly defensible positions. The well-preserved Wiltshire examples at West Dean (adjacent to the parish church) and Stapleford (adjoining a complex of fishponds) are good cases in point.

Against this background, it is most appropriate to understand the total distribution of Norman castles in Wessex not as some grand strategic master plan whereby a network of sites was superimposed on the landscape from a centralised authority so much as the result of a myriad of different decisions undertaken mainly at a more localised level. Specific tenurial factors, such as the consolidation of a network of estates, or the formation of a barony, were as likely to precipitate castle-building as much as specific military circumstances. Castles were estate centres and venues for the manorial court as well as residences, while some sites were in effect working farms. A further important point about the distribution map is that it did not progressively thicken through gradual accretion, as the late eleventh and early twelfth centuries saw castles abandoned, slighted and replaced as well as new ones built.

An obvious lacuna in terms of the archaeology of Norman castles in Wessex, as elsewhere, is accurate information about what sorts of structures stood within baileys and outer baileys and what sorts of activities these spaces housed. Excavations have commonly focused on defences and supposedly core features, so we have remarkably little understanding of these areas and have to turn to the handful of sites that have been thoroughly investigated elsewhere, but which may or may not be representative. The functions of outer baileys remain more mysterious still. Some larger outer baileys were created by re-purposing the defences of earlier sites, such as hillforts (see below, p. 44), but many more castles probably had outer baileys than we realise. Were these spaces intended to be used periodically, as refuges, or rather for the safe corralling of stock? Might others contain evidence of human settlement – either communities linked to the castle household and the workings of the manor, or even failed commercial plantations?

The likely existence of a second (outer) bailey at Marlborough castle was suggested by archaeological excavation of a defensive ditch within the precinct of Marlborough College in 1999. This revealed a broad ditch, V-shaped in profile and defensive in proportion, to the north-east of the known Norman earthworks.[45] Supporting this are documentary references that St Peter's parish, and by implication the church itself, lay in the 'Bailey Ward'.[46] The likelihood is that the outer bailey was a secondary addition, perhaps to separate the castle from the growing town. The town plans of Devizes and Trowbridge also suggest that Norman settlements accompanying early castles grew up within or around large outer baileys. In both cases, a crescentic configuration of curving streets emanating from the castle focus suggests that communities lay within what were in effect extensions of castle defences.[47] At Devizes (Fig. 2.10) the castle was bracketed on one side by the town and on the other by a deer park – completing a remarkably integrated exercise in Norman town and country planning.[48] The link between castles and early deer parks with combined economic, prestige and perhaps aesthetic value was strong.[49] The castles at Montacute and Sherborne were also accompanied by large lobe-like units representing early Norman deer parks that cut across the grain of the landscape. Scientific analysis of the remains of a Norman fallow deer from excavations on Trowbridge castle suggests a large first-generation import from somewhere such as Turkey or Greece.[50] If so, the beast seems likely to have lived – and died – in a park or menagerie associated with the castle, into which it was imported as exotica.

Re-use and Appropriation

In selecting locations for their castles, the Normans frequently re-purposed existing sites of significance, including power centres, ecclesiastical sites, burial monuments and fortifications. In some cases, this was driven by the pragmatic rationale of making savings in labour and resources by re-using existing infrastructure, while other instances may be purely coincidental, with castle-builders simply favouring the same sorts of prime topographical

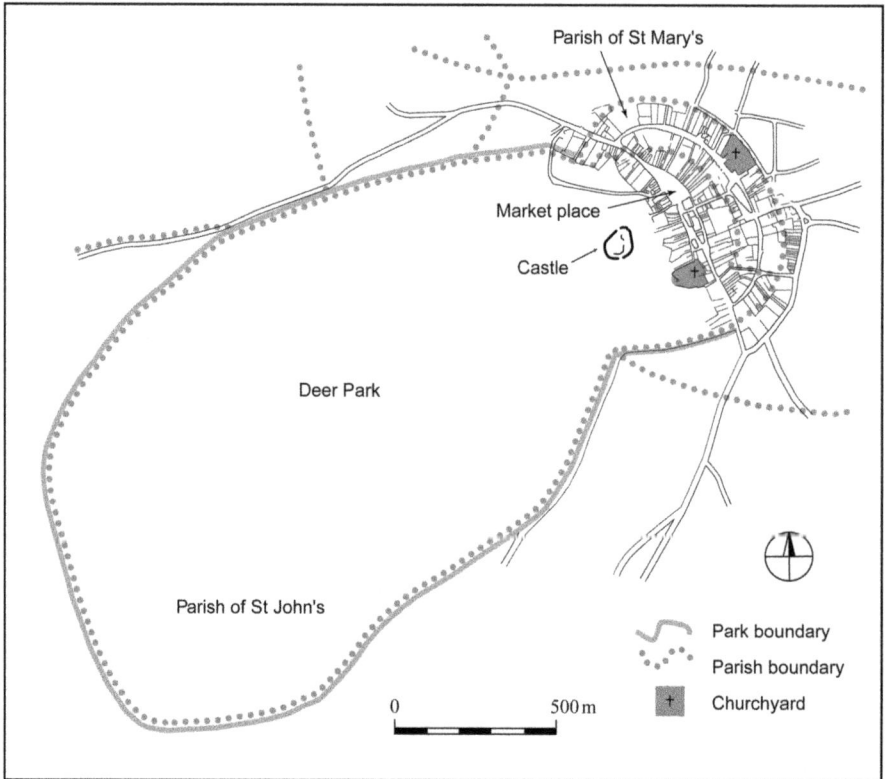

Fig. 2.10 Devizes: plan of castle and town.

locations as those who built earlier sites and monuments. However, there is also a strong argument that in some cases re-occupation equated to cultural appropriation, and that the Norman elite sought to draw power from the past by such actions in order to legitimise their position.[51]

The eleventh-century landscape of Wessex was already exceptionally rich in 'ancient' monuments and, as we have seen, there is considerable scope for confusion between the earthworks of early castles and prehistoric sites. There are several clear examples of Norman castles superimposed within hillforts (see below), but cases of mottes thought to have been raised on pre-existing burial or ritual mounds are rather more contentious. While the case of Marlborough's motte originating as a Neolithic mound is proven beyond doubt by modern archaeological investigation (see this volume, chapter 00), this level of analysis is unusual, and other sites present difficult puzzles. In the Wiltshire village of Ogbourne St Andrew, 3.5km north of Marlborough, for instance, in the corner of the churchyard of St Andrew's stands a small circular mound, little more than c. 1.5m high, from which excavations in the late nineteenth century produced evidence of Bronze-Age cremation and Anglo-Saxon inhumation, as well as later intrusive inhumations.[52] While the feature therefore seems likely to be a multi-phase burial mound, this has not stopped some castle scholars identifying it as a motte,[53] probably because of the strong association between early castles and adjacent parish churches that lay within baileys. Another good example is a heavily eroded mound in the grounds of Bishopstrow Farm, near Warminster (Wiltshire), which in its listing as a Scheduled Ancient Monument is identified as a motte but which is almost certainly the site of a mutilated prehistoric round barrow.[54]

The transformation of Iron-Age hillforts into Norman castles is a more common phenomenon, not least as the resultant earthworks are clearly diagnostic of re-use. The policy made sense at a variety of levels: the massive earthwork defences of hillforts formed pre-positioned baileys, while their sites typically commanded extensive viewsheds over wide territories. In most cases, we can only speculate on the more tantalising possibility that these places still held connotations of ancient power, and perhaps mystery, in the minds of local populations that Norman castle-builders might have seized upon.

Old Sarum is the classic example of hillfort re-purposed as castle. The castle mound of William the Conqueror's fortress was superimposed in the middle of a large multivallate Iron-Age hillfort. This was unusual, as in most cases mottes or ringworks were positioned on the edges of hillforts, but the arrangement presented a striking multi-tiered ensemble visible from every direction, with the mound (once crowned with masonry structures) rising from the very centre of the hillfort, which in turn rose from the natural hilltop. The hillfort lay adjacent to the site of the former Roman settlement of *Sorviodunum*, nodally positioned in the communications network, and was in the late Anglo-Saxon period a *burh* with a mint and probably the meeting place of the hundred.[55] An extensive and ambitious programme of geophysical survey led by the University of Southampton in 2014–17 has illuminated with exceptional clarity the complexity of the bustling 'lost' medieval city surrounding the castle and revealed evidence for structures, streets, suburbs and the zoning of the settlement.[56] The core of the city was embraced within the oval perimeter of the hillfort, some twelve hectares in extent and reinforced with a surrounding wall, meaning that it constituted in effect a vast outer bailey as well as the town defences. While the royal castle and town were topographically distinct in that the castle lay at the centre of, and rose above, the settlement on a great mound, the community effectively lay within the outer defences of the castle. An important point here is that 'castle' and 'city' need not be discrete and mutually exclusive entities.

At Ludgershall (Fig. 2.3), excavation and earthwork survey suggest that the castle's unusual 'double ringwork' plan, comprising two adjoining enclo-sures, resulted from the addition of a Norman ringwork, of either the late eleventh or twelfth century, to a hillfort that had been built a millennium earlier. A very interesting possibility is that the equally unusual double defences of the northern ringwork, with concentric banks and ditches, was a conscious attempt by the castle-builders to emulate the earthworks of the earlier site.[57]

Castle Combe, in north Wiltshire, is another clear yet relatively little-known example of a hillfort-cum-castle. Here, an Iron-Age hillfort occupying an immensely strong natural promontory site overlooking a tributary of the River Avon was given a medieval makeover when powerful defensive earthworks were built transversely across the promontory to convert it into an expansive castle comprising four or five bailey enclosures and a motte, which seems to have supported a small keep, set in the innermost of these (Fig. 2.11).[58] Geophysical survey reveals that the site was once packed with buildings, other than in the outermost enclosure, which was left open. The castle was probably built by the Angevin-sympathising Dunstanville family around *c.* 1140 as the *caput* of a locally based barony. Other examples of Norman hillfort re-use are less certain, including the case of Bincknoll castle,

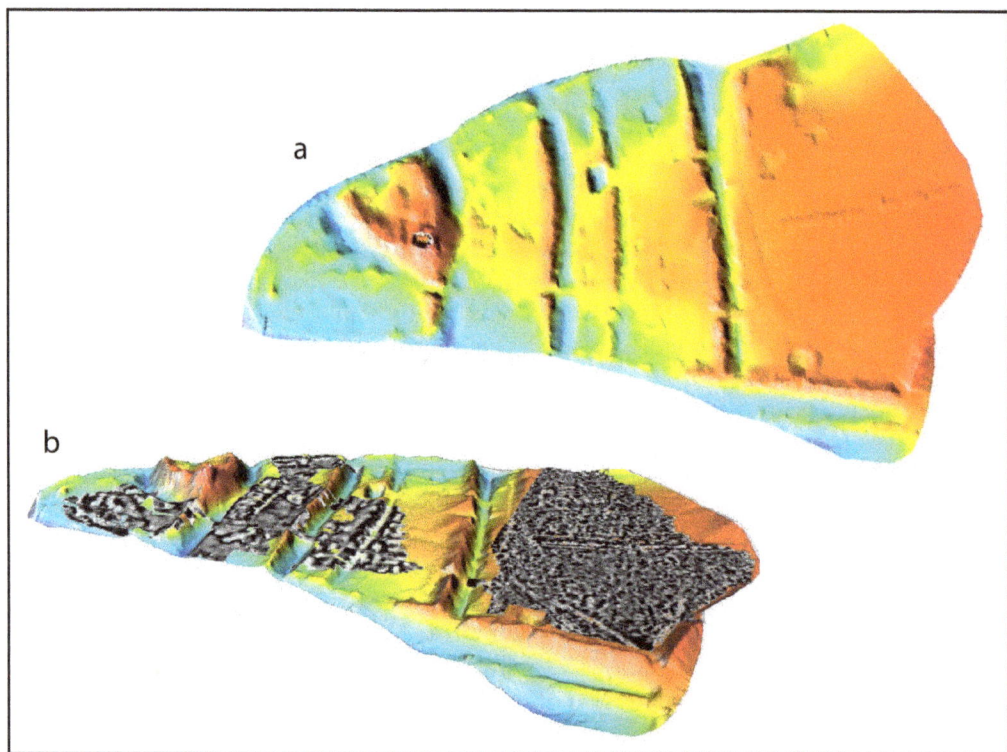

Fig. 2.11 Castle Combe: geophysical survey of a Norman castle superimposed within an Iron-Age hillfort: (a) digital terrain model; (b) 3D digital terrain model with draped geophysics.

Wiltshire (see above, p. 40). There is an enduring tradition of a castle site on Castle Hill, Calne. Here, a programme of geophysical survey and excavation by the Archaeology Field Group of the Wiltshire Archaeological and Natural History Society revealed likely traces of a castle superimposed into an Iron-Age hillfort, although the stonework, including a round tower, suggests a post-Norman feature.[59]

While these aforementioned examples of castles set within hillforts suggest that the earlier fortified sites into which castles were inserted were essentially derelict ancient monuments at the time of the Norman Conquest, a major area of controversy in castle studies remains the question of whether other castles perpetuated functioning Anglo-Saxon seats of lordship. A related question is whether some of these earlier seats of lordship were enclosed within their own 'private' defences and therefore, arguably, 'castles' of a fashion before the Norman Conquest. Several sites in the region are relevant here, of which the classic case study, and the most archaeologically secure in Wessex, is Portchester (Hampshire), where the Norman castle was built in the corner of a late Roman Saxon Shore fort re-purposed as a *burh*. Barry Cunliffe's large-scale excavations on the site identified a late Anglo-Saxon timber hall and adjacent stone tower within the outer bailey of the castle that probably equate to a thegnly (or aristocratic) 'church and dwelling' complex.[60] Given that a much-discussed Anglo-Saxon legal document lists the possession of a 'bell-house' and '*burh*-gate' as prerequisites of thegnly status, it might be significant that the tower commanded views over, and would have appeared to rise above, the gated entrances to the old Roman fort.[61] Domesday Book records a *halla* (hall) at Portchester, which could refer to either the Anglo-Saxon hall or the first Norman keep, although it is not entirely certain that the word should be equated with an architectural feature.[62]

A second archaeologically well-attested sequence of a Saxon aristocratic site converted into a castle in the region is at Trowbridge (Wiltshire). While nothing of significance survives above ground, rescue excavation in the late 1980s provided a clear mapping of the site's impressive defences and highlighted that the Norman castle of the mid-twelfth century was built on a pre-existing manorial site with an adjacent church or chapel (Fig. 2.12). While the castle perpetuated an existing seat of power, the excavations highlight the disruptive impact of fortress-building: timber buildings associated with the Saxo-Norman manorial site were levelled to make way for the fortification and the land surface sealed with a thick band of clay.[63] The inner bailey was defended with a V-shaped moat 10m wide and 4.50m deep and a clay rampart also 10m across, and may have had a motte erected in one corner, although certain evidence of this was not obtained, while the outer bailey ditch was 11m wide and 5m deep, flat-bottomed and probably water-filled.[64] The castle certainly existed in 1139, when it was controlled by Humphrey de Bohun and besieged by King Stephen.[65]

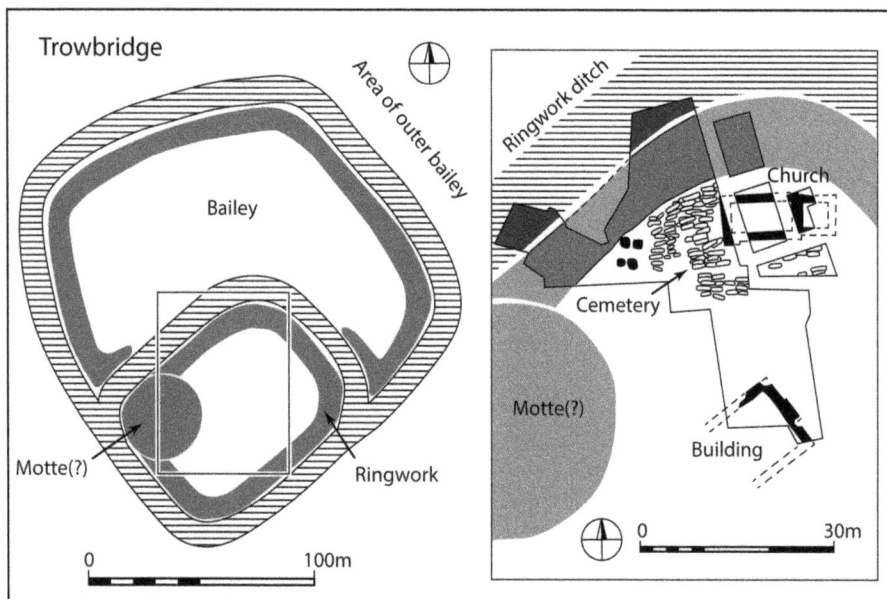

Fig. 2.12 Trowbridge castle.

Other sites are suggestive of pre-castle manorial occupation but not quite as clear. Excavations on the motte at Great Somerford, Wiltshire, while early and imperfectly recorded, suggest that the Norman earthwork was super-imposed over an earlier structure. In 1811, and again in 1910, investigation revealed substantial masonry remains encased within the motte, including a length of walling pierced by a doorway and two round-headed windows, as well as medieval pottery and evidence of burning.[66] It seems unlikely that the structure is a small Norman tower around which the motte was piled, because the architectural features would have been buried from view. Instead, the most likely explanation is that the building was part of a pre-existing thegnly site and/or church. Another likely example of a late Anglo-Saxon aristocratic site transformed into a castle is Castle Cary, Somerset; here, excavations on the Manor Farm site suggest that an oval enclosure – quite powerfully defended, with a ditch *c.* 10m across – forming part of the Anglo-Saxon settlement underlay the Norman castle, which comprised a keep and bailey, although the sequence isn't particularly clear.[67] At Castle Neroche, excavations by Brian K. Davison in the late 1960s suggested that the Norman motte was an addition to a pre-existing site and raised the possibility that this represented a late Anglo-Saxon pre-castle, although clear dating evidence for this was scanty and re-evaluation of the site suggests that the antecedent phase may be a prehistoric hillfort.[68]

The argument that the large, square, rubble-built tower known as St George's Tower within Oxford castle (Fig. 2.13) might be a late Anglo-Saxon aristocratic tower-nave rests mainly on the fact that it stood on the line of the *burh* defences, but dendrochronological dating of timbers within the structure did not reveal any pre-Conquest dates.[69] Another potential example of a Norman castle perpetuating a high-status Anglo-Saxon site in an urban context is Southampton, where excavations in the bailey in the 1980s

Fig. 2.13 St George's Tower, Oxford.

revealed a large underlying Saxon hall surrounded by a ditch or double ditch suggestive of enclosing defences.[70] If the castle was positioned to perpetuate this pre-existing seat of authority, as seems likely, this might account for its unusual positioning in the centre rather than in the corner of the town's defences, as was usual elsewhere.[71]

Castles and Conflict: Anarchy in Wessex?

Wessex was the epicentre of the conflict that raged in the middle years of the twelfth century between the forces of King Stephen (r. 1135–54) and the Angevin-sympathising supporters of his cousin and nemesis the Empress Matilda. Sometimes referred to as the 'Anarchy' (although this was not a contemporary term), this was a period of civil warfare and political turbulence in which castles featured prominently, although the exact levels of upheaval have been heavily debated, including in a recent project led by the author.[72] Campaigns criss-crossed the landscape, with the West Country generally and north Wiltshire and the Thames Valley specifically a focus for fighting and ravaging by armies that lived off the land and attacked the economic base of their rivals. For example, the chronicler of the *Gesta Stephani* comments how in 1139 raids between the castles of Devizes and Trowbridge had transformed the surrounding countryside into desert,[73] while in 1149 King Stephen and his son, Eustace, in a bitter scorched earth policy, 'raged with bestial cruelty' around Marlborough, attacked the hinterland of Devizes and laid waste to the 'fair and delightful' district around Salisbury (i.e. Old Sarum), plundering estates and burning houses, churches, fields and harvested crops.[74]

The conflict of Stephen's reign was a 'castle war', when fortresses dominated the strategic landscape.[75] Chronicles of the period are littered with accounts of castles built and strengthened as lords protected their assets and promoted their own interests amidst lawlessness and a vacuum of royal control, as well as others besieged, seized and forfeited in power plays between rivals.[76] Such was the insecurity and political turbulence that mints sometimes operated under the defensive shadow of some castle. For example, the discovery of a coin hoard at Box, Wiltshire, containing coins of unofficial 'rebel' issues, showed that Castle Combe, Marlborough and Trowbridge – all the sites of castles – operated short-lived mints in Stephen's reign.[77] Another probably operated from within the Angevin stronghold of Wallingford castle.[78] The coins corroborate the words of the late twelfth-century chronicler William of Newburgh, who stated that: 'Numerous castles had been raised in individual areas through the eager action of factions, and in England there were in a sense as many kings, or rather tyrants, as there were lords of castles. Each minted his own coinage, and each like a king had the power to lay down the law for his subjects.'[79]

Military installations built during the period that contemporary chroniclers styled as 'castles' did not necessarily equate to castles as understood by modern-day archaeologists and historians. A good example is the fortification constructed by King Stephen at Wilton in 1142–43. The account of Henry of Huntingdon has the king building a 'castle' (*castrum*) here although his men fled following a surprise attack by a large Angevin force.[80] However, the more detailed description of the struggle for the town in the *Gesta Stephani* has the king 'strengthening' a castle and then retreating to the town's nunnery.[81] We have no archaeological information on the nature of Stephen's fortification at Wilton, but the likelihood is that any defence-works entailed refurbishment of the Anglo-Saxon *burh* and occupation of the nunnery as a strongpoint and perhaps the royal headquarters. This occupation of an ecclesiastical site as a temporary campaign-base was repeated elsewhere in Wessex, including Wherwell Priory (Hampshire) in 1141.[82]

Another interesting case in point is Cricklade, the site of an Anglo-Saxon *burh* and another alleged Anarchy-period castle in north Wiltshire. Here, excavations in 1975 provided evidence for a late phase of re-fortification of the Anglo-Saxon rampart, including a massive palisade and concentric inner and outer ditches.[83] There is good reason to think that these works represent the 'castle' (*castellum*) built here by William of Dover in 1144, rather than this forming a separate fortification.[84] Archaeological excavations at Christchurch and Bath provide other evidence of Anglo-Saxon burghal fortifications given Anarchy-period upgrades.[85] All these examples remind us that contemporary chroniclers could see and describe a wide range of different types of fortifications as castles, including towns and ecclesiastical sites requisitioned as military bases.

A further important dimension to castle-building, which this chapter concludes by considering, is the prominent role of siege castles (or 'counter-castles') – temporary mini-castles built to besiege and blockade enemy strongholds – in twelfth-century warfare. Given the intensity of the conflict in Wessex, it is unsurprising that Wessex features a considerable number of attested or surviving examples, including at Malmesbury (1144), Corfe (1139), Castle Cary (1147), Faringdon (1145), Oxford (1142) and Wallingford (1139, 1146, 1152–53).[86] Many more probably await discovery. Wallingford was the most besieged castle in England and had a ring of siege castles around it from three successive sieges, although the chroniclers' accounts are difficult to reconcile with evidence on the ground.[87] The survival rate of siege castles is very poor, however. None of the sites survive as an earthwork, although one has been identified through development-led excavation (Fig. 2.16).[88] Another good case in point is Oxford, where one or more 'lost' siege castles from Stephen's siege of 1142 were depicted (but unnamed) on maps of the sixteenth, seventeenth and eighteenth centuries, but were later built over and lost.[89]

Fig. 2.14 Corfe castle, Dorset, showing the likely earthwork of a mid-twelfth-century siege castle known as 'The Rings' being surveyed in the foreground.

Only exceptionally do earthworks of siege castles survive, but where they do archaeological survey can shed new light on their forms, origins, contexts and purposes.[90] The earthwork known as 'The Rings' close to Corfe castle, Dorset (Figs 2.14 and 2.16) was, in common with most other surviving siege castles, built as a ringwork and bailey. Constructed *c.* 300m to the south-west of Corfe castle (and therefore beyond bowshot), it was clearly not a platform for direct assault or bombardment but was built to blockade, observe and intimidate its 'prey' and perhaps as a statement of resolve, as sieges of the period could be lengthy. While it seems very likely that the site was built during King Stephen's siege of 1139, we cannot be certain as no siege castle is actually documented.[91] We know very little about how siege castles were fortified, what went on within their defences, and whether they contained buildings. At Danes Castle, Exeter (probably built during King Stephen's siege of 1136) (Fig. 2.16), excavation revealed the ringwork interior to be featureless and archaeologically sterile, although there were signs that a timber gatehouse structure had been started but not finished.[92] At Cam's Hill, near Malmesbury (*c.* 1144), geophysical survey similarly shows furnishing of its entrance with a tower gateway (Fig. 2.15).[93]

Fig. 2.15 Aerial view of Cam's Hill, near Malmesbury, Wiltshire –
a likely siege castle of the mid-twelfth century.

A siege castle earthwork within parkland at Hamstead Marshall, Berkshire, is especially informative, as it seems to represent a partly completed work (Fig. 2.16). A marking-out ditch defined the circular perimeter of the castle earthwork, which was created by transporting spoil up an earthwork ramp on the north side of the site, and geophysical survey provides tantalising evidence of an internal tower-like structure.[94] The monument is one of three castle earthworks within the parish, lying 800m east of two adjacent motte-and-bailey castles, one of which seems to have succeeded the other.[95] The most likely context for the siege castle is King Stephen's 1152–53 siege of the 'lost' castle of Newbury, which he took by assault.[96] Archaeological excavation in the area of Newbury Wharf, where 'Newbury castle' was traditionally thought to lie, has identified no evidence of a fortification there,[97] and an alternative explanation is that the 'lost' castle is more convincingly associated with the remains in Hamstead Marshall Park.[98]

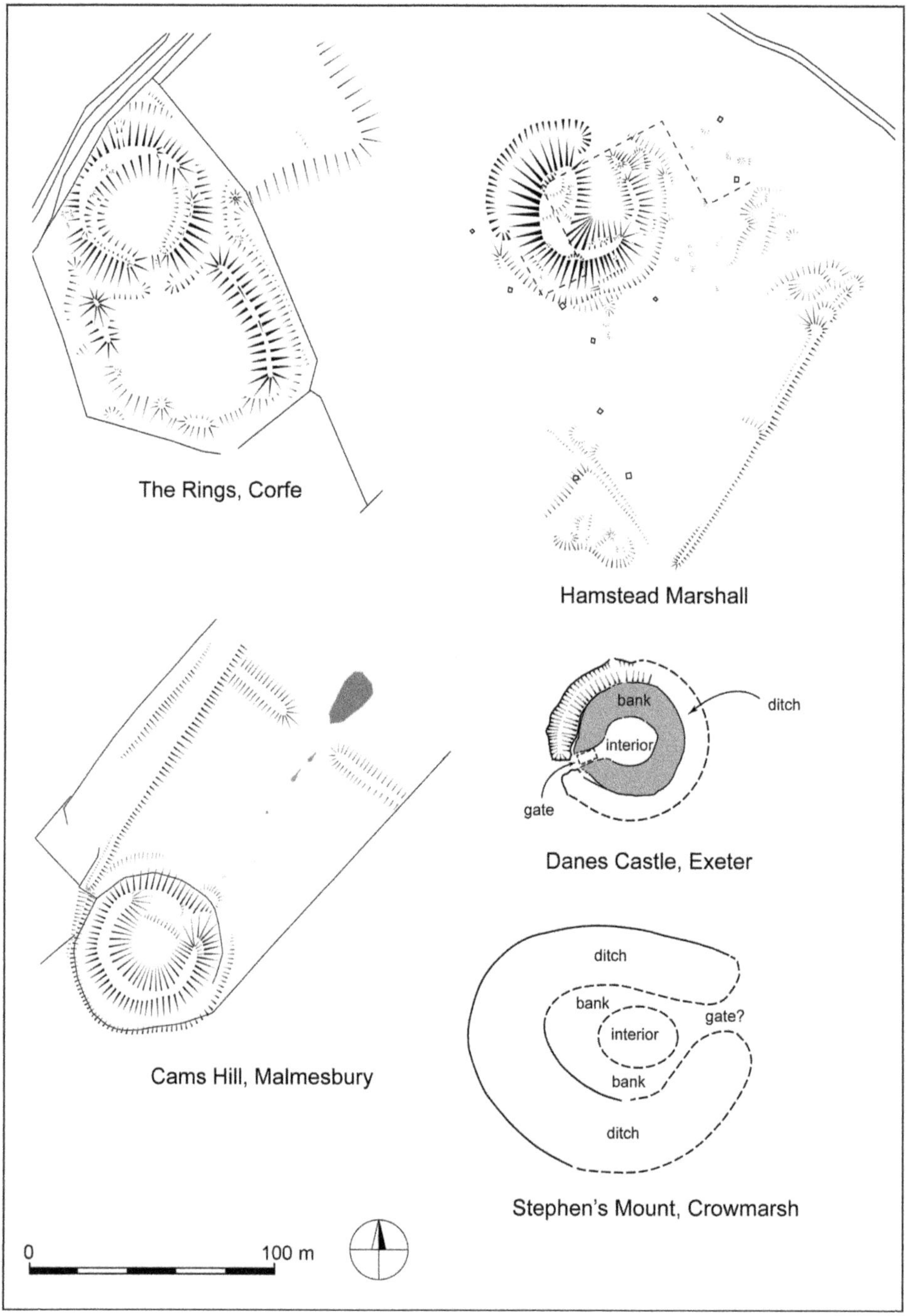

The Rings, Corfe

Hamstead Marshall

bank
interior
ditch
gate

Danes Castle, Exeter

Cams Hill, Malmesbury

ditch
bank
interior
gate?
bank
ditch

Stephen's Mount, Crowmarsh

0   100 m

Fig. 2.16 Siege castles: plans.

Conclusions

Through a survey of the archaeological and historical evidence for Norman castles in Wessex, this chapter has revealed great variety in the social standing of their builders and owners; in the chronology of their construction; and in the locations, appearances, technologies, planning, purposes and prehistories of the sites themselves. The discussion also underlines that we should not evaluate Norman castle-building in Wessex purely from the more impressive and better-known sites with standing remains that survive today. Some exceptionally grand masonry complexes have left no above-ground vestiges; earth and timber sites typically give a misleading impression of what could be impressive lordly edifices; and other sites are lost entirely. Indeed, so diverse are the castles in question – ranging from temporary and fleetingly documented military fieldworks to expansive quasi-palatial complexes built by the great and the good of the Norman world – that it might prompt us to question why we should indeed continue to identify them with the word 'castle'.

3

Marlborough Castle in the Middle Ages

Richard Barber

We now change focus from the broad context of the castles in the landscape of Wessex to the specific case of Marlborough. Where does Marlborough stand in the hierarchy of royal residences, and what features does it share with other contemporary royal castles? Was it militarily effective or simply for show? How frequently was it used by the kings? And how did it evolve between its creation in the eleventh century and the beginning of its decay in the late fourteenth century?

The recent discovery that the mounds at Marlborough and Silbury are almost twins is a contrast to their appearances today. Silbury rises out of its solitary valley, sharply outlined against the surrounding landscape, while Marlborough is hemmed in by buildings, and until recently was almost entirely masked by trees. Yet until the Norman Conquest their histories were very similar. The Romans settled near Silbury, but the mound seems to have played no particular part in the life of the small village at its foot. At Marlborough likewise, the mound was simply a feature of the surroundings for the small borough which had grown up next to it by the eleventh century, at the centre of a small royal estate.[1]

After 1066, Silbury remained undisturbed. In Domesday Book, Marlborough is not listed among the towns held by the king, though one-third of the taxes raised there were paid to the royal exchequer. This implies that it may have been a fief, rather than being held directly by the king, though it is not among the fiefs listed for Wiltshire. The charter in 1204 by which King John granted the growing settlement at Marlborough the right to hold markets twice weekly, and an annual fair at the end of August, is addressed to the 'borough and burgesses of Marlborough'. It also details the right of the borough to jurisdiction and liberties similar to that of towns such as Winchester and Oxford.[2] The borough had become an independent, if ill-defined, entity, and the 'men of Marlborough' paid an annual fee to the treasury. What is certain is that the status and wealth of the town in the thirteenth century was closely linked to the development of the castle. In many cases, castles were built in the context of existing large settlements, but Marlborough is nearer to the other extreme, where a town grows up around a newly built castle.

The Fortress, *c.* 1100–1216

The Norman kings, c. 1070–1135

When the first of the new Norman lords of England came to Marlborough, probably in the spring of 1067, they would have found a small settlement on the crossroads of two important roads. These were the Roman road from London to Bath and the later road from Cirencester to the religious centres of Wilton and Amesbury which continued to Salisbury and the port at Weymouth. What would have struck them immediately was the prehistoric mound, which towered over the modest houses beneath. Here was a ready-made castle motte of the kind which their fellow-invaders were laboriously building the length and breadth of England. Castle-builders had always taken advantage of natural features, particularly in mountainous areas, but in the rolling landscape of the Wiltshire downs there were no such opportunities. In his survey of 741 English mottes, D. J. Cathcart King classifies 'large mottes' as those over ten metres high, with a probable total of forty-seven in all.[3] Of these, four in the south-west use natural features, conical hills or tors reshaped to form the mound. Marlborough is among the very largest of all the mottes, at nineteen metres high, eighty-four metres diameter at the base, and thirty metres at the top.

The types of small fortifications found on eleventh- and twelfth-century mottes have been recently analysed in a substantial essay by Robert Higham.[4] Using this survey to identify possible parallels, and such details about the Marlborough motte as we have, we can make a tentative case that the original structure may have been in timber, either a timber palisade forming a defendable space where a garrison force could encamp, or a timber tower with a timber palisade.[5] In a region richer in stone than timber, the idea of a timber tower seems unlikely. However, any archaeological evidence which might indicate what the original castle was like has been destroyed by subsequent building activities on the mound.[6]

Historical sources do not specify directly that there is a castle at Marlborough before 1138. We know that the king kept Æthelric, bishop of the South Saxons, under guard here in 1070 after he was deposed at an unauthorised synod at Windsor held by Ermenfrid, bishop of Sion. His confinement would imply a secure building belonging to the king, but not necessarily a castle.[7] However, there is good reason to think that a castle may have existed from the late eleventh century onwards. In 1100, the first year of Henry I's reign, the king stopped at Marlborough on his return from a major royal council at Old Sarum, the predecessor of modern Salisbury.[8] Six years later, he was at Marlborough again en route to Salisbury for Whitsun.[9] He was waiting to cross the Channel to secure his claim to Normandy, and the Anglo-Saxon Chronicle notes that he did not hold the traditional Whitsun court because of his imminent departure.[10]

Four years later, in 1110, the Anglo-Saxon Chronicle records that courts were held at all three of the great feasts of the Church:

> In this year king Henry held his court at Christmas at Westminster, and at Easter he was at Marlborough, and at Whitsuntide he held his court for the first time at the New Windsor.[11]

The writer of this version of the Chronicle frequently notes where Henry is at each of these feasts, and also tells us when Henry was abroad or did not wear his crown on the feast day. The sites visited by Henry on the three great Church festivals are very restricted throughout his reign: Westminster is most frequent, particularly in the early years, followed by Windsor and Winchester. Three royal castles figure, at Odiham in Hampshire and the great fortresses at Northampton and Norwich. Two other places are not castles. Dunstable was a substantial royal residence, while Brampton in Huntingdonshire was a hunting lodge frequently visited by Henry I and Henry II. In the early thirteenth century, men remembered that Henry I and his queen had worn their crowns in the wooden church there at three festivals. In addition to these, Henry was at the great royal monastery at St Albans for one such occasion.[12]

The fact that a crown-wearing was held at Marlborough does not therefore mean that there was necessarily a castle here. The royal accommodation at Marlborough could have been a hunting lodge similar to Brampton, with Savernake forest nearby. Such royal houses could be substantial in the twelfth century.[13] At Marlborough it is the context of the mound which makes it almost certain that the royal residence was a castle, and possibly a substantial one.

From the Anarchy to the death of King John (1135–1216)

The Anarchy, which followed Henry I's death in 1135, brought Marlborough to prominence. When Stephen came to the throne in that year, he appointed John the Marshal as castellan of Marlborough. This is the first clear evidence of a castle here. John was the hereditary marshal of England, having succeeded his father Gilbert in that office in 1130, and an important figure at court. In 1138, after Robert earl of Gloucester's change of allegiance to the rival claimant, Matilda, daughter of Henry I, the chronicler at Osney Abbey, near Oxford, records that Bristol and Marlborough were the two best fortified castles in the south-west. He calls them *munitissima*, which implies that they were not only strongholds, but also that they were well garrisoned and provisioned, ready for war in every sense.[14] Both had been royal castles, and were given by Matilda to Robert, now the leader of her supporters in England.

Robert rebuilt Bristol as one of the grandest castles in the region, and indeed in England. Its donjon[15] was very large, measuring 29m by 36m, according to a fifteenth-century writer. It had towers at the corners, and was designed to reflects the earl's power. Marlborough's status was rather different. It was at this period a second-rank royal castle, and its donjon would in any case have been restricted in size by the pre-existing mound. The monk who wrote the annals of Winchester, a year by year record of important events, tells us that in 1138 numerous castles were built in the West Country. Henry of Blois, bishop of Winchester, younger brother of King Stephen, fortified his palace with a strong tower, and commissioned works on five other castles. Roger, bishop of Salisbury, built Salisbury, Devizes, Malmesbury and Sherborne. Robert earl of Gloucester was responsible for building or fortifying six castles besides Bristol. John the Marshal built or rebuilt Marlborough and Ludgershall, a small castle on the southern edge of Savernake forest.[16]

When Robert of Gloucester became the leader of Matilda's cause in 1138, John the Marshal soon followed, retaining his position as castellan of Marlborough after his change of allegiance. John seems to have decided to use the castle as a base for his own independent activities; the chronicler at Worcester thought he supported earl Robert, while another writer said that he was still the king's man. The author of *The Deeds of Stephen* says of John the Marshal that 'he built castles, designed with wondrous skill, in the places that best suited him'.[17]

Marlborough lay in a key position on the border between Stephen's supporters in London and Winchester and the lands of Matilda's supporters around Bristol and Gloucester. In 1139, King Stephen moved to retrieve the castle from John the Marshal. Marlborough was an important enough target for the king himself to lead the army attacking it. The siege began in July, but when, on 1 August, Stephen heard that Robert of Gloucester had landed in England and established himself at Arundel, he abandoned the operation and set out to attack Robert instead.

In the spring of 1140, Devizes castle was treacherously captured by Robert, a Flemish mercenary, who intended to use it as a base for dominating the countryside around, owing allegiance to no-one. He pretended to want an alliance with John the Marshal, but the latter was suspicious. When Robert came to Marlborough with a body of men, ostensibly for negotiations, John seized him and his companions, and imprisoned him 'in a narrow dungeon to suffer hunger and tortures'. John handed him over to Robert of Gloucester, who hanged him outside Devizes.[18] John was with Matilda when she besieged Stephen's brother Henry of Blois at Winchester. She was forced to retreat when he set fire to the city, and John was seriously injured in the fighting.[19]

Henry II and Richard I

When Henry II succeeded Stephen, John the Marshal was still castellan of Marlborough and Ludgershall. He seems to have lost Ludgershall castle at the beginning of the new reign, and in 1158, he also lost Marlborough, just before Henry left England for the best part of five years, to attend to his French territories. Soon after the king returned to England at Easter 1163, John the Marshal was in disgrace, along with various Welshmen, for saying that, according to 'an obscure pseudo-prophet', Henry would never come back from his expedition.[20] The prophet in question was undoubtedly Merlin: Geoffrey of Monmouth had written *The Prophecies of Merlin* in 1135, and the extremely 'obscure' predictions he attributed to Merlin were to cause political trouble for centuries to come, as a source of justifications for stirring up trouble.

At some time during the reign of Henry II, or possibly even as late as 1215, Marlborough was linked with Merlin. In Geoffrey of Monmouth's *History of the Kings of Britain*, Merlin transports Stonehenge from Ireland to its present site. He does so after the British have failed to move them after trying everything they can: 'Merlin laughed at their failure, then prepared contrivances of his own … when everything was ready, he took down the stones with incredible ease.'[21] Henry II was known to be interested in the Arthurian legends, and he may even have encountered them as a boy at the court of Robert of Gloucester, one of the dedicatees of the *History*, soon after the book was written. Richard presented Excalibur to Tancred of Sicily in 1191, and John claimed to possess Tristan's sword. The first identification of Marlborough as 'Merlin's barrow' is in a Latin poem by Alexander Neckam, abbot of Cirencester, and we know that he was at Marlborough on 8 July 1215, attending the royal court there.[22] It is just possible that this learned writer was the inventor of the story. In his poem *In Praise of Divine Wisdom*, which includes a passage on the mythical origins of English place names, he explains that

> The tomb of Merlin gave you, o Marlborough, your name;
> The English language is my witness.[23]

This derivation was picked up by later historical writers, though none of the Arthurian romances mention it.

John the Marshal died in 1165, but the office of marshal passed first to his son Gilbert, and then to the latter's brother William. By 1176, Gilbert appears to have been in charge of the castle.[24] He may have taken over from Alan de Neville, the king's chief forester, who died in that year.

It was at this time that the quarrel between Henry II and Thomas Becket, newly consecrated as archbishop of Canterbury, developed. Henry was at Marlborough for his Christmas court in 1164, and the following day the royal council, in session at the castle, issued the orders confiscating the properties of the see of Canterbury, because Becket had fled to France two months earlier. In the next decade, the king was at Marlborough in October 1175. He evidently decided that the castle needed improvement if he was to come here again. This is the moment at which the surviving royal records of building activity at Marlborough begin. For the year 1175–76 the annual accounts of the exchequer record the purchase of free stone, costing £43, and of seven hundred boards from Winchester to build the king's chamber.[25] He then visited three times between January and June 1177, when four hundred squared stones were procured for 'work at Marlborough, followed by 176,200 wooden roof tiles and 40,000 nails the next year. There were also twenty pickaxes, which implies general repairs as well as the roofing operation.[26]

Henry's last visit, in 1186, was a major occasion. He came to Marlborough on 6 September with William the Lion of Scotland, once his bitter enemy but now an ally, whose marriage had just been celebrated at Woodstock. A week later, a great council of the church was held here to elect the archbishop of York and the bishops of Salisbury and Exeter, at which most of the English bishops were present.[27]

Although Henry spent relatively little time actually at Marlborough, this part of England, the heart of the old English kingdom of Wessex with its capital at Winchester, remained important for the English kings until the fourteenth century. The Norman kings had inherited the royal estates of their Saxon predecessors, and the bulk of these were in this area. During the century after the Conquest, many grants of land from this royal patrimony were made to leading officials of the royal court. In the early years of Henry II's reign, we find his justiciar, Richard de Lucy, his chamberlains and the royal stewards among the beneficiaries. These men were frequently needed at court, and the proximity of their estates was a convenient arrangement.

The royal castles and hunting lodges in Wessex were those which Henry II and his immediate heirs most frequently visited when they were outside London.[28] Woodstock, near Oxford, was a site used by the Anglo-Saxon kings, and it was Henry I who developed it as a royal residence. It was, according to a contemporary chronicler, the 'favourite seat of his retirement and privacy',[29] and records show frequent visits by the king. Here Henry kept an extraordinary zoo, which attracted the attention of several other writers.[30] He may have built the 'spacious church-like hall' with two aisles of six pillars which is recorded by a visitor in 1634. Henry II retained his grandfather's affection for Woodstock, where he carried out an almost continuous programme of building works on the house itself, including a new chamber in 1176–77. His most substantial work there was a garden palace at Everswell close to the main house, the setting for his famous affair with Rosamond.[31]

Henry I and his successors also spent much time at Clarendon near Salisbury, where a modest hunting lodge in the New Forest, possibly founded by the Anglo-Saxon kings of Wessex, was developed into a palatial complex of buildings. These, like Woodstock, could house a large gathering, such as the famous council of Clarendon in 1164 at which Henry II's quarrel with Thomas Becket came to a head. Marlborough lay halfway between these two sites, and Winchester was also a day's ride away. It was frequently the stopping place on journeys between Clarendon and Woodstock: these excursions were for the royal sport of hunting. Both Clarendon and Woodstock had exceptionally large deer parks.

Henry's eldest son, known as Henry 'the young king', rebelled against his father in 1173; the revolt was quickly crushed, and in 1174 a charter setting out the terms of the settlement was sealed. Its terms included the provision that Henry II should be entitled to grant John, who as his youngest son had no great domains of his own, various lands in England, including the castle of Marlborough, and that the young king would not challenge these grants.[32] It is not clear whether the grant was actually made during Henry's lifetime.

At the beginning of Richard I's reign, in 1189, Marlborough was the scene of a royal wedding. Richard arranged a match between his younger brother John and Isabella, the heiress to the earldom of Gloucester. At the wedding, Richard either confirmed or executed the proposed grant of 1174.[33] The marriage was opposed by Hubert Walter, the archbishop of Canterbury, and when it had taken place, John's lands were placed under an interdict. John rebelled against his brother in 1194, and it was Walter who recaptured Marlborough for the king in anticipation of the return of Richard I from crusade. Walter had until recently been bishop of Salisbury and therefore a local magnate, and he was able to assemble a great army with ease. The siege lasted only a few days, and Walter went on to take two more neighbouring castles with little difficulty. The costs of part of the siege operations and the repair of the castle after it was taken were entered in the royal accounts:

> For 59 mattocks and one bundle of iron and 4000 crossbow bolts with bows, and cartage from London to Marlborough, 55s. 4d.; and for shields bought and sent from London to Marlborough, 12s. 6d.; and for one stone-thrower[34] brought from Marlborough to Salisbury … and for two carts hired to convey lime from Andover to Marlborough for the repair of the castle, 7s. 3d. And for the overhaul of the stone-thrower and mangonel which were at Winchester and bringing the same to Marlborough and taking them back again, and for 30 mattocks and 20 shields and 12 ladders brought from Winchester to Marlborough, and for the purchase of pitch and sulphur, 11s. 2d.
>
> And for the cost of bringing one stone thrower and one mangonel from Reading to Marlborough, 76s. 4d.
>
> And to the soldiers in charge of the engines at Marlborough, 4s.[35]

Another stone-thrower and mangonel were brought from Reading, transported in carts lent to Hubert by the abbot and monks of Reading; he wrote to them asking for their help on 14 February, very soon after the news of Richard's release from captivity and return to England had reached him.[36] The purchase of sulphur and pitch indicates that flaming missiles were used, and as most of the buildings in the bailey were timber rather than stone, this could have been very effective.

Following this escapade, John's estates were declared forfeit, but he was reinstated as count of Mortain and to the honour of Gloucester when Richard pardoned him later that year. It is not clear whether he regained Marlborough before his brother's death in 1199. Richard himself never visited Marlborough after 1189 in the short periods that he spent in England after returning from crusade.

The royal records

From 1200 onwards, the records kept by the royal exchequer increased very rapidly, and a large number of these survive. The nature of these records is critical to what we know about Marlborough castle, and a brief explanation is needed. The best illustration of the change in culture is to look at the phrase 'time immemorial' used in English law. In 1275, it was declared by statute that if anyone had owned or occupied property since before 1199, they did not need to prove ownership by producing documents, but could rely on witnesses. From 1200 onwards, documents were declared essential. This marks the watershed between a primarily oral culture and a world where writing was paramount.

Both the chancery and the exchequer respectively kept a record of royal transactions and finances in four forms, and these were written on parchment sheets stitched at the head into bundles, which were then rolled up: almost all records were kept as rolls of this kind. Copies of letters with the royal seal attached at the foot were open or 'letters patent', in effect public declarations, while letters which were sent privately were 'letters close', for the addressee only. Both of these types contained orders from the king; in the case of Marlborough these would be sent to the constable of the castle.

The constable would then submit an annual account to the sheriff of Wiltshire, who would summarise it and pass it on to the exchequer. These annual accounts survive as far back as 1130, and are called 'pipe' rolls, from their similarity when rolled up for storage to a pipe. When the order from the king and the corresponding pipe roll entry both survive, we can see the actual work completed by the constable. On occasion, there would be repeated instructions from the king about works which had not been carried out.

A rarer and intriguing survival are the detailed accounts submitted to the constable by the clerk of the works. These specify precisely what the workmen employed did on a daily basis, and one such document for 1238–39 is printed in Appendix B. This covers the wages and activities of everyone from the skilled workers making padlocks for the windows to the women who acted as water-carriers for the masons.

Finally, there are the *liberate* rolls, where the money delivered to the sheriff in payment of his account is recorded. The entries marked 'contrabreve' duplicated the king's instructions recorded on the rolls of patent and close letters, and include items which do not appear on either of these. On the other hand, they only record specific payments (headed *allocate*) or settlements of whole accounts (headed *computate*).

Jeremy Ashbee emphasised the value of these documents in his lecture at Marlborough in 2015 as follows:

> Henry III's documentation for sites all across England runs to several thousand instructions of this kind: about buildings, decoration, furnishing, provisioning with food, and sometimes stern reprimands when the king found the results unsatisfactory. Little wonder that Henry III has the reputation he does today:- of someone whose political ineptitude was counter-balanced by deeper interests in the material trappings of kingship. And we are very fortunate that the documentation for Marlborough Castle occasionally runs to an even greater height of prolixity.[37]

King John: the castle as royal centre

John continued the tradition of extensive royal journeys based on the kingdom of Wessex. These tours amounted to about 15 per cent of the time he was in England during his reign. After Winchester, Marlborough was the place he visited most often, followed closely by Woodstock and Clarendon. Like his father, he loved hunting. Nineteen of his fifty-one visits to the castle were preceded or followed by a stay at either of these royal houses or at Ludgershall, and were therefore likely to have been hunting expeditions.

However, it was under John that Marlborough became a major administrative centre. This was in part due to the fact that the castellan of Marlborough was Hugh de Neville, who held the office of chief justice of the king's forests. The Neville family had been associated with Marlborough since 1158, when Alan de Neville was given land there, the year before he was first mentioned as the king's forester. He may have been Hugh's grandfather. Hugh, like Alan, presided over the forest exchequer, which was independent of the main royal exchequer, and its proceedings were on occasion held at Marlborough. As a young man, Hugh had been a close companion of Richard I, and had accompanied him on crusade. Richard appointed him as forester in 1198. His first action had been to hold a tyrannical inspection of the forests, described as 'a torment that confused the men of the kingdom' following as it did hard on the heels of an oppressive enforcement of other laws, with correspondingly large fines, by the royal justices. The forest laws were highly restrictive and unpopular, and his predecessor Alan had had an even worse reputation.[38] John confirmed Hugh in his office, and despite a stormy relationship with the king, Hugh remained on John's side during the negotiations over Magna Carta in 1215. The establishment of a treasury at Marlborough castle, discussed below, was clearly connected with the collection of forest fines by Hugh. During this period substantial sums were drawn by the king, for example 'various large sums' in 1208 and 4700 marks (£3133) in January 1209.[39]

At two moments in John's reign, Marlborough castle was centre stage. The first was just after the pope had placed England under an interdict in 1209 because John refused to accept the pope's candidate for the archbishopric of Canterbury. Fearing that this interdict might lead to a rebellion, 'in great ceremonies around the country, climaxing in one at Marlborough, all the freemen of the kingdom were summoned to do homage to the king and to Henry as the king's heir.'[40]

The gathering in 1209 for what has been called 'the Oath of Marlborough' is particularly interesting because of its scale. There is scant mention of it in the chronicles, but John Maddicott rescued the event from obscurity by collating a number of different sources which mention it and give a number of separate details. He concludes:

> Though we have only an inadequate knowledge of the identity of those appearing at Marlborough, the sources point to a huge gathering: the *universitas* of England, according to the London annalist. It almost certainly included the Londoners, quite probably other townsmen (to judge by the pipe roll evidence) and quite possibly additional numbers of rural freemen. On no other occasion that we know of in the history of medieval England was there a comparable mass assembly at one central place; nor, with the possible exception of army musters, are we able to recall any other occasion when a king appeared in person before a multitude of his ordinary subjects. … It is again hard to avoid the conclusion that this was another aspect of 1209 that was unique.[41]

Although John was a frequent visitor to Marlborough, he did not make any major changes to the castle. In 1205, he ordered new kitchens to be built at Marlborough and Ludgershall 'for making the king's meals, each to include a fireplace for cooking two or three oxen'. There are also occasional entries concerned with the defence of the castle. In 1199, immediately after Richard's death, knights and foot soldiers were sent to Marlborough and Ludgershall and two other castles; their wages amounted to £40.[42] Several records concern the garrison: there is a letter from John to Hugh de Neville about arrangements for the manning of the castle while the king was in Yorkshire in 1207.[43] The provision of weapons was secured by installing a resident maker of crossbows in 1205: Peter the crossbowman was given a house in the castle for making crossbows, and was allowed 6d a day for his wife and servant; like other castle servants, he was given robes annually, from 1207 onwards. His successor, William, seems to have replaced him by 1225, when the constable was instructed to buy crossbow staves at Southampton, evidently from a shipment which had just arrived, for William's use at Marlborough.

From the death of Henry II to the accession of Henry III, there is only one year when substantial building work was done, namely 1211–12. Much of it was to do with strengthening the defences in a time of trouble: the stockades and drawbridges were overhauled, and the motte was given a surrounding wall. The entry to the motte was reinforced with a barbican in front of the gate. The 'great chamber' was given a lead roof, the castle walls were mended, and the accommodation in the bailey was repaired.[44] When matters came to a head in 1215 before the signing of Magna Carta, John organised the defences at Marlborough. On 10 May, he wrote to Peter de Chanceaux, constable of Bristol castle and one of his 'corps of strong-arm agents' who were specifically named in Magna Carta to be 'utterly removed from their offices',[45] to send him all the helmets and iron hats and half the armguards which he had in his stores, as well as ten thousand crossbow bolts and all the crossbows, leaving only enough of the latter for his garrison.[46]

Three days later, John rejected the proposals which the barons had put forward at Oxford six days earlier, and on the same day he went from Wallingford to Marlborough. Here he summoned troops to join him from Devon. On 14 May, eleven crossbows, ballistas and stones, three helmets and an iron hat arrived from Peter de Chanceaux. John also ordered fifty horn crossbows to be supplied from elsewhere: forty one-foot bows, ten two-foot bows 'and all the quarrels you can get' (Fig. 3.1). He then moved on to Trowbridge, and it was here that he issued instructions to Richard de

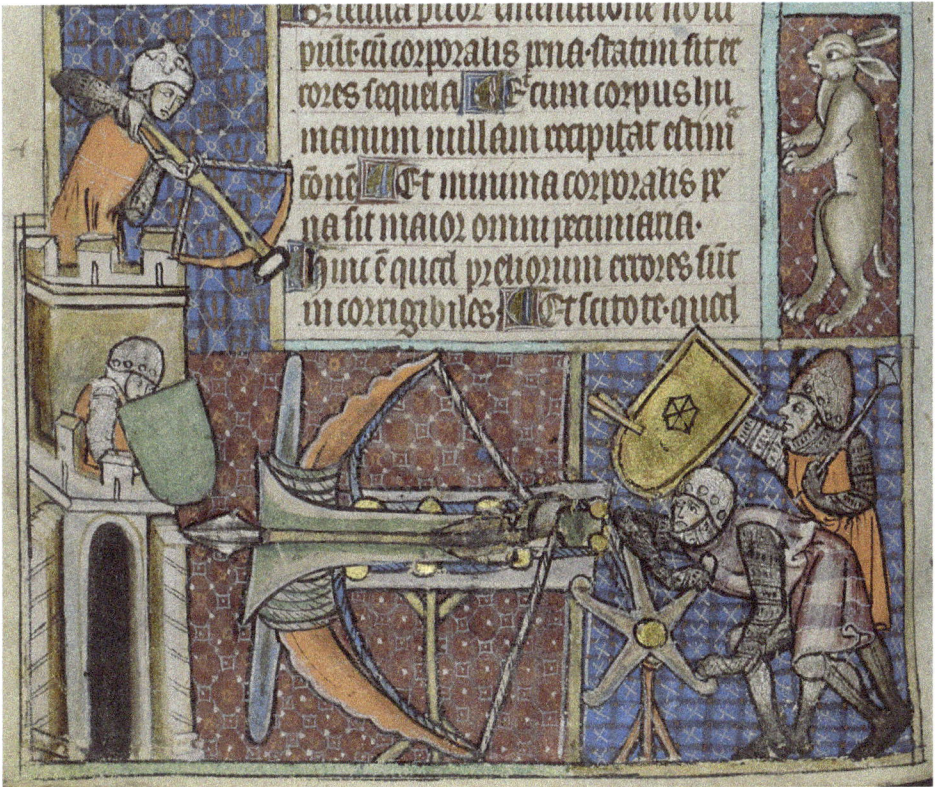

Fig. 3.1 Ballista (in centre) and crossbow (upper left) from Walter Milemete's treatise on kingship, 1326.

Mariscis, the chancellor, and Hugh de Neville, then at Winchester, telling them to send the queen and prince Henry, escorted by William de Faleis and Maurice de Turville, to Marlborough immediately.[47] The king was back at Marlborough on 15 May; two days later he heard that the barons had taken London and he then left to establish himself at Windsor. It is not clear how long the queen and prince Henry were at Marlborough, but it was obviously regarded as a safe refuge for them while the king rallied his forces.[48]

After the death of John in the autumn of 1216, the barons who had opposed him offered the throne to prince Louis of France. When Louis invaded England, the castellan of Marlborough surrendered the castle to Louis and joined his supporters. It is at this point that William Marshal, the son of John the Marshal, castellan of Marlborough, having served Henry II and his sons loyally, reached the peak of his career. On John's death, William Marshal, already earl of Pembroke, became regent of England, and took command of the campaign against Louis. Early in 1217, William Marshal's son William besieged Marlborough castle; the biographer of the elder William reports that while he was besieging Rochester, his son came to him and said: 'Truly, sire, I say we should be more concerned with taking Marlborough, for it is ours by right.'[49] John the Marshal's tenure of the castle was still clearly remembered: the younger William seems to have taken the castle on his own initiative. The garrison put up a strong resistance, and only surrendered after a siege lasting a month, not knowing that prince Louis was on his way to relieve them. A safe conduct was issued for Hugh Grosso and his men who had held the castle against him on 27 April, expiring five days later, which probably gives us the date of surrender.[50] William the elder, fearing that Louis would recapture the castles his forces had recently taken, is said to have had them all demolished, with the exception of the key fortress at Farnham in Kent.[51]

There is no other evidence about this demolition, which would have included Marlborough. The author of the biography of William Marshal uses the word 'trebuchier' to describe the operation: a contemporary poet used it in the context of the total destruction of Troy. This may be confirmed by an entry in the royal accounts in 1238 when a lime kiln was installed for 'finishing the great tower of the castle'. If the twelfth-century tower was still more or less intact, this work would have been described as repairs to an existing structure. Rather, the implication seems to be that major rebuilding had already taken place.

The Royal Residence

Royal court and household

Medieval kings travelled with their court, which was an impressive sight on its travels. Even the early royal visits would have involved large numbers of people, a crowd such as the spectators had probably never seen before. Until the beginning of the thirteenth century, most government officials remained in attendance on the king, wherever he might be. The treasury was of course an exception to this rule, and after 1200 other departments of state began to be permanently based in London. The real change came after the death of King John in 1216. John had travelled extensively because he used his journeys to raise revenue, in ways which were often oppressive, and which were part of the abuses ended by Magna Carta in 1215. From 1216 to 1226, before Henry came of age, he and the government spent half their time in London, as against an average of less than 10 per cent during John's reign.[52]

The travelling court consisted of a great mixture of people, and the arrival of a train of twenty or more carts, dozens of riders and two or three hundred people on foot would have had an enormous impact. At the centre was the king and his personal entourage, the household knights, who were part bodyguard, part household officers. There were clerks who sang in his chapel and administered the day-to-day transactions of the household. Then there was the manpower needed for the handling of the dozens of carts in the convoy, and the servants, from cooks to the squires who served at table. And there were the camp followers, such as the poor men who hoped to be fed by the king's almoner. Finally, there were the hangers-on, from heralds and musicians to the prostitutes. In the French court, the man in charge of this rabble was called 'king of the ribalds'; in England, he was 'master of the whores'.[53]

Visits to Marlborough castle might be irregular, but when the court did arrive, this mass of people had to be housed and fed. It is hard to estimate how many they were in total. John's court was probably smaller than that of either his father or his son. At the core of the royal retinue were the household knights. These were both the king's bodyguards and the core of his army; a fair number of them would have been in attendance at any given time. The total number is hard to estimate, since even when the knights were mustered for the army, where they formed a separate group, not all of them would have been present. Estimates for John and for Edward I are put at about one hundred knights, but at the maximum under Henry III, we find two hundred listed on the livery rolls for 1236 and 1237. Many of these may have received robes, but were not paid. Certainly, the group of knights regularly with the king on his travels was nearer to forty or fifty; the size of the chamber built for the knights in 1270 would seem to confirm this.[54]

A better overall measure of the official members of the court is that of the number of people who were entitled, as members of the household, to receive new clothing every year. Based on this, the royal court, from the most senior official to the humblest porter – all of whom would have received clothing – varied between three hundred and four hundred people, depending on whether the queen was also with the king. Not all of these would accompany the king and queen on their travels. And, of course, there is no way of estimating the number of those present who were not part of the court itself. Magnates would have their own attendants with them. Then there were those who followed the court. Anyone whose business was with the king on legal and administrative matters which only he could decide might have to follow the court for weeks on end before they could obtain a hearing. For a great assembly, such as that for the Oath of Marlborough in 1209, the numbers could be in the thousands. A total of 1800 people may have attended a similarly important gathering at Clarendon in 1164, and the scope of the Marlborough occasion was potentially much wider.[55]

The *Constitutio Domus Regis*, a handbook on the king's household compiled in 1135, is of particular interest if we are trying to look at the king's companions on his travels. The *domus* in this case is not the entire royal household, but those members of it who usually accompanied the king on his journeys. It lists over 150 individuals and their positions at court, from the king's chancellor to the bowmen who are part of the royal hunt, and gives their wages and perquisites.[56] The writer describes the four marshals and their servants who 'arrange lodging' under the direction of the officials and clerks of the household. They form the advance party, together with two of the bakers who 'travel ahead' taking with them enough wheat to bake 440 loaves. An essential part of the court's mobility were the carters, who travelled separately along the king's route, keeping within reasonable distance of him but not necessarily stopping at each place at which he stayed. The same must have been true of the bulk of the court, so that the arrival of the whole court at Marlborough would have consisted of different groups arriving in the course of a day or two.

The marshals' job of finding accommodation was not an easy one. At Marlborough, it is very probable that some houses in the town belonged to the king, as the chambers in the castle itself were occupied by the king and his family and the people employed in the castle, from the constable down to the gatekeeper. There may also have been specific houses which could provide lodgings for the court's use: but we have no records of transactions with the townsmen, and they do not figure in the castle's history except as recipients of royal gifts, usually timber with which to repair their houses. Many of the king's retinue were probably housed in tents, which would have been carried with other provisions and equipment as the court moved around the country. Entries about tents are rare in the records, and often refer to the tents needed for the army. The king had a 'pavilioner' who was responsible for them, but for at least part of Henry's reign they were kept by John Mansel, his tailor.[57]

We do know that quarrels over lodgings were a commonplace of court life, and on one occasion when the court arrived at Marlborough, a serious fracas broke out. Geoffrey de Mandeville, earl of Essex, sent his serjeants ahead to find lodgings. But shortly afterwards, the serjeants of William Brewer, who was constantly in attendance of the king and one of his most trusted officials, arrived and ejected Mandeville's men. When Geoffrey came to claim the lodgings, a fight ensued, and one of Brewer's servants was killed. Geoffrey, who was not in favour with the king, realised that he was in danger, and fled; it took several years for him to obtain the king's pardon.[58]

The size of the household was quite small in the years when the king was frequently at Marlborough: it is very hard to estimate, although we can follow the increase and decline from the total costs on the household's annual accounts. These start modestly during the king's minority and rise sharply in the 1230s, only to be cut back in the 1250s when money was being set aside for a proposed crusade.

We also know a good deal about the two royal stewards who ran the household, because they were regular witnesses to the charters issued by the king as he moved round the kingdom; one or both of them would usually have been with Henry when he was at Marlborough.

The actual work of feeding and housekeeping for the court was divided into a series of departments. We have the rolls for 1259–60, with the daily accounts which were audited by the stewards, and which include a visit to Marlborough from 15 September to 23 September 1260, when both Henry and Eleanor, his queen, were here.[59] We know that the queen was present because there are separate entries for her stable costs: she left a day earlier than the king. The kitchen costs are divided into pantry, buttery, kitchen, scullery, saucery and hunting larder. Food in general was purchased and prepared by the kitchen, the largest of these departments; venison from the hunting larder was the one exception. The pantry dealt with bread and linen for the table; the 'buttery' was in fact the butler, where wine and ale were provided. The scullery was so called from the dishes (*escuelle*) stored there, while the saucery provided the ingredients for the sauces which were central to medieval cookery.[60] In these accounts, fuel and other domestic expenses are listed for the hall and chamber. We can tell that the weather obviously turned cold while the court was here. No fuel was used in the chamber on the first two days, but five days later nearly 20d-worth of wood was needed. Stable expenses follow; entries for the queen's horses imply that she had roughly a quarter of the total recorded for the king.

There is just one occasion when we have details of a major feast at Marlborough. December 8 was the feast day of the Immaculate Conception of the Virgin Mary, 'that most English and controversial of Marian feasts.'[61] Both Henry and Eleanor (probably under his influence, as she was only twelve when the wedding took place) were devotees of the cult of Mary, and on this day he sometimes visited Walsingham, the chief shrine dedicated to the Virgin in England. In his absence, he would order thousands of candles to be sent there for the occasion. In December 1236 he was at Marlborough. Instructions were sent to his chamberlains in London to send supplies to him to await his arrival on 3 December. The first item was two thousand pieces of wax for candles, and these can only have been for the feast day, on 8 December. The rest of the list is food and linen appropriate to a feast: 40 pounds of dates, 6 baskets of figs, 25 boxes of raisins, 4 dozen napkins, 4 linen cloths, and 5 or 6 packets of good ginger. These were luxury items which would not have been held in stock at Marlborough; the rest of the food would have been obtained locally.[62] If the king was not present, instructions for supplies were sent by the king's clerks: in 1256, during the queen's extended stay here, there are orders in January, July and November for forty to fifty deer to be provided by the keeper of Savernake forest. Herrings and a hundred salted eels were supplied from Southampton in February, for Lent, as well as raisins, figs and almonds from London. The bulk of the latter were sent separately to the king, who was visiting Norfolk and Suffolk.[63]

Royal Administration

From the reign of Henry I onwards, the major departments of government gradually came to have permanent offices at Westminster. The king had a travelling staff of personnel who dealt with the business of the different sections, and only occasionally were there local offices at the royal castles. Marlborough had two of these, the treasury and the almonry.

The treasury[64]

The development of local treasuries under John is an intriguing story, which can only be outlined briefly here. Technically, all revenues came into the exchequer at Westminster, and all payments were made out of the exchequer. John, however, was always on the move, even more than his notoriously much travelled father. Taking money to London and then sending it out again to wherever the king might be was a cumbersome business. If cash was needed, the official procedure, established in Henry II's reign, was that a writ would be sent to Westminster or to the subsidiary treasury at Winchester requesting the cash, silver pennies in sacks or barrels of £100 each.[65] These had then to be transported by cart to a point on the king's journey, however distant.

This might suit the officials who ran the treasury, but its practical disadvantages meant that John wanted to short-circuit the system. The officers travelling with John collected money from debts and fines owed to the king, and paid it into the king's chamber. This was paid out again as needed, and the chamber accounted for the balance to the exchequer. However, this still meant that cash had to be obtained from the exchequer if there was a shortfall, and from 1200 onwards, John had experimented in Normandy with local treasuries in the ducal castles there, run by the constables.[66] After the loss of Normandy, a similar system evolved in England. Here there were three treasuries: Westminster, its subsidiary at Winchester, and the independent 'treasury of Ireland' at Bristol. In 1213, the latter held £80,000 (120,000 marks) in cash, equivalent to more than half the average annual revenue of

England.[67] Treasure at Bristol was held in the inmost vaults of the castle, only accessible by the constable in the presence of his co-custodians, who were burgesses of Bristol.

From 1207, 'half a dozen of [these castles] became permanent, standing reserves for the king's wars and journeys.'[68] As an opening deposit in July 1207, 10,000 marks were to be sent to Hugh de Neville at Marlborough; but it looks as if there was not enough cash available as, in April 1208, there was a general order that as revenue came into the exchequer it was to be diverted to the treasury at Marlborough.[69] From then on profits collected on the king's journeys were sent to the nearest provincial treasury, 'most commonly to the premier of all such centres in the south, to John's most favoured castle of Marlborough and its castellan Hugh de Neville.'[70]

This initial payment represented something like 2 per cent of the average annual revenue of the exchequer. The use of the treasury at Marlborough as a large-scale depository comes to an end with John's death; Henry III, who spent the fortune that his father had amassed, is only on record as using it once in this way, for money coming from Ireland which was probably on its way to Westminster.

King John's treasure

Before this treasury for royal revenue was established, John seems to have brought together his personal treasure at Marlborough, drawing up a list in the presence of witnesses, a *testamentum* or solemn declaration which was recorded on the charter rolls. The occasion took place at Marlborough on 28 April 1204, at a time when it was clear that Philip Augustus of France was about to drive John out of Normandy. The record was signed by Simon of Wells, bishop-elect of Chichester, at Winchester on 18 May.[71] It implies that Marlborough had somewhere secure in which to house the immense wealth that the list represents, perhaps in the keep. The treasury is not mentioned in the records as a separate place, and was probably, like that at Bristol, in the vaults of the keep or another building. Security would have been tight: at Bristol, the constable could only access the treasure by showing the citizens who were his fellow-custodians the king's writ, before removing the seals. It was then sealed again by all those present.[72]

It is not clear from the Marlborough document whether the various holders of royal treasure actually brought it with them. Because it was held in the presence of witnesses it seems likely that it was a physical audit, and it is the first such surviving list for any English king.

Five men close to the king were named as those responsible for bringing the royal treasure. Aimeric of St Maur, master of the Knights Templar in England, was the first, and had in his care the largest section of John's jewels, including the royal regalia. The Knights Templars were in effect the greatest bankers of the period; because of their wide network of priories throughout

Europe, they could transfer funds and lend money on a scale unrivalled by any of the merchant systems. St Maur was with John eleven years later when the king died. Robert, treasurer of the Knights Hospitaller in England, held another substantial collection, while John, abbot of Ford in Dorset, the king's confessor, and William, prior of Bradenstoke, a house of which Richard I had been a patron, brought much smaller quantities. The six jewelled belts from Waltham Abbey were brought by Geoffrey fitzPeter, earl of Essex, who had acted as regent of England when John was absent in Normandy in 1203.

The list is very detailed. The royal regalia consist of 'a great gold crown made at London, followed by a mantle, of red samite [the richest kind of silk] bordered with sapphires, cameos and pearls, with a great clasp on the front; a dalmatic, a vestment worn under the cloak, of the same stuff, with embroidered and jewelled trimmings' and other items of dress, including a belt of the same samite studded with cameos and other precious stones, concluding with the sword made for the king's coronation with a scabbard with embroidered decoration. The majority of the rest of the treasure is made up of the great clasps and belts which fastened the loose overgarments of the period, a few magnificent mantles, seventeen rings, and a 'crown which came from Cyprus', a total of some eighty items in all. The treasure was taken to Reading by two Knights Templar on 18 December.

Two weeks after the sealing of Magna Carta in June 1215, in anticipation of possible civil war, John ordered a dozen abbeys and half a dozen priories to deliver up the treasure which they were holding for safe-keeping.[73] Some of this was deposited at Winchester, and small quantities were received at other major royal houses and castles, but the majority of items came to Marlborough, where a list of the plate which was kept here was also drawn up.[74] This is the last we hear of the treasury at Marlborough: this may be due not to its closure, but to a change in the way records were organised after John's death.

There was also a mint at Marlborough, probably transferred from Great Bedwyn soon after the Norman Conquest, and active until the end of the eleventh century. Moneyers, however, were independent workers licenced by the king, and the mint would have been in the town rather than the castle.[75]

The Almonry

The royal almoner, responsible for the royal acts of charity, is first recorded at the court of Henry I in about 1103. At first, he was usually an important official with other duties, but from the later years of Henry II's reign until 1255, the post was filled by a Templar brother who would have had the necessary financial skills.[76] As almsgiving in the form of systematic feeding of the poor in large numbers was a daily ritual, there were almonries, offices which enabled these ceremonies to be carried out, and which held the necessary supplies, at major royal castles.

The first occasion when we have a record of almsgiving at Marlborough was in 1205, when John instructed Hugh de Neville to feed a hundred paupers at Easter, as the king's penance for not eating fish on Good Friday.[77] Henry III's household accounts for 1260 show that 150 paupers were fed by the court every day, including ten days at Marlborough in September of that year.[78] The daily total cost varied from 6s 3d to 17s 1d. Shortly afterwards, at the feast day of St Edward on 13 October, patron saint of Westminster, to whom Henry was specially devoted, the record shows a total of no less than 5016 paupers fed.[79]

On special occasions, such as the commemoration of the anniversary of the death of a member of the royal family, we find instructions to the almoner. On 28 May 1250, the keeper of the royal manor at Marlborough was reimbursed for a payment of 50s made to 'brother Roger [de Cramfield], the king's almoner, at Marlborough … to perform the anniversary of the king's mother'.[80] This was Queen Isabella, who died on 4 June 1246, and for whose soul a daily mass was said in 'the queen's chapel'; her daughter Joan was also remembered in the same way.

History of the Castle, 1216–1548

Henry III 1216–72

In August 1216, at John's instigation, the pope annulled Magna Carta, and by October there was open warfare once again. The barons who opposed John offered the throne to prince Louis of France. Louis invaded England in May of that year, and Hugh de Neville went over to his side. He had remained castellan of Marlborough, but with the death of John in October 1216, the political situation was once again reversed: Henry III was crowned at Gloucester cathedral, and it was at this point that William Marshal, son of John the Marshal, became regent of England.

William Marshal the elder held Marlborough until his death in 1219, when the castle passed to his son. William the younger held it until 1221, when he surrendered it to the king, in return for a marriage with the king's nine-year-old sister Eleanor, which took place in 1224, probably at Marlborough; Eleanor seems to have been here from August 1223 until the end of the year.[81] Thereafter the castle was once again the king's own possession, and the Knights Hospitaller, who acted as royal administrators and bankers, were given custody of it.[82]

It was in 1222 that another royal Eleanor came to Marlborough – Eleanor of Brittany, a tragic figure who spent most of her life in political confinement.[83] She was the sister of Arthur of Brittany, whose claim to the throne as the heir of Henry II's third son Geoffrey was a serious challenge to King John. However, Richard, fearing the effect of a regency if the thirteen-year-old Arthur succeeded, had named John as his heir on his deathbed in 1199.

Nonetheless, Arthur was recognised as the rightful heir to England by Philip II of France, and war broke out. By the Treaty of Le Goulet, John was recognised by the French in return for a large payment. When war broke out again, John captured Arthur, and nothing more was heard of him after he was imprisoned at Rouen in 1203. A reliable contemporary chronicle describes his murder by John himself, but there is no other evidence as to when and how he died.

Eleanor of Brittany had been with the Angevin royal family since her father Geoffrey died in 1186, and was with John when he returned to England just before the loss of Normandy to the French in 1204. As Geoffrey's daughter, her claim to the English throne was less secure than that of Arthur, but she was nonetheless a potential focus for any rebellion against John. She spent much of John's reign confined to Corfe castle, where John kept several of his political prisoners, and which was heavily guarded. She was however with John, his wife Isabella and his second son Richard when they went to western France in 1214.

After John's death, she remained at Corfe until 1222. She was then moved to Gloucester, Marlborough and finally Bristol in that year. She remained in Bristol or Gloucester for the rest of her life, dying in 1241. The nature of her imprisonment and the thinking behind Henry III's attitude to her are not clear. She described herself as a prisoner, hoping for freedom, in 1208. She was perhaps less at liberty than if she had been a hostage, simply because she remained a focus for rebellion.

There is some evidence that she was well treated, and accorded the respect due to her rank, with gifts of robes and occasional luxuries from the king, but this is intermittent. She was guarded, but not closely, though her transfer to Marlborough indicates some concern: in 1223, at the time of her move to Marlborough, for example, the council ordered reinforcement of the guard, to include horsemen and crossbowmen.[84] Instructions were given for the deployment of the guards, and provision was made for watches both day and night, and similarly detailed orders seem to have been given once she moved to Bristol.

Marlborough continued to be the setting for major councils and assemblies, though none were on the scale of that of 1209. In 1234, the quarrelling magnates of Ireland were summoned to a great council here in an attempt to reach a settlement.[85] Once again, the Marshal family were to the fore. Richard Marshal had succeeded his brother, William the younger, in 1232, but had been mortally wounded trying to recover the family possessions in Ireland. He was succeeded by yet another brother, Gilbert, who had taken holy orders. Gilbert in turn was seeking revenge for Richard's death, and the council was called to try to reach a settlement. Nine years later, in 1241, Henry was at Marlborough when news of Gilbert's death in an illicit tournament reached him. Gilbert, as a cleric, had only recently taken up arms, and was reputed to be 'inexperienced and useless as a knight'.[86] He was unable to control his

Spanish tournament horse, which threw him: his foot caught in the stirrup, and he was dragged the length of the lists and mortally wounded. Within four years, both his younger brothers had died, leaving as heir Joan, titular countess of Pembroke.

Marlborough retained its role as a major royal fortress throughout Henry III's reign. In 1258, his son prince Edward sided with rebellious barons against his father. Anticipating civil war, Henry ordered weapons to be sent to Robert Walerand, keeper of the castle, on 13 and 15 March 1261. Ten crossbows with a single foot stirrup, and five with two stirrups, were to be supplied, with 8000 bolts and 2000 bolts respectively; the bolts were to be sent from St Briavels in Gloucestershire. The following month, the pope released Henry from the oaths he had sworn when he came to terms with prince Edward and Simon de Montfort in 1259. Again, in 1264, the castle was put on a war footing in anticipation of Simon de Montfort's open rebellion. Roger Clifford was constable, and spent £86 16s 8d on the wages of a garrison of four knights, sixteen serjeants at arms and fifty-four foot soldiers, who were here from 25 March until 1 June.[87] Montfort took control of the government after his victory at Lewes at the end of May, and ordered that all the royal castles were to be put under the control of his supporters. Clifford seems to have complied with this order, on the evidence of this entry in the royal accounts. By September, however, Henry III was in control of the castle again.[88]

It was to Marlborough that Henry III came to convalesce in 1265, after the death of Simon de Montfort at the battle of Evesham, fighting against prince Edward. Henry himself was wounded in the mêlée in which Montfort was killed, and went first to Gloucester for three weeks, before spending ten days at Marlborough.[89] The political and legal consequences of Edward's victory over his father were hammered out first at Kenilworth in the early autumn of 1266. The statute produced by a parliament held at Marlborough on 18 November 1267 was designed to ensure implementation of the agreement at Kenilworth, and to punish those who had taken the law into their own hands in recent months.[90] It is a hugely important and wide-ranging document, and parts of it are still the law of the land. Ironically, it is the last major political event to have taken place at Marlborough.

In 1272, Henry III died when prince Edward was in Palestine, and the lieutenants whom Edward had left in charge of his affairs put the major castles on alert. Four crossbowmen were sent to Marlborough from the day of Henry III's death, 16 November 1272, and stayed until Whitsun the following year.

During Henry III's reign, Marlborough became the king's favourite royal castle after Windsor. Indeed, Henry spent more time here than at any other of his castles and houses outside London. The records for his father and grand-father, admittedly incomplete, show that stays of more than a week were rare. In January 1226, Henry spent the entire month at Marlborough due to illness, and in 1229 he stayed for three weeks in March and April. In total, he was at the castle for about a year and a half of his 56-year reign; his visits were less frequent after the beginnings of the baronial revolt in 1258 and the civil war that followed.

In 1256, Queen Eleanor was here for a long period,[91] probably with her two-year-old daughter Katherine, whom both Henry and Eleanor loved dearly, but was evidently very disabled. In March 1256, Henry had a silver image of her placed on the shrine of St Edward at Westminster; three days later a messenger arrived from Marlborough from the queen to say that she was better.[92] She was the first of their children to die, on 3 May the following year. The chronicler Matthew Paris described her after her death as 'mute and incapable but very beautiful in face'.[93] Her mother was so grieved by her death that she became seriously ill, such that 'neither human consolation nor medicine' could comfort her.[94] An effigy by William of Gloucester, of oak covered in silver-gilt plates, was placed on Katherine's tomb in Westminster Abbey two years later.[95]

The queen's castle: 1272–1399

Edward I only came occasionally to Marlborough before his father's death in 1272, nor did he have any particular attachment to it. Its strategic importance had sharply diminished, and in 1273 he gave Marlborough to Eleanor as queen mother.[96] This was to be her dowry, and Marlborough's status therefore changed from that of a king's castle to become a perquisite of the queens of England. The original gift may well have been because Eleanor was fond of the place, on which her husband had lavished money to create comfortable surroundings for both of them. We rely heavily on the king's charters and other acts to map out his journeys and sojourns; the queen's records are much slimmer, and we only catch occasional glimpses of her whereabouts. As a result, the detailed picture we have of Marlborough castle in the thirteenth century disappears in the next hundred years. Most of the records about it are to do with its transfer back to the king on the queen mother's death, and its reassignment, often after a lapse of some years, to the king's wife. We do know that Eleanor was here quite frequently, as a considerable number of original letters from her written at Marlborough survive in the National Archives.[97]

The change in the castle's status did not mean that the king could not use it, and he stopped here occasionally en route for Clarendon or when he hunted from Ludgershall. He also stayed at Marlborough before his ceremonial visit to Glastonbury at Easter 1278, when the supposed remains of Arthur and Guinevere were transferred to a splendid new tomb which he had commissioned.

If indeed Eleanor had some special affection for Marlborough, it may have been reflected in the arrangements made when, in July 1286, she retired to the nunnery at Amesbury. The house at Amesbury had been founded by

Henry II; several other members of the royal family had taken the veil there, including Eleanor's granddaughter Mary. Edward stayed at Marlborough in January that year, to make the arrangements for her retirement; a grant was issued declaring that Eleanor could keep her lands, specifically including the town, castle and manor of Marlborough, even if she entered a nunnery.[98] In April 1290, Edward was at Marlborough before he went on to Amesbury to visit his mother. After this, they only met again once before she died at Amesbury on 24 June 1291.

Edward was a widower when his mother died. When in 1299 he married Margaret, daughter of Philip III of France, Marlborough once again became one of the queen's castles. The deed of grant is dated 10 September 1299 at Canterbury, the date and place of her wedding to Edward.[99] The following year, the chapel and 'the three great chambers within the castle' were repaired, and, in 1304, 140 great oaks were ordered for mending the houses within the castle, as if the queen was likely to use the castle.[100] But there is no evidence that she ever visited Marlborough. In 1308, Edward II appointed Hugh Despenser constable and keeper of the castle.[101] On Margaret's death in 1318, it passed to Isabella, wife of Edward II.

Isabella, like Margaret, is not known to have visited Marlborough. It was granted to her very shortly after Margaret's death on 14 February 1318; the entry on the patent rolls is dated 5 March.[102] It is part of a list of grants in settlement of the dowry agreed on her marriage to Edward II in 1306. The reason for the delay was that many of the properties intended for Isabella had belonged to her stepmother-in-law.

However, on 2 May 1321, the custody of the castle was once more given to Hugh Despenser the elder, together with Wallingford, which was also in Isabella's possession.[103] The Despensers were Edward's favourites, hated by Isabella, and matters had come to a head earlier in 1321. By May, open warfare was imminent, and Edward's grant to Despenser came two days before the barons attacked the Despenser estates in Wales. In August 1321, Isabella and her supporters succeeded in driving the Despensers into exile. In the process of ejecting him from Marlborough, Hugh Despenser claimed that he had been robbed of goods valued at the huge sum of over £6000, including gold vessels, vestments, the contents of his chapel, and valuable cloth of gold from his wardrobe. His entire wardrobe was carried away both at Marlborough and elsewhere.[104] The custody of the castle passed, with the queen's agreement, to Oliver de Ingham in December that year. Ingham had been instructed to assemble the local cavalry and infantry from Wiltshire and Berkshire to join Edward's army in Wales, where the king was launching a campaign against the lords who opposed the Despensers.[105] Marlborough was one of sixty-seven castles where Edward II ordered the reinforcements to garrisons sent 'in the late disturbances in the realm' to be disbanded in February 1322.[106]

In 1330, Isabella and her co-regent Mortimer were removed from power by Edward III, and her estates were confiscated; she was sent into comfortable exile at Castle Rising in Norfolk. Three months after her downfall, Philippa of Hainault, Edward III's queen, became the last royal holder of the castle. The grant was made on 1 January 1331, and she held it until her death in 1369; there is no direct evidence that she ever came here, though she may have visited Marlborough with the king.

During the reigns of Edward II and Edward III, the castle was little used by the kings. Edward II spent six days in and around Marlborough in June 1308, and four days in April 1321; these visits were part of a journey round the West Country, as were two short stays in May and June 1326. He did spend Christmas and New Year here in 1320–21, but without his family: gifts were taken to his three children by a messenger, Llewellyn ap Madoc.[107]

Edward III seems to have been here chiefly for hunting in the earlier part of his reign, as his visits were almost always linked to a stay at Ludgershall. As the Black Death receded in the summer of 1349, he ventured down to Marlborough and the surrounding area in July, August and September. In 1357, when both the kings of France and of Scotland were his prisoners, he chose to spend Christmas at Marlborough, between the two great tournaments at which the captive kings were paraded, at Smithfield in September and at Windsor the following April. His final visit, in August 1371, was marked by a sudden and serious illness. Mark Ormrod, Edward's biographer, gives this account of it:

> While the royal household was in residence at Marlborough Castle in August 1371, Edward III was suddenly taken ill at the nearby village of Everleigh. The king's regular physician, John Glaston, being absent, messengers were despatched to Oxford and London to summon no fewer than five medical experts – the physician William Wymondham, the surgeons William Holm, Adam Leche and William Stodeley, and an unnamed friar – to deal with the emergency. Glaston himself arrived a little later with various newly acquired potions for the relief of his royal patient. No-one recorded the experts' diagnosis, and there is no detail in the medicaments to give clues to the nature of Edward's indisposition. If we read back from the end of his life, it is tempting to suggest that he had suffered a minor stroke. But it is just as likely that he had taken a bad fall while out hunting. After three weeks of enforced rest, the king was judged well enough to move, though it took a whole ten days for Edward, travelling by litter, to reach the security of Windsor.[108]

In October, the members of the medical team were thanked for 'labouring and dwelling upon a good cure for the king when he was ill' and presented with *ex gratia* payments of between ten and twenty-five marks each. And with this moment of drama, the royal visits to Marlborough come to an end.

Essentially, the castle reached its final form in the middle of the thirteenth century, and thereafter the picture is one of occasional repairs and fairly rapid decay. Once it was no longer one of the king's own residences, the king's resources were directed elsewhere. And there was a much more general trend, beginning about the start of Edward I's reign, for castles to become permanently inhabited. Castles belonging to lesser lords were obviously already in this category, but the great lords and above all the king concentrated on their chief seats. The first indicator of neglect at Marlborough is that cattle were grazed on what had been the castle's main garden in the 1280s.[109]

Edward I also had other priorities in terms of castles, such as the fortresses in newly conquered Wales. The disturbances of Edward II's reign meant that by 1327, when Queen Isabella became regent, an urgent and widespread survey of the king's castles was needed. On 15 May, an order was issued for the appointment 'in all possible haste' of good and sufficient persons to carry out the survey.[110] This was followed by instructions for setting up the operation on 16 July, by which Adam de Herewynton, chancellor of the exchequer, was made responsible for surveying all castles in Gloucestershire, Worcestershire, Herefordshire, Shropshire and Staffordshire, along with Marlborough and Devizes.[111] The report on Marlborough, dated 11 September 1327, was undertaken by local people and addressed to Adam.[112] It is the most detailed description of the castle which we possess, and makes depressing reading. Two bridges into the castle needed to be rebuilt, at a cost of £40, and the gate and walls of the castle, parts of which had been battered down, required a further £125. Within the bailey, a number of the chambers, as well as the almonry and the bakery, were damaged or even ruinous, but the worst damage was to the keep itself, 'half of which has been destroyed for a long time'. Other buildings on the motte and the walls around the motte were in a bad way, and the total cost for that area was estimated at £300, not allowing for cost of timber. The inspectors reported that the damage dated from as far back as the reign of Edward I, some twenty years earlier, and had continued since then, naming the constables who had been responsible for the castle at the time.[113]

No serious action seems to have been taken about the report; all that is recorded is a series of surveys between 1327 and 1403. When it belonged to Queen Philippa, a survey was undertaken in 1339, four years after it was granted to her,[114] but action was only taken in 1354, when 'as many carpenters and workmen, not in the king's service, as are required to repair' the castle were to be recruited.[115] Five years later, modest works, needing £10-worth of timber, were undertaken, followed by more general repairs in 1361 overseen by Nicholas, the rector of St Peter's, next to the castle, who had been appointed surveyor of the works. His account reports the employment of sawyers, carpenters and tilers to work on the great hall, chambers and queen's chapel, as well as the great gate, and chapel.[116]

But these efforts were not enough: a writ issued in August 1367 declares that 'the king understands that [the defects] are due to the negligence of the keepers … of the castle'.[117] Repairs in 1371 to the chambers in the castle seem to have been ineffectual.[118] When John de Roches was appointed custodian in 1382, the question was both what had happened to money supposed to be spent by his predecessor, and what was its present condition?[119] Four years later, the keepership of the castle was granted for life to William de Ashthorpe; he was ordered to take masons and carpenters to work on repairing it, with the power to imprison anyone who refused.[120]

In 1371, Nicholas, the rector of St Peter's, the surveyor in 1362, was accused of having built two houses in Marlborough with materials he had removed from the castle, consisting of both new and old timber, 20,000 wooden shingles worth over £5, £6-worth of lead and 1000 slates. Many buildings were reported as damaged; it is not clear whether this was due to plundering or to natural decay. The jurors who reported on the castle declared that they did not know 'the amount of damage to walls, gates, turrets, loop-holes, watch-towers, bridges, barriers and ditches because they can hardly be repaired without a complete rebuilding'. The cost of the rebuilding 'belongs to the king', who was hardly likely to spend money on what was little more than a ruin.[121] There were further inquests in May 1390 and in September 1391. In 1391, the clerk who wrote the order for the inquiry seems to have thought that there was some military equipment left in the ruinous castle, but the report that came back paints a picture of ruin and plunder. There was lead, scrap iron and bells lying in the chapel worth £10, the only objects of any value. The military value of the castle was now relatively slight compared with the fortresses in Wales or on the Scottish border, and there was no real incentive to make it good for warfare. Nor was it needed as a residence.

The castle remained an important asset because of the revenue derived from the estates attached to it, and it was for this reason that it was granted by Henry IV to his son Humphrey duke of Gloucester in 1403. Another inquest at the time of the grant found that the castle had been 'injured and wasted in many ways' under the last three constables.[122] At his death in 1447 it became once more part of the queen's dower, when Henry VI granted it to Margaret of Anjou. It passed in turn to Elizabeth Woodville, Edward IV's queen, then to her daughter Elizabeth, wife of Henry VII, and to each of Henry VIII's six wives. Finally, Edward VI granted it to Edward Seymour, duke of Somerset, and in 1548 the castle ceased to be part of the royal estates.[123]

The Castle Buildings

Marlborough castle as a stronghold

Our general lack of information about Marlborough castle until the thirteenth century means that we have no other evidence for the chronicler's claim (which may well be true) that it was very strongly fortified by 1138. The layout of the castle is likely to have been established by this time, but again there is no evidence about the size of the bailey, apart from the assumption that it is probably much the same as the line of defences which are just traceable on recent ground-penetrating radar maps. We can however say that the height of the motte was a point of strength, as was the castle's site, in a relatively broad valley which meant that it was out of range of siege engines on the hills to north and south. And we can deduce a little more about the castle's strengths and weaknesses from the sketchy details we have of the three sieges between 1139 and 1217.

The usual purpose of a castle keep is to act as a secure refuge in which the garrison could hold out for some time, even if the outer bailey was stormed and captured. It was the strongest structure within the castle, usually built of good stone. In the late twelfth century, keeps were typically square, though experimental octagonal examples, as at Orford in Suffolk, and round towers are also found. Keeps are defensive structures and could withstand considerable bombardment by the stone-throwing machinery which was the attacker's chief weapon. Siege machines could also be used by the defenders. The use of the prehistoric mound meant that the slope which enemy soldiers had to climb was unusually steep.

A successful assault depended on the enemy's ability to do sufficient damage to the castle to weaken its defences, or to mount a massive attack by scaling the walls. Until the introduction of the trebuchet in the early thirteenth century, which was capable of firing accurately and used heavier stones, bombardments were moderately ineffectual. The earlier stone-throwing machines (*petraria*) relied on sheer muscle-power, rather than the counter-weight which propelled the stone from a trebuchet, and were smaller and weaker. Fighting during a siege consisted mainly of a duel with crossbows, which could be pre-loaded and fired instantly. This gave the advantage to the garrison. And Marlborough had ceased to have much military value by the time that longbows, which had a greater range, came into general use.

Taking a castle by assault was a rarity during this period. A fortress fell either because the garrison was unable to obtain new supplies because of an enemy blockade, or because too many of the garrison were killed or injured to continue the defence. And surrender was even more frequently due to political considerations, when the garrison decided that they could no longer expect relief or even simply wished to change sides. The first siege of Marlborough, in 1138, was abandoned as a result of outside events. The second, in 1194, probably contained an element of political calculation, given that the defenders were fighting a king who was about to return and reclaim his kingdom. The third, like the first, depended on outside events. In this case, in 1217, the garrison thought there was no hope of relief, not knowing that Louis of France had in fact returned to England.

The keep and the towers

At the beginning of this essay, we saw that we can only speculate as to the original building on Marlborough Mound. By 1100, when the king is first recorded as visiting the castle, it was probably a stone building, and there is little doubt that John the Marshal's 'very strongly fortified' castle was stone rather than wood. An entry in 1211–12 reads as if there was a tower on the motte, as it is an order for the building of 'a barbican before the gateway of the tower'.[124] In 1226–27, 'the walls and battlements of the towers and bailey of the castle of Marlborough' were repaired, probably meaning the small towers of the curtain wall.[125] It seems, however, that the great tower was being rebuilt at this point, because in June 1229 the king wrote to John de Eston, the constable, ordering him to make urgent repairs to the tower, currently covered with a false roof, so that it was not damaged by the coming winter.[126] This work was completed in 1238; the entry in the accounts reads: 'And for finishing the tower of the castle of Marlborough, and making a lime kiln for the works on the same tower, £126 7s 8d.'[127] This major building operation may confirm the report that William Marshal, during the civil war after the death of King John, had all the royal castles under his control partly demolished to prevent them from falling into the hands of the rebels who had invited prince Louis of France to invade England.[128]

H. C. Brentnall, who taught at Marlborough for many years, made an extensive and scholarly study of the Mound, culminating in a plan of the castle as it was in the thirteenth century. This was published in 1933, in his article '*Castellum Merlebergensis*' in the journal of the College's Natural History Society,[129] and Christopher Hughes based an oil painting on it (Fig. 3.2). Brentnall revised it slightly to illustrate a further article in the Wiltshire Archaeological and Natural History magazine for 1938.[130] (Fig. 3.3).

The most striking feature of all three depictions is the great round tower on the mound which dominates the castle as a whole. It is also the most controversial feature. Brentnall's painstaking plotting of the buildings in the bailey using the descriptions in the account records is as good as we are likely to get. Because of the lack of archaeological evidence, and the lack of detail in the historical records, we know very little indeed about the original structure on the mound.

We have to start with the basic assumption that a tower of some sort stood on the motte. These donjons or keeps were generally designed as a defensive structure into which the garrison could retreat in a siege. Many of the castles built on large mottes have a surprising amount of accommodation in the donjon, and the buildings often occupied the entire top of the motte. The combination of a steep slope with a high wall at the top was a powerful obstacle to any besiegers.

The first evidence we have of a tower in the castle is in 1211–12, when a barbican was added to the 'gateway to the tower'; at the same time a *cingulum* or curtain wall was built around the motte.[131] H. C. Brentnall believed that there was a continuous moat around the motte itself, and that this *cingulum* was around the moat, though he noted that Stukeley's drawing dated 6 July 1723 clearly indicated that this was not the case at that date (Fig. 1.3).

Fig. 3.2 Reconstruction of Marlborough castle in the mid-thirteenth century; painting by Christopher Hughes.

Brentnall also showed the tower as rectangular, but if there was a curtain wall as suggested, the keep within was very probably circular. Furthermore, recent archaeological work has found no trace of this moat around the southern end of the Mound, and *cingulum* is therefore much more likely to refer to a wall around the top of the motte.[132] The 'turris' could then logically be a tower within that wall: this term is used in the royal records both for a simple tower and for a 'shell keep', consisting of a ring wall with buildings attached to the inner wall. This combination of a circular curtain wall and a circular keep within it can be seen at Launceston (Fig. 3.4). Launceston was built by Henry III's brother Richard of Cornwall, on a motte very similar in size to that of Marlborough. Its appearance may be the nearest we can get to an idea of what Marlborough Mound would have looked like in the mid-thirteenth century.

The only other clue we have as to the layout on the motte is an entry in the accounts for 1238–39, which tells us that the 'stables and houses *infra turrim*'

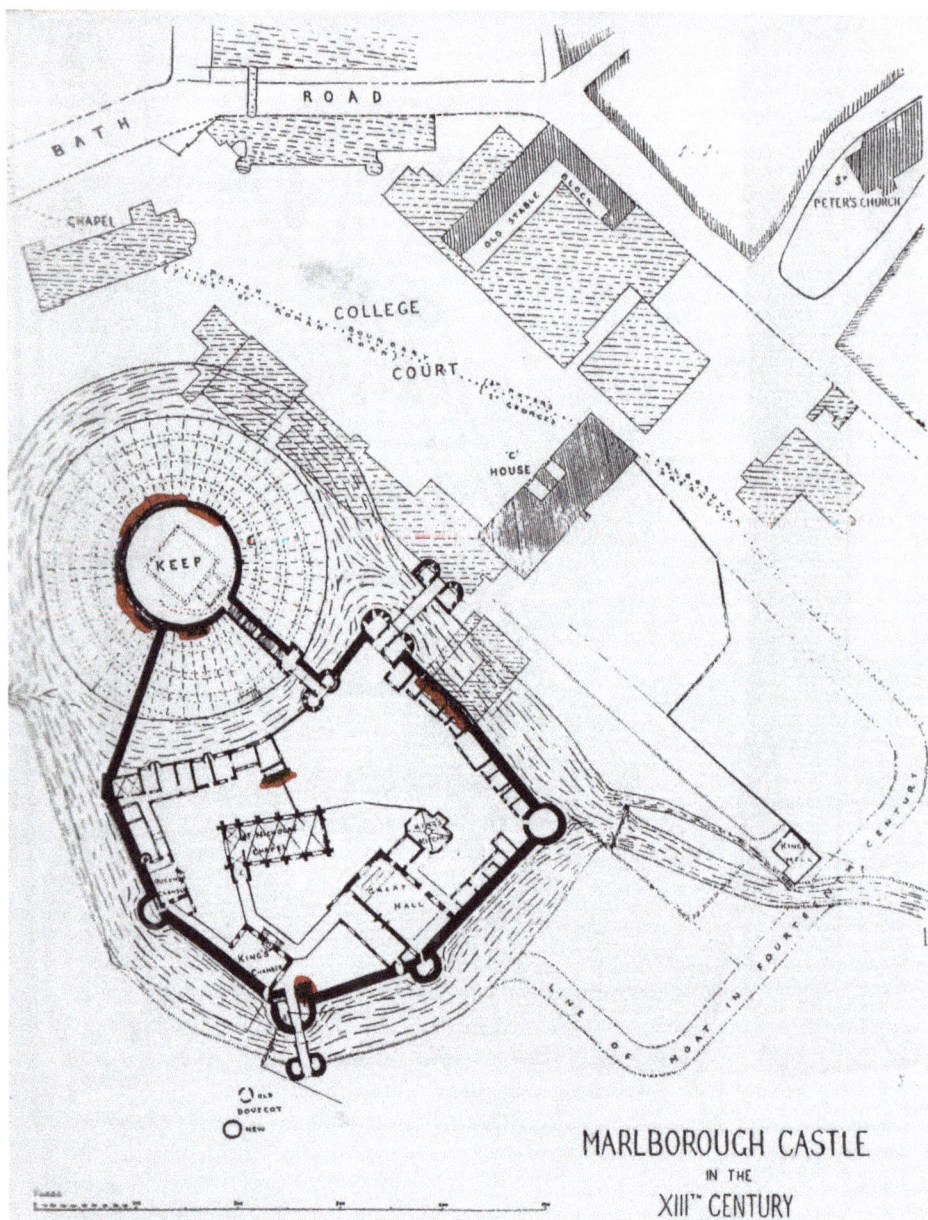

Figure 3.3 Reconstruction plan of Marlborough castle in the thirteenth century. H. C. Brentnall wrote: 'This is a conjectural plan only. Nothing can be affirmed except the existence of mediaeval foundation where shown in red. The suggestion of building within the Keep means only that some sort of *donjon* stood there, but no details survive.'

Fig. 3.4 Launceston castle: a keep within a cingulum.

were re-roofed.[133] Now *infra turrim* can mean both 'below the tower' and 'within the tower'. It is highly unlikely that there were stables at the top of the mound (though not impossible). Stables and houses certainly existed in the bailey, and they may well have been at the southern foot of the motte, and therefore 'below the tower'.

What did the tower on the motte contain? Jeremy Ashbee in his 2015 lecture noted that, at Clifford's Tower in York, what actually happened inside the tower was not the residence of a king, but the storage of his valuables, a base for the clerks of his treasury, and occasionally the imprisonment of sensitive but high-ranking captives. For Marlborough, we have even less information.

H. C. Brentnall suggested that the chapel of St Leonard's was in the tower because he was the patron saint of prisoners.[134] In fact, this link is unlikely: St Leonard – for whatever reason – is one of the most common dedications for English churches in the twelfth century.[135] A further problem is that the first entry relating to this chapel is in 1231–32,[136] before the great tower had been completed. This document puts it in the context of the king's chamber, in a list of repairs: '... the gallery of the king's chamber, and for leading all the windows of the king's chamber and the chapel of St Leonard, and mending the porch before the doors of the king's chamber ...' The chapel dedicated to St Leonard in 1232 had three gabled 'upstanding windows'. It was therefore quite spacious, and its interior was provided with lecterns, lattice screens and a painted tablet in front of the altar.[137]

However, we know that there was definitely a chapel, not necessarily that dedicated to St Leonard, on the mound at Marlborough: in 1246, in what the clerks called 'the tower of the king's castle at Marlborough', a chaplain was paid to celebrate commemorative masses for the soul of Eleanor of Brittany, the king's cousin. It was not unusual to have several chapels within a castle, and while it is clear that the chapel of St Nicholas is the most important, it is possible that St Leonard's was the queen's chapel and that there was a third chapel in the tower.

The buildings in the bailey

The layout of castles with a raised keep, whether on a natural outcrop or a motte, tended to use the keep and its eminence as one corner of the defences, forming part of the fortifications surrounding the bailey. This was the pattern at Marlborough, and we can trace the extent of the bailey fairly easily. Recent surveys have shown the probable existence of a long stretch of the foundations of the outer wall to the south-west of the mound. A stretch of wall to the east was discovered in 1936 and was re-excavated in 2017; this is the only archaeological dig that has taken place in the area. The space occupied by the bailey is roughly that of what used to be known as 'the Wilderness', which has been substantially built over since 1950. The most recent buildings have been subject to archaeological watching briefs, but no finds of importance have been recorded. This is partly because many of the buildings would have been timber structures; but we know that there were substantial stone buildings as well, and it would seem that these have been entirely quarried for their materials – beginning, as we have seen already, in the late thirteenth century. It was not unusual for even the foundations to be dug out. At Windsor, when the unfinished 'house of the Round Table' started in 1344 and abandoned in the 1370s was excavated, it revealed a robber trench for this purpose, and only fragments of the stone which had been the base of the building were recovered.[138]

In the absence of archaeological evidence, how can we form an idea of what Marlborough castle looked like in its heyday under Henry III? The only possible approach is to look at comparable buildings, and here we may be fortunate. Relatively few thirteenth-century castles survive substantially intact, and one of these is Chepstow, the great fortress on the west bank of the River Wye at the point where it flows into the Severn. At the Norman Conquest, it came into the possession of William Fitz Osbern, the childhood friend and intimate counsellor of William I. He held it for less than five years, and it was in the king's hands from 1074 onwards. In 1115, Henry I gave the castle to Walter de Clare, whose family were among the most important lords of the Welsh marches. At the end of the twelfth century, William Marshal, whose central role in the history of Marlborough we have already described, married Isabel, heiress of the Clare domains, and thus came into possession of Chepstow.

Chepstow survives more or less in its thirteenth-century form, and much of it can be dated to the period when the Marshal family owned it.[139] William used Chepstow as the base for his operations in the southern marches of Wales; he also acquired Pembroke by this same marriage and used his already considerable wealth to carry out extensive building works in both places.

The most prominent marker of these fortresses is the style of the outer fortifications, with straight stretches of wall joined by round or D-shaped towers at the angles. The towers have plain battlements, without the overhanging pentices of later thirteenth-century castles, and the overall effect is of relative simplicity. The height of the walls is modest and there are relatively few arrow slits, except on the south, where the lie of the land made it vulnerable. There would have been similar considerations at Marlborough, in this case because of the proximity of Granham Hill, which rises steeply above the Kennet.

The outline of the bailey of Marlborough castle is markedly similar to that of the slightly larger lower bailey at Chepstow (Fig. 3.5), and the buildings against the bailey walls would also have been present at Marlborough. The plan drawn up by Brentnall in 1938 has been confirmed by recent geophysical surveys, and to a lesser extent by the recent excavations.[140]

The twin towers of the gatehouse (Fig. 3.6) were to be found in numerous contemporary castles, varying only in the degree of architectural decoration. The windows in the gatehouse at Chepstow are a later insertion, but again, it is quite probable that similar improvements in the amenities would have taken place at Marlborough. The Chepstow gatehouse door (Fig. 3.7) has recently been dated to the late twelfth century and is a rare survival.

The hall at Chepstow was within the Norman great tower, whereas that at Marlborough seems to have been a separate structure within the bailey, given what we know about it from the account records discussed later. The best parallel here is perhaps the hall at Winchester, contemporary with Henry II's hall at Marlborough. It is on a grander scale, but the exterior

Fig. 3.5 Chepstow castle baileys from the air.

Fig. 3.6 (above) Chepstow castle gatehouse.

Fig. 3.7 (right) Chepstow castle gatehouse door.

Fig. 3.8 Drawing of exterior of Winchester Hall, c. 1780, by Francis Grose.

Fig. 3.9 Chepstow castle great hall.

would have been similar (Fig. 3.8). The surviving interior of the Chepstow hall does show us something of the kind of architectural decoration which was added in the mid-thirteenth century at both sites (Fig. 3.9). One further detail comes from the Templar manor at Strood, where there is a reconstruction of an external staircase: at Marlborough in 1225 just such a staircase is mentioned outside the king's chamber, with instructions that it is to be roofed in stone (Fig. 3.10).[141]

These physical parallels can only be conjectures. The royal accounts are our only reliable source of the small amount of information about the structure of the castle. The development of the castle beyond the motte itself must have begun in earnest with its transformation into a heavily fortified site during the Anarchy of Stephen's reign forty years earlier, which implies a resident garrison. This in turn means that the prime purpose of the bailey would have been as an area containing the necessary stores and facilities to support this garrison.

The first buildings in the bailey of which we have a record are Henry II's great hall and the king's chamber, in 1175. Whether the combination of stonework and carpentry which the accounts record in that year was in fact for a new king's chamber in the bailey, we cannot tell. In 1211, there was a 'great chamber', probably the king's chamber, which, along with the other

Fig. 3.10 External wooden staircase, Strood, Knights Templar Manor.

chambers, was re-roofed in lead.[142] This would definitely have been outside the keep, as it evidently had a separate roof. The first queen's chamber was probably created for John's wife Isabella, who was at the castle on several occasions in 1204, and the first queen's chamber may date from this period: a payment for 'necessary expenses on works for the queen on various occasions' amounted to £44.[143] It was this chamber which was repaired extensively in 1225–26, seven years after the widowed Isabella had returned to France.[144]

The royal quarters under Henry III

John made Marlborough castle an important administrative centre. It was Henry III who gave the castle its final shape, recreating it as a royal residence. Henry's great enthusiasm was his pious devotion to the cult of his predecessor, Edward the Confessor, who had been canonised in 1161.[145] His other preoccupation was building, which was for the most part the remodelling of existing buildings. His major work was of course at Westminster, where both the abbey and the palace were the focus of his attention. He undoubtedly loved the decoration and furnishing of rooms; in addition, and in line with a change which can be seen throughout Europe, his palaces, houses and castles were made more comfortable.

In the twelfth century, broadly speaking, much of the king's life would be spent in public, in the great hall, and the royal quarters would be relatively modest. When his grandfather, Henry II, adopted the custom of retiring to his chamber to read or to hold private conversations, his courtiers saw this as a new departure. Henry III began to create royal lodgings on a much more extensive scale, in which the chamber had become as important as the great hall in the daily life of the castle. It was no longer simply a bedroom or private room, but had become the place where the king lived during the day. He would meet most of his visitors and officials there, and would often dine there rather than in the great hall. The costs attributed to the chamber, particularly for firewood, are nearly always the larger. At Marlborough, on 2 January 1226, which was not a feast day, wood for the hall cost 16d and for the king's chamber 16½d.[146] On days of great feasts, however, the hall came into its own, and on these occasions its costs frequently exceeded those of the chamber.[147]

Marlborough was in the king's hands from 1221 onwards, and the first of a very substantial list of entries in the royal accounts for Henry III's reign was made in 1224. For the next three years, repair work, particularly on the 'king's houses', the domestic buildings within the castle bailey, was carried out. This was routine maintenance, during Henry's minority. The royal quarters were relatively simple when Henry III first visited Marlborough, and consisted of little more than the hall and the king's chamber. Modest works were undertaken two years later, in 1234, and a new gate, 'in woodwork, ironwork and stonework', was installed at a cost of 72s 10d.[148]

It is only in 1236 that serious building activity began at Marlborough, which effectively transformed the castle into a moderately luxurious royal residence over the next twenty-five years. The reason for this was Henry's marriage to Eleanor of Provence in January 1236. David Carpenter, Henry's biographer, writes that 'Henry's enthusiasm for building and decoration was now poured into providing worthy accommodation for his wife.'[149] At Windsor, new royal quarters for the queen and her children were built in the lower ward in January 1240, and over £10,000 was spent over the next twenty years. Nottingham, the headquarters of the government in the north, and Dover, the main gateway to the continent, were also extensively remodelled and redecorated, even though Henry himself spent relatively little time at either place.[150] In February, March and April 1236, Henry and Eleanor visited all the castles and houses which were to be their main residences: Winchester, Clarendon, Marlborough and Woodstock, followed by Westminster and Windsor. When Henry visited one of these places, an order for works to be carried out there usually followed very quickly.

Marlborough was no exception to these rebuilding activities. Like Henry's other favourite castles, palaces and houses, it was designed to be a place for leisure as well as both a fortress and a centre of administration. There were secluded places where he and Eleanor could relax in private, and the chambers, with their views over the valley, comfortable fireplaces and fine wall paintings, were pleasing to the eye. Indeed, Henry's personal priority as far as castles were concerned was definitely aesthetic and luxurious rather than political and military.

The towers in the lower bailey

By 1225, there was a small tower behind 'the king's leaded chamber', and by 1241, the king's tower appears in the accounts.[151] An outer chamber 'in the high tower', thatched with straw, is mentioned a decade later, which refers to one of these towers, as it is in the context of work on the king's chamber and the kitchen.[152] And there is an enigmatic direction in 1270 'to build a chamber, 50 feet by 24 with fireplace, in front of the castle tower for the king's knights'. As the king's knights were his personal bodyguard rather than part of the garrison, this is likely to have been part of the complex in the bailey.[153]

The chapels

The existing great hall and the chapel of St Nicholas formed part of this complex, and possibly, as we have seen, that of St Leonard as well. Both chapels were refurbished in 1231–32; the king had issued a very detailed description of what he wanted, as was his usual habit with anything to do with both religion and decoration:

93

erecting an altar in the chapel of St Nicholas in the castle of Marlborough, and in wainscoting beyond the same altar, 20s 10d; ... for making three gabled windows in the chapel of St Leonard, and on wainscoting in the chapel of St Nicholas, above the two altars and the crucifix, and for renewing the painting which is in the same chapel, 76s 3d; and on paintings in the chapel of St Leonard in the castle of Marlborough, and in making chairs, benches, latticework, lecterns and a certain painted tablet before the altar in the same chapel, and in buying a crucifix and images and placing them in the chapel of St Nicholas in the same castle, and in decorating the chancel of the same chapel, and renewing the painting of the same chapel, 104s 7½d ...[154]

Henry ordered the building of private chapels adjoining the king's and queen's chambers in several of the castles he frequented, and indeed both a 'king's chapel' (which may have been that of St Nicholas) and a 'queen's chapel' are mentioned in the accounts, though with little detail about them. In other castles, such chapels adjoined both chambers, and were the forerunners of the private oratories found from the fourteenth century onwards. At Marlborough, there was a covered passageway from the king's chamber to his chapel;[155] at Woodstock, a similar passageway was installed so that Eleanor could go from her chamber to the chapel 'with dry feet', a reminder that the ground in the bailey was almost certainly unpaved, and probably frequently muddy.[156]

The great hall and king's chamber

The first major redevelopment, in 1238–39, largely concerned the refurbishment of the great hall. The account for this reads:

> ... for making four large windows in the hall of the castle at Marlborough, and wainscoting from above the king's seat to the fourth bay, and making two wooden smokeholes in the same hall, and for whitewashing the hall, and repairing the doors of the same hall, and the gallery of the king's chamber, and for leading all the windows of the king's chamber and the chapel of St Leonard, and mending the porch before the doors of the king's chamber, and for repairing the king's barbican and the bridge towards the king's dovecot, and for repairing the damaged buildings of the same castle, and for making two glass panels for the newly-built great window in the said hall, towards the west ... £50 5s 4d, by the King's writ. And in painting a certain curtain above the king's seat in the hall of Marlborough, and in making and decorating certain wainscoting in the king's chamber, leading there above the king's bed, and decorating a certain hanging there at the head of the king's bed, and re-roofing the same chamber, and repairing the walls of the castle where necessary, £56 9s 3d.[157]

We also have the very detailed account for a small part of these works, which paints a remarkable picture of the team of builders at work (Fig. 3.11). The

Fig. 3.11 Drawing of builders at work by Matthew Paris, *c.* 1250.

day's wages for the different craftsmen and their helpers, ranging from the skilled masons to the four women who carry sand and water, are recorded. The cost of materials is also detailed; perhaps the most surprising discovery is that stone was relatively cheap, but the cost of carting it could be up to ten times the value of the stone. Most of the operations are maintenance rather than new building, some of it 'against the coming of the king before Christmas'. Henry arrived at the castle on 3 December and stayed until 7 December, but then went to Clarendon, and to Winchester for Christmas.

The queen's rooms

Henry ordered the queen's rooms, which were presumably his mother's old quarters, to be made more spacious and with large glazed windows. Henry and Eleanor were at Marlborough twice in 1238, spending a week here in March, and it was at this point that a major building campaign was ordered. This included repairs to the queen's chamber due to decay, as well as the rebuilding of the gable and a new stone window, with a lock. The wooden windows were replaced and fitted with padlocks.[158] In 1241 an oriel window in the latest fashion was added to the queen's chamber.[159]

In 1241–42, the constable accounted for further extensive works, largely for the queen's benefit:

> a new gabled and glazed window before the door to the Queen's chapel and a new fireplace in the storeroom before the Queen's chamber, and in wainscoting, plastering and whitewashing that storeroom, and making a large window in the same storeroom with one column, and barring it with iron; and making a porch between the Queen's chamber and her chapel, and a new gate in the entrance to her chamber.[160]

He had also been instructed to provide 'a good wardrobe for the queen by the chapel of St Nicholas, replacing the old one, with fireplace and privy chamber', but this had not been done, and the instruction had to be repeated in 1244.[161] This was carried out at the same time as a new order in 1245 specifying that the queen's chambers should be rebuilt with

> two storeys, with a fireplace below and above, the chamber to contain 24 feet in width within the walls, with four large and well placed windows with columns, two in the gables and two on the two sides of the chamber; the passage between the king's and queen's chambers to be likewise in two storeys.[162]

This implies that the chamber probably lay on the west side of the bailey, with a view down the Kennet valley, over the dovecot and lawn which lay outside the walls. These were reached by a separate barbican and gate near the king's chamber which guarded a bridge over the moat. This work was billed in 1246–47; it was expensive, costing a little over £235.[163] The connecting passage between the king's and queen's chambers was a feature at Henry's other residences. A new two-storey chamber similar to that at Marlborough had been built at Woodstock by 1350; it was here that Henry escaped an assassination attempt at night because he was sleeping in the queen's chamber;[164] and at Windsor the queen's chamber was 'to adjoin our chamber' when it was built in 1240.[165]

And after Eleanor had spent some time at Marlborough in 1256, the apartments were remodelled yet again. The constable accounted for

> ... removing the chamber and walls which were between the King's chamber and the Queen's chamber in the castle of Marlborough, and building a certain chamber there, and for extending a certain privy chamber for the use of the king, and a privy chamber for the queen.[166]

We do not know whether the royal children – or even some of them – travelled frequently with their parents, but if they did, there were five of them by 1256, which in itself would have required more space in the queen's rooms. They might equally have had separate accommodation, as at Clarendon.

Alongside Henry's enthusiasm for interior decoration and architectural improvements, there is another underlying trend, towards better amenities and a generally higher standard of comfort. Fireplaces were now almost standard. Chimneys were repaired in 1238,[167] and in 1241 the almonry was pulled down and replaced by a new one with a fireplace.[168] A fireplace was even added to the storeroom next to the queen's chamber in the same year.[169] After 1244, any new chamber was usually specified as having a fireplace. In 1268, the fireplace (and presumably the chimney) in the queen's chamber had to be repaired because it had come down in strong winds.

Before the thirteenth century, communal latrines seem to have been the normal arrangement in castles.[170] By 1240, private chambers for the king and queen and their attendants were becoming the norm: a 'wardrobe with a private chamber' was ordered for Eleanor in 1241.[171] The order was repeated in 1244, with two further privies added, one for the chamber of her attendant Alpeys.[172] Privies were carefully positioned: in 1250 two rooms were rebuilt so that a privy could be positioned over the moat surrounding the motte.[173] And both the royal privies were rebuilt when the walls between the king's and queen's chambers were removed in 1256–57.

Domestic offices

The great kitchen was built in 1205, and it was given a lead roof in 1212. In 1225 it caught fire, with dramatic results. Two records on the same day, 26 July, give instructions for repairing the damage:

> Order to John de Fostebir and his fellow foresters of Savernake, to deliver to the men of M as underwritten, rafters for rebuilding their houses, which have been consumed by fire, namely [*list of 38 men and women, and the timber to be delivered, plus materials to the abbot of Stanley, the keeper of the hospital of St John of Marlborough, and the prior of St Margaret's of Marlborough*].

> Order to Robert de Meisy, constable of M, that from the money he has received from selling the K's grain … he should … rebuild the kitchen of the castle, which has been burnt.

This information about the fire also tells us that there must have been houses built close up to the castle walls, and that the modern separation between the mound and the town was filled by streets. The mound and the site of the old bailey now stand well separated from the nearest town buildings.[174] However, it is very likely that the medieval town stretched right up to the moat on the east side of the castle. Flames and sparks could easily have been blown across the moat into the huddle of thatched timber buildings on the far bank. The 'great kitchen' was a sizeable building, probably at least 36ft square, like other kitchens of this period (Fig. 3.12).[175] Because of the fire risk, a position away from the royal apartments on the town side of the castle would be logical.

Fig. 3.12 The abbbot's kitchen at Glastonbury.

After its destruction in 1225, the kitchen was rebuilt with a fire-resistant stone roof.[176] Thirty years later, a chimney was installed, instead of the original smoke-hole.[177] There was also a separate kitchen attached to the king's chamber, built in 1246,[178] and in the 'new tower'.[179] Beside the kitchens, there were the usual ancillary offices: a saucery, a buttery and a pantry or bread store.[180] There were further storehouses, and a considerable space would have been needed for the wine, which often came in loads of as much as forty tuns or 45,000 litres. The wine often came from Southampton. It was stored in cellars, as the accounts specifically record amounts taken from or placed in the king's cellars. A new door was made for the cellar in 1254. The contents of the cellar fluctuated hugely; there appear to be no deliveries in some years when the king was here, and the figures do not correspond directly to the amount of time he spent here in any given year. In 1256, when Queen Eleanor was here for a long period, no less than eighty tuns were delivered. In 1257, on the other hand, all the wines in the cellar were sent to Windsor, 'as the king has stayed longer than expected in London and Windsor'.[181]

The 'great stable' was also probably within the bailey. In 1255, a new stable was ordered by the king, but what actually seems to have happened is that an existing stable was rebuilt and the great stable was repaired.[182] Stables required a lot of space: the specified area for a modern stall is thirteen square metres. Even though those stables elsewhere which have been excavated or surveyed indicate a much smaller size of stall, it seems likely that only the horses required by the king and his close companions can have been inside the bailey. A separate stable for the queen was built in 1248–49, which also seems to have been within the castle walls.[183]

There were probably also stables elsewhere, simply because of the large numbers of horses needed, both for riding and for transport. There are examples from much smaller households for the division of stables between two adjacent places,[184] and the obvious place for such stabling would have been Ludgershall, fourteen miles away. The additional stables at Marlborough may well have been part of a second bailey, lying to the north-east of the castle. This has to be purely conjectural, and the evidence for it is very slight.[185]

When the court was at Marlborough, the large numbers of horses involved may have been managed in the same way as an army on campaign. We know surprisingly little about horse management at this period. The modern methods of picket lines and hobbling, where horses are tied to a fixed rope and have one foot strapped to prevent them from moving too far, do not seem to have been used before the sixteenth century. Even tethering to a single point is unlikely to have been used, as the word 'tether' is recorded for the first time in 1376. An alternative is that enclosures like the royal deer parks, of which a large number are recorded, were available nearby. There were parks at Ludgershall and notably at Clarendon and Woodstock, but there is no record of one at Marlborough.

The treasury and almonry

There seems to have been just two offices at the castle related to the royal administration. The almonry, where charitable gifts were distributed, was a separate building, containing the almoner's stores, almost certainly in existence by 1205, when we have the earliest record of royal almsgiving at Marlborough. At least a dozen almonries were to be found in royal castles before Henry III came to the throne.[186] Ten trees were needed to repair the Marlborough almonry in 1231, and it was subsequently demolished and rebuilt in 1241–42. The whereabouts of the treasury is unknown.

The king's houses

The king's houses are a recurrent feature of the accounts from 1222 to 1238, but only in terms of repairs; we have little indication of where or what they were. The phrase seems to refer to buildings which are otherwise individually unnamed anywhere within the castle. There are just three entries where the term has a different meaning, referring to all the accommodation within the castle. In the first two instances, the intention was to provide secure accommodation for someone with royal connections, because the castle was unoccupied. Edward I did this on two occasions for men who were going abroad in his service. The first was Amaury de St Amand; when the king was assembling his army at Portsmouth for a campaign in Gascony in 1294, a writ was issued for Amaury giving him custody of the castle so that his wife Mary could live here.[187]

The second writ brings us back to the Marshal family, who had been closely associated with the castle from the reign of Henry I onwards. William Marshal the younger surrendered the castle in 1221, and he and his brothers had no male heirs. His granddaughter Joan was regarded as countess of Pembroke in her own right. Her son Aymer de Valence was asked in 1297 to accompany Edward I to Flanders. His wife Beatrice, whom he had married in 1295, was still living with her mother-in-law, as Aymer had no residence of his own in England, although he had just inherited his father's French lands. For whatever reason, Aymer petitioned the king to grant him Marlborough castle so that Beatrice could set up her own household here; he would pay the costs. This was agreed, and his mother came to her estate at Swindon at the end of May 1297, evidently to help her daughter-in-law to establish herself. She left Swindon in early August, and the king's order to hand over the castle was issued on 21 August. It was seventy-five years since a member of the Marshal family had occupied it.[188]

The king's houses also served as a safe haven in troubled times for the royal family. In February 1325, Edward II assigned them to Roger de Monthermer, his cousin, as he and his wife Isabel were to look after Edward's daughters, Eleanor and Jeanne, aged seven and four. Monthermer died that spring, and Isabel was given sole charge of the houses in July, and of the castle in February 1326.[189] These entries stem from a famous love story. Monthermer's father Ralph had been in the service of Gilbert de Clare, earl of Gloucester, who died in 1295. His widow Joan, daughter of Edward I, fell in love with Ralph, and persuaded her father to knight him. She then married him privately early in 1297, but when this came to light, the king had Monthermer imprisoned at Bristol, while Joan was sent to Marlborough, where her eldest daughter was born.[190] Ralph was freed that summer and became earl of Gloucester during his wife's lifetime. His son's guardianship of the king's daughters has to be read in the context of Edward II's downfall. A month after the first writ to Monthermer appointing him as guardian was delivered, Isabella, the children's mother, left for France, and only returned at the head of an army in September 1326. Again, there was an echo of the past: Edward II sent his daughters to Marlborough for safety, just as John had sent the young Henry III in similar circumstances in the troubled year of 1215.

Defences: walls, gates, bridges

The outer wall of the bailey was probably laid out during John the Marshal's fortification of the castle in about 1138.[191] A castle without a strong bailey is unlikely to have been described as a very strong fortress. The main gate was probably on the eastern side, towards the old Roman road and the town. By 1241, this 'great gate' had towers which were given lead roofs.[192] The walls and battlements needed constant maintenance, and one order to the constable instructs him to 'prop up walls and bridges' as if temporary measures were all that could be done.[193] Occasionally a specialist was brought in: 'Elias the engineer', based in Oxford, came to Marlborough after the castle had been recaptured following the siege of 1197, probably to deal with damage caused by the attackers. He seems to have been part of a team who maintained royal castles in southern England. Elias was highly paid, and was keeper of Beaumont palace in Oxford.[194]

Gardens

In 1250, a new barbican was built behind the king's chamber, with a bridge over the moat which led to the dovecot. Beyond this were a lawn (*pratellus*) and the king's garden. In 1203, this garden was enclosed,[195] but it would have been primarily a practical garden rather than a pleasure garden. Most castles would have had such gardens, but very few had a *herbarium*. Now *herbarium* is often wrongly translated 'herb garden', but it is not a medicinal herb garden such as might be found in a monastery. The word comes from the French *herbier*, a place where *herbe* (grass) grows. The *herbarium* was an enclosed lawn or arbour (Fig. 3.13). In modern English 'arbour' means a sheltered seat or place within a pleasure garden, so the medieval English 'herber' is used to distinguish these small courtyard gardens from the familiar 'arbours' of more recent times. The herber at Marlborough is first recorded in 1230–31, when there is an entry on the accounts 'for repairing the herber in the castle of Marlborough, 21s 7½d'.[196] In 1239, the herber was enclosed by planked walls with an entrance gate, which would have given greater privacy, at a cost of 26d for the labour, excluding the materials.[197] The result would have looked like the garden shown in Fig. 3.13. There was a pleasure garden outside the walls at Windsor, and only three of Henry's other favourite castles, Gloucester, Nottingham, Winchester and Marlborough, had herbers. The major herbers are not found in royal castles but in the king's houses or palaces, such as Clarendon and Woodstock.[198]

Winchester had three herbers, and one of these was reconstructed in 1986 as 'Queen Eleanor's garden'. Herbers filled small courtyards within the castle, or were placed in enclosed spaces between the buildings and the outer boundary, and this was probably the case at Marlborough. The specification for the herber at the king's manor at Guildford in 1251 gives us a clear picture of this. The herber was outside the king's bedroom, with a door into it from the adjoining passage: it was a small enclosed area, as an existing wall was to be demolished and moved back fifteen feet in order to create it. At the same time, the large window in the queen's bedroom was to be glazed,

Fig. 3.13 A herber similar to that at Marlborough, from a fifteenth-century manuscript.

presumably so that she could see the garden.[199] The placing of the modern reconstruction of the herber at Winchester lacks this sense of a private space within the royal apartments, a kind of outdoor extension of the king's or queen's chamber, because the layout of the buildings has changed since the thirteenth century. (It now abuts the wall of the law courts.) Quite frequently, the herbers are specified as being below the chamber, as a foreground to the view. The Guildford specification shows us that views were important; indeed, appreciation of the landscape influenced the siting of windows and the alignment of the buildings. Within the herber there would have been turf seats, a fountain, trees and perhaps a tunnel arbour, and a water channel. Sylvia Landsberg, who designed the Winchester garden, chose the plants following the instructions of a German writer, Albertus Magnus, who wrote a detailed description of a herber about 1260, soon after Henry III had created them in many of his houses and castles.[200]

Eleanor's love of gardens is demonstrated by an episode after she was widowed. One of her dower castles was Gloucester. The priory of Llanthony Secunda lay below the castle, on the banks of the Severn, and its book of charters records that in 1277 the queen thanked the prior for allowing her to build a bridge down to the priory garden so that she and her ladies could walk there.[201]

Other Activities at the Castle

Royal recreations

Hunting

One of the great attractions for the kings at Marlborough was its proximity to Savernake forest, together with the castle at Ludgershall, fourteen miles away on the southern edge of the forest. The Anglo-Norman kings loved hunting and hawking in equal measure. Here, hunting came first: the royal hawks were kept near Northampton, and hawking was not a pursuit for forests – open country with meadows and rivers was much more suitable.

Henry II was famous, indeed notorious, as a hunter; Gerald of Wales, who was hostile to the king, portrayed it as one of his vices: 'He was addicted to the chase beyond measure. At crack of dawn, he was off on horseback, traversing the wilderness, plunging into woods and climbing the mountain tops.' William of Newburgh, another chronicler, noted that he had inherited his enthusiasm from his grandfather, but the younger Henry delighted in it 'more than was right'.[202]

John was also a passionate hunter, and one surviving roll of the accounts of the king's hunting expenses survives from 1212. It shows us a large hunt which followed the king round England on suitable journeys, a cavalcade which in itself would have been very striking (Fig. 3.14). There were as many as sixty-four handlers and 325 hounds, and they usually stayed a few miles away from where the king was, since the addition of this group would only have placed further burdens on the feeding and accommodation of the royal court.[203] When the hunt came to Marlborough, the problem was easily solved by housing the hounds at Ludgershall, within easy reach of the castle, ready for a day when the king wanted to ride out with them.

Indeed, hunting seems to have been one of the prime reasons for the timing of John's visits to Marlborough. The classic work on medieval hunting, Dame Juliana Berners' *Boke of St Albans*, specifies a close season when no activity should take place in woodland; this is from 25 March to 24 June, to avoid disturbing deer with their young. Only two of John's nineteen visits during his reign fall within that period.

Fig. 3.14 King John hunting, from a thirteenth-century manuscript.

Henry III seems to have much preferred falconry to hunting, but Edward I was a keen hunter. However, he preferred the attractions of the New Forest and of the hunting around Clarendon. He moved round the kingdom much more frequently than his father, and Marlborough was only occasionally visited; this is confirmed by the state of repair of the castle.[204]

Prison

In 1070, Aethelric II, bishop of Selsey, was uncanonically deprived of his office, and, although innocent according to the chronicler, was soon afterwards 'kept under guard' at Marlborough by the king.[205] Assuming that the castle was in existence by then, this does not imply that there was necessarily a prison within the walls. There was a 'narrow dungeon' here in 1140, as described earlier in the account of John the Marshal's imprisonment of Robert the Fleming.

The Marlborough prison may have been outside the system of county gaols established by laws passed in 1166.[206] It was perhaps under the king's direct control, as the main Wiltshire prison was at Salisbury. It was only used by the sheriff occasionally, but remained on the official list of prisons until 1504. A sample of the years 1236–86 shows eighty-nine writs committing prisoners to gaol for the whole of Wiltshire, of whom seventy-seven went to Salisbury and five went to Marlborough. The most important prisoners on record were indeed royal prisoners, Templar knights held here in 1309. This was shortly after the Templars began to be persecuted for the supposed crimes of heresy and blasphemy which led to their dissolution in 1312.

Fishery

When Chaucer portrayed the pilgrims in the prologue to his *Canterbury Tales*, he singled out the Franklin, whose name defined him as 'a freeman not of noble birth', as an example of a man who was climbing the social ladder, lavish with his hospitality. He could feed his guests well because 'he had many a bream and many a luce in stew [pike in his pond]'.[207] One of the more surprising aspects of Marlborough castle was that it was one of the most important royal fishponds (Fig. 3.15).[208] It probably existed in the late twelfth

Fig. 3.15 A medieval fishpond, from a fifteenth-century French manuscript.

century, since in 1205 William de Cornhill was paid the substantial amount of 43s 8d for transporting fish from Marlborough to Farnham in barrels.[209] In the light of later entries, this looks like a consignment of breeding stock from the royal ponds to the bishop of Winchester's stews at his great castle at Farnham. Freshwater fish were very much a status symbol, and this was a suitable present to the newly elected bishop, Peter des Roches, who was to be Henry III's tutor and guardian, a controversial figure from the royal household who proved to be as much at home on the battlefield or exchequer as in his cathedral.

This transaction is typical of the dozens of such orders to the constable or bailiff at Marlborough during Henry III's reign. The fish involved are predominantly freshwater bream, with some pike and occasionally eels, shad and lampreys.[210] Marlborough supplied the king's houses at Woodstock and Clarendon, the castles at Windsor and Winchester, and the palace of Westminster itself:[211] in 1262, the king wrote urgently from Canterbury to tell Robert de Walerand, the constable at Marlborough, to send thirty cooked bream to Westminster, to arrive by 4 January.

Bream were not very exciting eating, and probably the reason why the king declared to the sheriff of Gloucester in 1237 that he wanted lampreys because he and the queen found all other fish 'insipid'.[212] Bream were usually prepared in a pie with a kind of aspic; they are not to be confused with sea bream, and do not appear in modern cookery books. Eels, pike and shad do have a place there, and pike, in the form of *quenelles de brochet*, is a speciality of French provincial restaurants. Lampreys are indeed very different from any of these white fish. They are still eaten in south-west France, where they are stewed in a red wine sauce, and have a very meaty taste. Eleanor came from Provence and was certainly fond of them: when she was convalescing at Marlborough in 1256, ten lampreys were sent to her from Gloucester when the king was away in East Anglia.[213]

The 'king's great fishpond of Marlborough' lay along the River Kennet between the town and 'the bridge of Okeburn'. Okeburn is Ogbourne St George, and the bridge must be that at the east end of the town on the Ogbourne road.[214] The whole enclosure is usually called the *vivarium*, a general term for a place where living things are kept.[215] Within it were ponds, the most important being the king's great pond. This seems to have been divided up into 'bays', sections which could be drained individually. The maintenance of these ponds was a continuing task, and in 1272, the year that Henry died, Edward I ordered no less than a hundred oaks to be provided to the constable at Marlborough for repairing the king's great pond.[216] It implies that the bays were substantial timber structures; there were also sluices and the ponds may well have been enclosed by oak stakes as a revetment. Part of the pond appears to survive on the east bank of the Og at its junction with the Kennet; the Ordnance Survey map marks it as an ancient structure. Sadly, a recent visitor to the site reports that the pond has been filled in, though the grass field which has replaced it shows markings which make the placing of the pond evident.

The stocking of the ponds was done by transporting fish from other royal ponds or estates under royal control, as well as by gifts from individuals. Once the ponds were established, gifts of breeding fish were as frequent as gifts of fish for eating. Pike, which were not very numerous at Marlborough, could be transported on wet grass or rushes for places within a day's journey, while the bream were put in canvas-lined barrels of water. As to catching the fish, one method was to drain the bay and simply collect them if a large number were needed. Otherwise standing nets were used, and possibly netting from a boat. Many households had fishermen attached to them, but curiously there does not seem to have been a royal fisherman at Marlborough, despite its prominence in the supply of fish.

* * *

Any survey of Marlborough castle in the Middle Ages is inevitably very partial, without meaningful physical remains to help us, and with records which provide us with a series of vivid flashes of illumination and as many tantalising blanks. What is indisputable, and which previous writers on Marlborough have only partly discussed, is the undoubted importance of the castle as both a regional stronghold and a royal residence in the twelfth and thirteenth centuries.

4

The Mound as a Garden Feature

Brian Dix

The Crown's grant of Marlborough Castle to Edward Seymour, Protector Somerset during the reign of Edward VI, and its subsequent restoration to the family after his execution and attainder, led his successors to develop the site as a country residence.[1] The castle had already fallen into disrepair by the late fourteenth century[2] and was in ruins when John Leland came to Marlborough in the mid-1540s.[3] The sheer bulk and prominence of the Mound, however, meant it inevitable that it would become a garden feature.

The artificial hill, either specially created or utilising an existing feature as at Marlborough, provided an elevated position from which to view the garden and look out upon other surroundings. Although partly influenced by the viewing platforms and low mounds in some late medieval gardens,[4] advances in military architecture and engineering were undoubtedly a major factor in the design and development of later, more monumental examples, together with related earthworks like garden terraces.

Mounts (*montagnola*) or 'little mountains' (*montagnette*) of natural rugged appearance or with spiral paths winding around smooth sides were introduced into Italian Renaissance gardens from at least the mid-fifteenth century onwards.[5] The fashion had spread to England within a century. In 1533–35, for example, Henry VIII buried the basement of an elaborate banqueting house within a specially constructed mound in one of the gardens at Hampton Court Palace. The main doorway was reached by means of a spiral path lined by rosemary and a series of heraldic beasts mounted upon painted poles.[6] At about the same time, John Leland, visiting Wressle Castle in East Yorkshire, described two mounts in the orchards there that were 'writhen about with degrees like turninges of cokilshilles, to cum to the top without payn'.[7]

The attraction of the mount as a vantage point, either with a deliberately built belvedere from which to look outwards or with the summit left bare yet still affording a prospect, was subsequently developed in Elizabethan times.[8] Whilst usually circular in plan, such features might also be square or pyramidal with stepped sides needing stairs for ascent rather than the more usual spiral path. Both types are still to be found in the earthwork remains of the gardens that Sir Thomas Tresham laid out at Lyveden in Northamptonshire between 1594 and his death in 1605, when work stopped.[9] High-ranking courtiers William Cecil, Lord Treasurer Burghley, and Christopher Hatton, Lord Chancellor, both built so-called 'snail mounts' at their properties and others quickly followed, either simply copying fashion or motivated by rivalry.[10] Some were even incorporated into pageants like the entertainment that Edward Seymour, 1st Earl of Hertford, staged for the queen at Elvetham in 1591, which included an island made in the form of 'a *Snayl-mount*, rising to foure circles of greene Priuie [privet] hedges, the whole in height twentie foot, and fourscore foote broade at the bottome'.[11]

The fashion for creating prospect mounts continued in the seventeenth century. Contemporary commentators like Salomon de Caus advised that the finest view of a garden was to be seen from above,[12] with Sir Francis Bacon going so far as to recommend that a mount with a banqueting house should be set in the middle of broad walks.[13] His cousin Robert Cecil created just that in his gardens at Hatfield, but today no trace remains.[14] Examples of mounts constructed in Jacobean and Stuart times do however survive at Kirby Hall, Northamptonshire[15] and Lords Place on the site of the former Lewes Priory, East Sussex,[16] in addition to that which was built in the grounds of New College in Oxford during the 1640s.[17] A number of mounts re-used relict mottes, as at Warwick Castle and Dunham Massey among other places,[18] and in the 1680s the antiquary John Aubrey knew of plans for a similar appropriation of another mound at Hamstead Marshall, Berkshire, which 'is a hill like Silbury hill … on which Capt[ain] W[illiam] Winde designes to make a Skrew-walk, as at the keep of the Castle at Marleborough, at the Lord Seymours'.[19]

The Marlborough mount

Sir William Seymour inherited the Marlborough property in 1621 and seems immediately to have conveyed it to his brother Francis, who may already have been living there in a new house.[20] Whilst this incorporated the former motte into its grounds, it is unclear exactly when any formal gardens were laid out or when the castle mound may have been remodelled to create a visual attraction with a spiral walk to the summit. It appears to have been used during the Civil War, suggesting that there was some means of access to the top, although this need not have been a formal path. A few years later, John Evelyn recorded in his *Diary* that 'at one end of this town we saw my Lord Seymour's house, but nothing observable save the Mount, to which we ascended by windings for near half a mile …'.[21]

Evelyn further recalled the Mound when considering such structures for a projected study of gardens, *Elysium Britannicum*, which was still in manuscript when he died. He wrote that the length of the path 'is sayd to be a mile from the foote to the summit' and he might even have had Marlborough in mind when describing how the top could be treated: 'where the area would be flatt & sufficiently spatious {either} for a smale Coronarie Garden & a Speculatory Towre built Fortresse like with battlements where {amongst other Mathematicall Engines} two or three smale pieces may be mounted to be shott off upon Triumphs & Sollemnitys, or else, a peruq of Trees be planted, such as are … the pine, firr & other perenniall Greenes, (plants & simple) lovers of prowde & loftie situations.'[22]

Evelyn also commented how the summit could serve 'to take a universall {vista &} prospect not onely of the Gardens, but of the whole Conutry [*sic*]'. Visitors like Celia Fiennes and Daniel Defoe would later testify to the fine views that existed from the top of the Marlborough Mound, particularly over the adjacent town.[23]

Sir Robert Moray, one of the founders of the Royal Society, read a paper to members in 1664 that described the Mound as 'a spiral of 4 entire turns and about a quarter making a very insensible ascent of some 700 yards in all, the walk being some 6 foot broad handsomely gravelled [with] a fine quickset hedge on the outside with fruit trees of severall kindes set in it and at orderly and convenient distance on all sides of bankes of the sloping hill in spiral footpaths, thereof being green everywhere. About the end of the third turn there is a pretty arbor [*sic*] or resting place of hewn stone covered and at the top a pretty green compased with the quickset hedge and fruit trees as the rest of the spiral walk, and in the Middle a very fair and handsom Octagonall arbour or room so[me] 24 foot wide with a pair of stairs of one side, rising some 15 or 16 foot to a platform leaded, with a fair cistern in the middle of some 18 foot over, and 4 foot high into which there is water forced up by a water mill and force pump in lead pipes of some ¾ inch bore and between 3 and 400 yards long [from] the Mill set upon a brook.'[24]

Whilst the cistern would have provided water for the house, the building that contained it was clearly also used for recreation, being described both as a 'banquetting howse' and summer house in subsequent accounts of expenditure upon its maintenance and repair. Other costs were incurred by the occasional planting of fruit bushes together with the need to fill in gaps that arose in the hedges that lined the spiral walk and from renewing turf on parts of the slope; the 'belvedere' or arbour on the side also required occasional repair.[25] Archaeological investigation in 2004 revealed vestiges of an early gravel path that pre-dated the construction of the belvedere and may have been revetted into the slope, but no evidence survived from the hedge planted on the outside.[26]

Apart from the eventual collapse of the cistern-house, little seems to have changed by the time that Celia Fiennes visited at the start of the eighteenth century, just as Charles Seymour, 6th Duke of Somerset, was replacing the old mansion with the current building or 'C House' now at the heart of Marlborough College.[27] She described how from 'the bowling green; you go

Fig. 4.1 Reconstructed arbour towards the summit of the Mound
photographed in July 2016.

many stepps down into a grass-walke with quick sett hedges cut low, this leads to the foote of the Mount and that you ascend from the left hand by an easye ascent bounded by such quick set hedges cut low, and soe you rise by degrees in 4 rounds ... in the midst of the top of the mount was a house built and pond, but that's fallen down; halfe way down is a seate opposite the dwelling house which is brick'.[28]

William Stukeley depicted the seat as a round-arched arbour and it was still sufficiently recognisable in the 1840s to be recorded in the Preshute Tithe Map.[29] It appears to have been approximately three metres wide and two metres deep, and the surviving sarsen stone foundation may originally have supported a timber superstructure that was subsequently replaced in brickwork.[30] The feature was reinstated in 2000–02, albeit without its former shellwork and in a modern form that recreates a semicircle of four niches connected by a continuous seat below an open metal roof (Fig. 4.1).[31]

The continuation of the hedge around the summit was 'cut in works' and thus had an ornamental form, as shown by Stukeley, who drew a crenelated parapet in his elevation of the Mound (Fig. 4.2).

Marlborough Mount

Fig. 4.2 Elevation of the garden mount shown as part of plate 1 in William Stukeley's *Itinerarium Curiosum* (1724).

Fig. 4.3 The Mound in the early nineteenth century: views by Samuel Prout in 1804 (top) and Philip Crocker c. 1814 (bottom).

By that time there was a new 'octagonal summerhouse' at the top.[32] Both the building and the hedges around the sides were 'all apparently still in good order' almost a century later, as noted by Sir Richard Colt Hoare.[33] There had also been tree planting on the summit, as seen in contemporary illustrations and witnessed by visitors in 1785, who noted 'a small quincunx of young trees on the top'.[34]

Drawings of the Mound from towards the end of the eighteenth century also show the development of tree cover around the sides, initially growing in the increasingly unkempt hedges beside the spiral path as illustrated in a view of 1788 by S. H. Grimm[35] and afterwards extending onto the grass slopes as depicted by Samuel Prout and Philip Crocker in 1804 and *c.* 1814 respectively (Fig. 4.3).[36]

A charmingly naive painting showing boys at play in front of the buildings during the College's early years also depicts the side of the Mound, where several groups of pupils can be seen walking behind the hedge that bordered the spiral path leading to the top (Fig. 4.4). The summit is planted with broad-leafed trees which can be identified from their shape and colour as English elm. These may have formed the quincunx recorded in 1785. The quincunx still exists, but the trees are limes, planted in about 1910,[37] evidently as a replacement for the elms.

Fig. 4.4 The Mound in the context of the newly established College, *c.* 1850, by an unknown artist.

By contrast with the summit, the slopes of the Mound are largely planted with what appear to be tall-stemmed larches and possibly other conifers. A tall leaning tree behind a wall at the base cannot be easily identified, but seems to be of a deciduous kind. A nearby row of trees beside the forecourt is presumably formed of common lime, but two taller trees opposite are most likely horse chestnut, particularly if they are being shown in flower. Two tall cypresses visible at the rear of the Mound may be growing on its far side or planted in the Wilderness beyond. Whilst they might have arrived in Britain comparatively recently, most of the species are either native or earlier introductions.[38] Until their recent cutting, the mature tree population almost entirely obscured the shape of the Mound and provided cover for illicit smoking by generations of schoolboys.[39]

House and gardens

Marlborough House, as it was then known, was settled upon Algernon Seymour, Lord Hertford, after he married Frances Thynne in 1715.[40] In due course William Stukeley became their friend and, rather than simply visiting to view the house, we may expect that he most likely stayed there whilst on

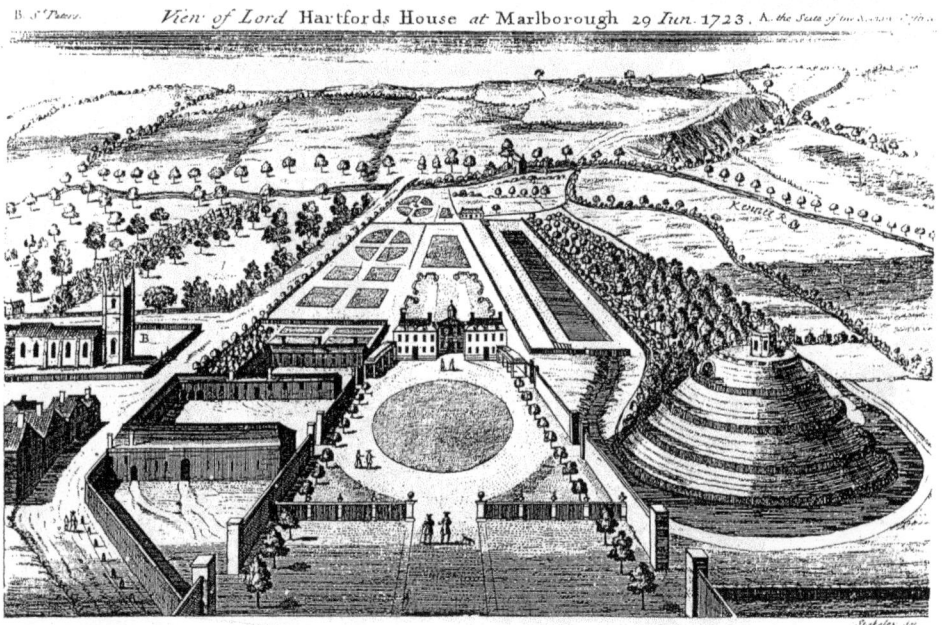

Fig. 4.5 Overview of Marlborough House and its gardens, plate 3 of Stukeley's *Itinerarium Curiosum* (1724).

116

his way to study neighbouring monuments in early summer 1723.[41] Indeed, three of his drawings are dated 29 June that year,[42] which was the day before he started working at Avebury.[43] He believed that Marlborough was the site of Roman *Cunetio* and seems to have confused the earthwork of part of the medieval castle's outer bailey ditch with the defences of an earlier fort. Although still faintly visible today, the remains are now largely filled-in as the result of later garden landscaping.

Stukeley undertook numerous tours or journeys to study ancient monuments and other antiquities at first hand, making drawings wherever he visited and noting the date when they were drafted.[44] Engraved versions of some were included in a printed collection of some of his tours published as *Itinerarium Curiosum* in 1724. A further selection of dated drawings was published posthumously in a second edition in 1776. They include a town plan of Marlborough showing the house and Mound at the western end.[45]

Whilst differences between the individual illustrations of Marlborough might lead us to question their reliability, some of the discrepancies probably arise from engraver's error and the limitations of technique or may be due to misrepresenting details which may not have been completely clear in the drawing that was being copied. It is nevertheless difficult to reconcile the representation of the gardens in Stukeley's quasi-bird's eye view dated 29 June 1723 with their portrayal in the wider prospect of the town that he made the same day and his subsequent ground plot.[46]

The series of parterres depicted to the south of the house in the aerial view (Fig. 4.5) are not shown in the plan (Fig. 4.6), which he dated a week later on 6 July, on the very day that Lady Hertford visited him at Avebury.[47] Perhaps she provided the results of a previous survey to serve as a base map for his own plan? Stukeley's version appears to record the situation when the site was still constrained by the course of an old road leading to the river. His earlier drawing could therefore have been intended to demonstrate the potential for extending the grounds once this lane was removed and the garden could be enlarged up to the new road beyond (the present Pewsey Road). It remains uncertain how much of his proposed layout was taken up or if the arrangement of parterres is simply an indication of what might be achieved. The inclusion of the design as a plate in *Itinerarium Curiosum* published in the following year, however, suggests an element of confidence on the part of its author.

Taken together, the series of illustrations can be used to demonstrate the main characteristics and prominent features of the former Hertford property at Marlborough. The house was approached from the Devizes or Bath road, passing through an outer forecourt along a central roadway with lawns at either side before entering the main court with its broad carriage-sweep around an oval grass plat. William Stukeley's plan shows the division between the two courts as the mirror image of the linear arrangement of house façade and quadrant colonnades, but his aerial view depicts a straight boundary,

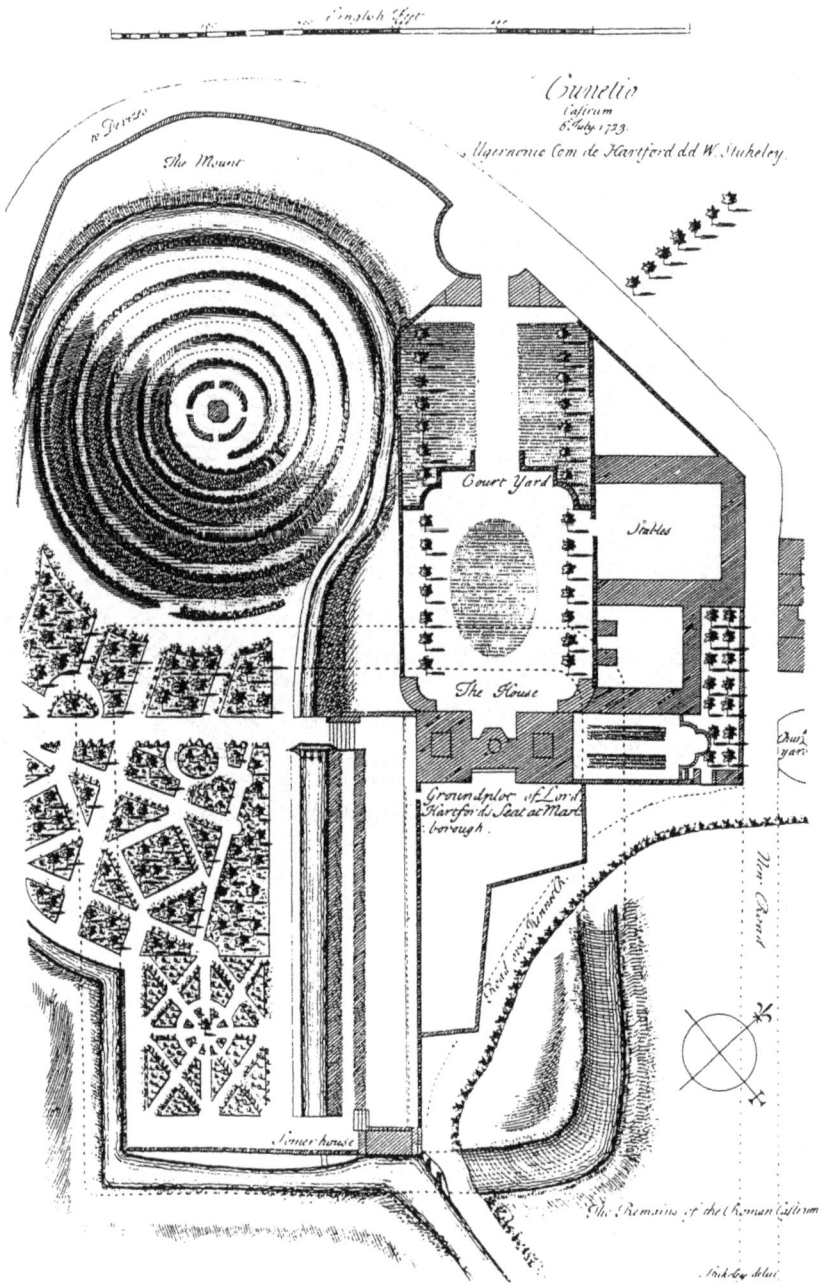

The Mount

Cunetio
Castrum
6° July 1723.
Algernono Com de Hartford dd W. Stukeley.

Court Yard

Stables

The House

Groundplot of Lord
Hartfords Seat at Marl
borough.

Somer house

The Remains of the Roman Castrum

Stukeley delin.

Fig. 4.6 William Stukeley's plan of the gardens at Marlborough published as
plate 62 in his *Itinerarium Curiosum* (1724).

apparently with a wooden palisade or iron railings between individual piers. A row of trees lines the sides of each court in both illustrations.

Other regular planting on the edge of the property beyond the stables and service block to the south and east presumably denotes an orchard or possibly a combined fruit and vegetable garden, since there is no other obvious area for growing kitchen stuff. The plan shows a group of buildings around an entrance at the far end but there could also have been a passageway leading into the service court (Fig. 4.6). It seems that the area was largely hidden from the house, with which there is no direct connection because of a separate walled garden in-between. This was of a rectangular shape with an elaborate *demi-lune* or half circle at one end and contained a series of parterres, or possibly flowerbeds; it may have been a 'privy garden' directly accessible from the house.

Both Stukeley's plan and his prospect of the town show an awkwardly shaped plot of ground beyond the house, where the property was bounded by the road or lane that led southwards to the river. We should expect such a prominent location directly in front of the house to be laid out as the principal garden, usually known as the great or best garden,[48] and it is telling that the wider view appears to show some form of planting, albeit very sketchily.[49] It is therefore possible that Stukeley's aerial view incorporated some extant elements. Indeed, the curlicues he depicts to be seen from the main windows suggest the presence of a scrollwork parterre of the type that was fashionable in the opening decade of the eighteenth century when the house was being rebuilt.[50] The generic nature of the series of rectilinear and circular parterres that lie beyond may be intended however to show how the space could be filled.

The canal

There are no surface remains to indicate the extent to which any of these works were carried out and today much of the garden area has been altered by landscaping and changing soil levels, or is covered by tarmac or otherwise built upon. Rather than being removed, the boundary wall beside the old lane was retained within the enlarged garden, presumably because of the differences in the height of the ground on either side. It is shown in most subsequent surveys, for example in connection with the tithe apportionment of Preshute parish between 1843 and 1847,[51] together with later Ordnance Survey mapping, and remains to this day, although it has been rebuilt or renewed in several places.

The least altered length of walling, formed out of bricks nine inches long and almost two and a half inches thick, acts as a revetment or 'breast wall' to retain the higher ground of an artificial terrace raised along its western side. The terrace forms a broad earthwork some 13m wide with a grass *glacis* slope, which was presumably created using the upcast from digging out an adjacent canal.

The feature was originally straight-sided and was presumably the 'fish pond' which Celia Fiennes described being supplied with water from the 'cannal' around the base of the Mound.[52] This appears to have utilised the existing ditch or moat, which presumably was freshly scoured and stabilised or strengthened at the edges, as suggested by the discovery of a seemingly seventeenth-century wall during the construction of new science laboratories in 1956.[53]

The continuation of the watercourse as a straightened channel was depicted in 1706 in J. Hutchinson's *Map of Marlborough* but only along part of its eventual course, since it turned west through a right angle to flow towards a mill-house at the junction with the main encircling moat.[54] Neither this connection nor the mill were recorded by Stukeley, who showed the canal aligned simply to the south, along a course that continued to be delineated in subsequent maps and surveys until about the middle of the nineteenth century (see below). It was presumably then backfilled and the site grassed over, so that it is scarcely visible today and survives only as a very faint depression without clear edges.

Frances Hertford, writing to her friend the Countess of Pomfret in 1739, mentioned the canal being widened together with the construction of cascades that created 'a rushing noise, which is heard in every part of the garden, and, in a hot day, sounds peculiarly cool and refreshing. The uppermost cascade passes betwixt two artificial rocks which are intermixed with so much earth as to allow the periwinkle and other greens that love the water, to creep upon them. The lower one where the stream falls into the main river, has the ruins of an arch built over it which, being composed of flints and unhewn stone, makes a very Gothic appearance. Betwixt the stones are here and there interspersed tufts of the house-leek and moss; which, from their appearance, might be supposed to have grown there at least a century.'[55] Whilst William Stukeley's plan might be thought to show a cascade at the point where the canal broadens out beside the terrace, it is simply a representation of the struts of the bridge at its head (Fig. 4.6).[56]

A culvert at the far end of the canal would have enabled the water to flow out into the stream or channel at the edge of the garden. Although precise details are lacking, particularly regarding the nature of a sluice or other controlling measures, part of the arrangement may survive in the remains of a brick-lined conduit that has been left accessible following recent discovery. Stukeley's illustrations show an adjacent single-storey building closing off the terrace, which he labelled a 'Somerhouse', or summer house as it was previously described in Hutchinson's 1706 map. Such places were often used for quiet afternoon activity, such as fishing in the adjacent canal or simply reading and writing, or even taking a nap.[57]

The wilderness

Lady Hertford clearly enjoyed the pleasures of the garden and in summer 1741 wrote further to Henrietta Pomfret, '... I find my own garden full of sweets, and I have a terrace between a border of pinks and a sweet briar hedge ... [which] perfumes the air for a long way ... Whether it is because this was the first habitation I was mistress of ... or because almost every little ornament has been made either by my lord's or my own contrivance, I cannot tell, but I certainly feel a partiality for this place ... The flowers to me appear painted with brighter colours, and the hayfields and elder bushes breathe more fragrance than the same things do any where else. When I am sitting near the cascade upon a favourite seat by the side of a little wilderness of flowering shrubs, I cannot help thinking, or almost saying to myself, "Lady Pomfret would not dislike this shade".'[58]

Hutchinson's map in 1706 labelled a wooded area at the foot of the Mound as 'Wilderness', the only named area of the gardens apart from 'the Mount' and a separate straight alley called 'the Green Walk'.[59] This last had disappeared by the time that William Stukeley published his plan, which shows the area in great detail (Fig. 4.6).[60] In particular, he locates a rectangular *bosquet* or grove in the south-west corner of the garden. This lies opposite the lower end of the terrace and straight-sided canal and, like them, is aligned parallel to the axis through the forecourt and house. A series of hedge-lined paths divided the enclosure into quarters, which may have contained a variety of trees and shrubs in addition to other, intersecting, diagonal pathways that all converged upon a large tree planted within a circle in the middle of the garden. The northern end of the garden adjoined a larger wilderness area, meeting its paths at an angle since they were not aligned with the main garden axis.

In Stukeley's plan this part of the wilderness comprises a symmetrical arrangement of compartments at either side of a central path running between the western edge of the garden plot and entry into the spiral path that winds clockwise up the side of the Mound. A skewed cross-walk projecting outwards as part of the orthogonal pattern of walled courts and paths set around the house emphasises the close visual and spatial relationship between the wilderness and the Mound. It further demonstrates how best use was made of the site within the constraints imposed by the bulk of the Mound itself and the remnants of its surrounding ditch or moat. The Mound was thus an integral part of this section of the garden layout, in which the wilderness was surely designed deliberately to be viewed from the summit.

It was usual for the individual divisions within such gardens to be planted up with elms and other trees behind tall hornbeam hedges or 'palisades' with gravel walks in-between.[61] Several later eighteenth- and nineteenth-century views show how these trees had grown out to give the appearance of a densely wooded area with further trees either colonising or being purposely planted around the sides of the Mound.[62]

The grotto

The wilderness garden and adjoining mount provided a suitable setting for Lady Hertford to combine her personal sensitivity and philosophical leanings with contemporary trends in developing feelings for Nature. All these found expression in the construction of a shell house or grotto that was set into the base of the Mound at the point where the spiral path begins to ascend (Fig. 4.7).

Inspired by classical antecedent, grottoes have been added to buildings and gardens to provide places for contemplation, recreation and social activity from the Renaissance onwards, ranging from subterranean or cavernous excavations to specially made above-ground structures.[63] Except where occurring as part of a special kind of fountain, the earliest grottoes in England date from the 1620s and were chiefly located inside the house, as in the remaining examples at Woburn Abbey and Skipton Castle.[64] Whilst later grottoes continued to use indoor rooms, purpose-built structures soon began to be developed, often taking advantage of a natural spring or a source

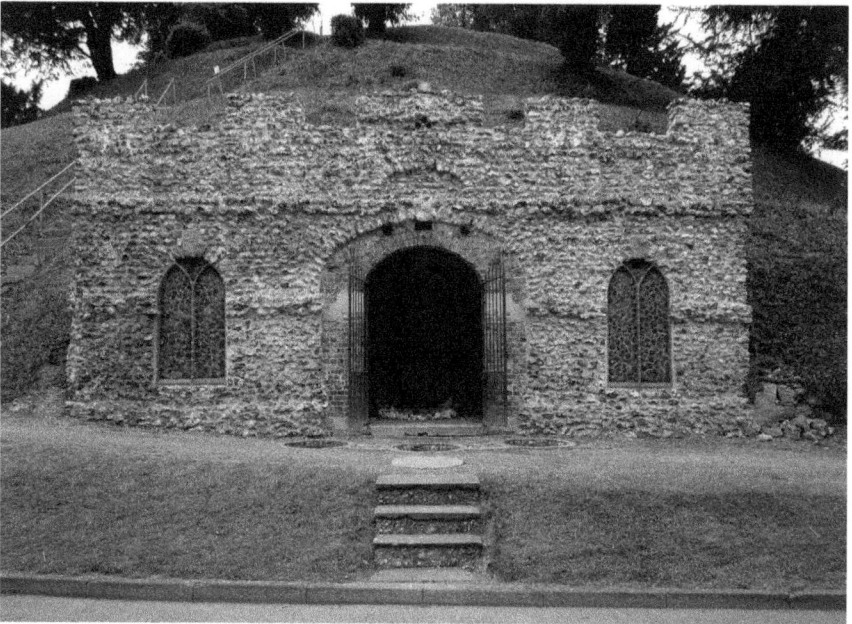

Fig. 4.7 The restored grotto, July 2016.

of water piped into them. They could be either free-standing or take the form of caves and tunnel-labyrinths cut to various depths into a hillslope or excavated in the underlying ground.[65]

The elaborate waterworks and astonishing effects of the early grottoes, such as automata and other hydraulic devices, were eventually abandoned as fashions changed with different taste and new outlook. In particular, in the early eighteenth century there was a shift of emphasis to 'follow Nature' and bring forth the 'genius of the place'. Initially promulgated by Anthony Ashley Cooper, 3rd Earl of Shaftesbury,[66] the idea was taken up and widely promoted by the poet Alexander Pope. Between 1720 and 1725 he constructed a grotto in the cellars of his house beside the River Thames at Twickenham, conceiving it as a place for meditation and creative writing, wherein the spirit of the inhabiting muses would inspire the imagination. The original decorative scheme of shells, flint and iron ore interspersed with fragments of mirror to provide *camera obscura* and other glittering effects was reworked from 1739 onwards to include a variety of rocks and minerals, chosen more for their natural beauty than rarity. By 'imitating Nature' the grotto developed a museum-like didactic purpose that was well suited for study by the *virtuosi*.[67] That Pope now considered this preferable to the whimsical shellwork already adopted in other places is shown by his admiration for Ralph Allen's wife upon the grotto being made at Prior Park, where she had 'begun to imitate the Great Works of Nature, rather than those Baubles most ladies affect'.[68]

Frances, Countess of Hertford belonged to that group of 'poetical ladies' whom Joseph Addison would have had in mind when recommending they decorate small shell grottoes as an amusing alternative to needlework.[69] As well as writing poetry herself, she was a strong supporter of budding mainstream poets like James Thomson and Stephen Duck, so the notion of a grotto as a haunt of the Muses must have had particular resonance. Indeed, it would not take a great leap of imagination to transform the Mound into the mythical Mount Parnassus and fabled home of Apollo where he brought the nine Muses, as told by Ovid in Book Five of the *Metamorphoses*.[70]

Some modern commentators have suggested that the frontispiece which William Kent produced to illustrate 'Spring' in the 1730 subscriber's edition of Thomson's *The Seasons* shows an idyllic version of the Marlborough landscape. Since the poem was dedicated to Lady Hertford, it is argued that a mountain in the background of the drawing should be thought of as Silbury Hill, while a lesser but nearer knoll might represent the Mound, possibly with the grotto beside it, although the classicised building shown there could as easily be intended for the Seymour mansion.[71]

We do not know precisely when the shell house or grotto was built. The poet Stephen Duck, who benefited from the Countess' patronage, hinted that it may still have been in the process of being worked on in the late 1730s when he wrote, in *A Description of a Journey to Marlborough*,

Within the Basis of the Verdant Hill
A beauteous Grot confesses Hertford's skill;
Who, with her lovely Nymphs, adorns the Place;
Give ev'ry polish'd stone its proper Grace;
Now varies rustic Moss about the Cell;
Now fits the Shining Pearl, or purple Shell.[72]

Presumably its decoration was complete by 1739, as in a letter written in June that year Lady Hertford mentioned 'The grotto which we have made under the mound ... without partiality I think is in itself much prettier than that at Twickenham.'[73] As with Pope's own grotto, we should expect construction and other works to have taken place over a period of time, with additions made here and there in accordance with changing enthusiasm and as different interests evolved. The extent of direct influence from Pope's grotto cannot be established beyond the applicability of its underlying philosophical notion, which may have encouraged widespread imitation. Indeed, in August 1733 while visiting the Lisle family at Crux Easton, near Highclere on the borders of Hampshire and Berkshire, the poet composed some lines in celebration of the owner's nine daughters and the grotto which they had decorated with shellwork in a wood on the estate. Although not published at the time, Lady Hertford is nevertheless likely to have known about the achievements of the 'maiden ladies' since their brother succeeded Lord Hertford as the sitting Member of Parliament for Marlborough for fifteen years from 1727.[74]

The surroundings of the wilderness provided a suitable sylvan setting for the Marlborough grotto, as shown by its only known historical depiction in a drawing of *The Enterance to the Mound at Malbro* made by John Baskerfield *c.* 1792 (Fig. 4.8). This shows a rugged façade with gothic-style pointed windows of simple Y-tracery at either side of a round-headed arch of dressed stone that forms the central doorway. A pair of doors or double gates made up of either open slats or vertical rods are opened outwards to reveal a glimpse of the interior, where a large niche dominates the back wall in the main room.

The building has been restored to something like its former appearance, mixing archaeological evidence with various levels of speculation and artistic interpretation (Fig. 4.7). Whilst Baskerfield's view might show a battlemented parapet like that which has been rebuilt, the evidence is ambiguous and he may unintentionally have created a wrong impression by his way of depicting the sweeping branches of overhanging trees. Likewise, the present gates are made of iron, albeit after an eighteenth-century pattern,[75] but the originals could equally have been of wood or decorated with twig-work to provide a rustic appearance.

Despite some details not being entirely accurate and others, such as the creation of new basins or pools, clearly not authentic, the modern recon-struction seeks to remain true to the spirit of the original and indeed conveys a good sense of what it may have been like. The work was largely carried

Fig. 4.8 John Baskerfield's view of the grotto and its setting, *c.* 1792.

out between 1980 and 1986 but not finally completed until 1990.[76] It marked the beginning of a series of collaborative projects between Diana Reynell, a former teacher at Marlborough College, and Simon Verity.

The rectangular structure, roughly eleven metres by four metres, with its back wall built into the slope of the Mound, is constructed of red bricks clad on the outside with large unworked flints. The interior is divided into three rooms with small equal-sized chambers at either end beside the central room containing the external doors. The walls with their alcoves or recesses, together with the vaulted ceilings, were originally covered with a variety of shells, pieces of rough stone and iron slag, through which white 'snail trail' patterns of baked flint meandered in an apparently random manner (Fig. 4.9). The late Diana Reynell, who worked extensively upon restoring the grotto's decoration, felt able to detect 'different hands and different materials' used in the end chambers.[77]

Patches of surviving shellwork and cladding, together with rusted iron cramps that were used to hold the heavier materials in place, were recorded diagrammatically[78] and helped to guide the present restoration where some of the missing shells could be renewed by matching replacements with the impressions that the originals had left behind. As in other contemporary grottoes, they included both freshwater and sea shells, combining exotic specimens from the West Indies with types from the Mediterranean and British shores and rivers.[79] Where some of the original choices of shell, like the ormers (*Haliotis tuberculata*) from the Channel Islands, are now protected against farming because the species has become endangered, a close relative

Fig. 4.9 'Snail-trails' and other decoration inside the grotto.

was substituted for reconstruction. Similarly, missing areas of recycled furnace slag have been repaired using material gleaned from the site of an eighteenth-century ironworks in order to match the blue glassy appearance of the original.[80]

The floor appears to have been covered by a brick and tile pavement, but it is unclear how much of the pattern is original due to the extent of late twentieth-century reconstruction. The removal of a concrete floor within the central chamber at that time revealed no evidence of an earlier surface, with only subfloor features surviving. A related series of photographs taken in 1983 were subsequently annotated with a few details.[81] They show a culvert or drain running across the room from the base of the niche towards the doorway. It appears to have been of simple construction, less than one foot wide between walls a single brick thick and capped by other bricks laid lengthwise across the top. An almost parallel lead pipe, one and a half inches in diameter, could be related to similar pipework shown in other photographs to run vertically down the mid-line of the niche, but it is no longer possible to establish a direct connection.[82] It is possible that the pipes could have supplied water from a cistern above.

The remains of a circular basin lined with slag and shells were discovered at the foot of the rear wall of the main room, although unfortunately the

Fig. 4.10 Central niche within the restored grotto, July 2016.

surviving photograph of it is out of focus due to 'hands trembling in excitement'.[83] It has been restored together with the niche above, where the broad band of rich shellwork surrounds a modern centrepiece of a stone urn carved by Simon Verity after an eighteenth-century original at Petworth House, West Sussex (Fig. 4.10).[84] The vessel is placed in such a way that water can divide around it and fall onto the open half of a giant clam (*Tridacna gigas*) before spilling into the floor basin. This large shell is another modern intro-duction, acquired through 'begging' at the food hall of Harrods in London, where it was being used in a display.[85]

In today's scheme, water flows from the basin below the niche into a new flint-edged pool set in the middle of the floor, where it is surrounded by inscribed flagstones and polished horses' teeth before continuing outside to three interconnecting flint and pebble-lined basins placed in front of the grotto. Photographs show them being constructed in 1983 above the modern flight of steps that rises up the remodelled bank at this point.[86] The top step is inscribed in memory of Harold Brentnall, who was a former history master at the College and early authority on the medieval castle.[87]

Later history

Despite a dearth of contemporary visitors' descriptions, the garden and its features would surely have impressed any who saw it. Indeed, in 1742 Lord Hertford reported upon the favourable reaction of his son-in-law, Sir Hugh Smithson, who through his marriage to Lady Elizabeth would eventually become 2nd Earl and then 1st Duke of Northumberland. While marvelling at the garden's variety, he looked upon the Mound 'as one of the noblest and most surprising works he ever saw' and was also 'quite charm'd' by the grotto.[88]

Together, the grotto and Mound remain the most tangible elements of the historical gardens. Whilst their individual importance is recognised by the designation of the Mound as a Scheduled Ancient Monument[89] and the grotto being a Grade II Listed Building,[90] the site of the garden as a whole, including its twentieth-century additions, is also deemed important and registered Grade II.[91]

Following the death in 1750 of Algernon Seymour, who had succeeded as 7th Duke of Somerset two years previously, Marlborough House was leased out to become the Castle Inn.[92] It would appear that the garden was already no longer intensively maintained, presumably having started to decline sometime after 1739 when the Hertfords acquired Lord Bathurst's old estate at Riskins or Richings, which they renamed Piercy (Percy) Lodge.[93]

The state of the gardens at around this time was recorded by the Reverend George Woodward, rector of East Hendred near Wantage, twenty miles from Marlborough. He stayed at the inn in autumn 1754 when, he says, the gardens had lost some of their earlier elegance: 'for now they are filled with useful things, and sheep are the only mowers of the bowling green.'[94] It appears that the summer house, now called a greenhouse, was being used for storage, and although the canal still contained fish, its ornamental rockwork had 'all gone to decay'. The approach to the Mound through the wilderness or grove of trees passed 'a temple in the middle of it' – the only reference to such a building – while the grotto is described as having an iron gate. The summit of the mount was still dominated by the octagonal pavilion at its centre, where 'the broad grass plot' was not yet planted with trees.

The continuation of a programme of simple upkeep in the early nineteenth century would explain how the basic structure of the eighteenth-century gardens was still apparent when the College took over the property. The

General plan of the premises of the Castle Hotel Marlborough as proposed to be altered, which its architect J. M. Nelson prepared in 1842, shows much of the previous layout of paths surviving in the wilderness and the geometric garden to its side, together with other historical details.[95] It was not long, however, before the canal or moat was largely filled-in and new school buildings began to appear.[96]

The backfilling of adjacent parts of the surrounding ditch as early as about 1850 may have been in response to their increasingly insanitary condition forming a noisome hazard so close to the school.[97] However, a section beside the western edge of the former wilderness was left open for use as a 'Bathing Place' and remained available for swimming until the late twentieth century.[98] The intervening area was gradually developed for building. From being largely confined around the old mansion, individual structures have spread progressively closer to the Mound and wilderness so that they now cover much of the area, as indicated in successive editions of the 1:2500 scale or 25.344 inches to one mile Ordnance Survey plan.[99] Whilst the extent of building and the need for associated infrastructure of water and power supplies, pathways and service roads, together with grounds landscaping, may have destroyed many earlier garden deposits, isolated pockets of material might yet remain.[100] The potential impact of any proposed future development should be carefully assessed.

Road-making and subsequent widening, together with occasional building, have also encroached upon the Mound. The lower parts of its slope have been shaved off and truncated by the insertion at different times of a retaining wall or revetment of sarsen, re-used stone and occasional brickwork which skirts the base in two sections of varying construction and quality.[101] In 1892 the corner of a cart shed that was built over the backfilled moat or canal clipped the Mound's northern edge, and in 1912 a new pumping house was built into another part of the base.[102] An inclined flue cut through the monument to connect with a chimney at the summit. This was demolished only recently and the site made good; a sunken area remains, however, where a modern water tank removed at the same time had replaced an earlier reservoir on top of the Mound.[103] A series of concrete steps introduced to access the summit in the late twentieth century became redundant following the latest restoration of the spiral ramp and have now been covered over and the accompanying handrail removed.

At the same time, maintenance works continue at the grotto. Until its restoration in the 1980s it had served to store swedes and other vegetables, before becoming a bicycle shed and suffering the further ignominy of use as a smokers' den.[104] In 2013 work involved rebuilding the roof as well as removing previous inappropriate repairs.[105] Fittingly, a stone inscription was installed in front of the grotto to commemorate the late Eric C. Elstob, whose role in the Mound's history is described in the Epilogue.

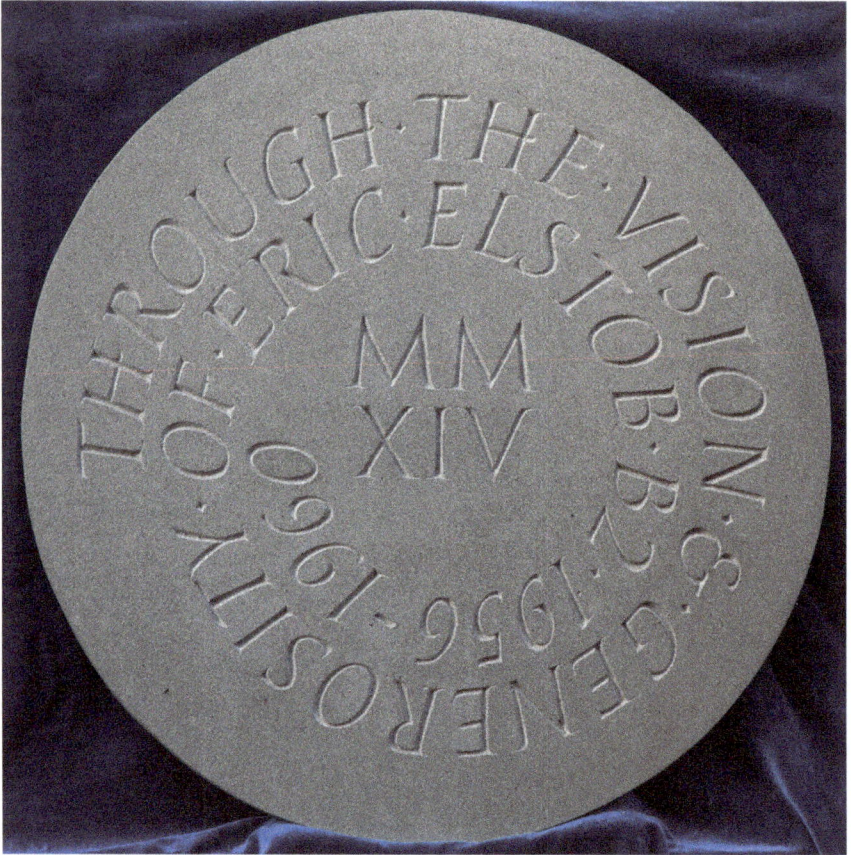

Fig. 5.1 Memorial inscription to Eric Elstob
in front of the grotto at the foot of the Mound.

5

Epilogue: The Marlborough Mound Trust

The Mound Trust was the idea of Eric Elstob, who was at the College from 1956–60. It was established in January 2000, and its objective was defined as being 'to restore, conserve, preserve and maintain the Mound at Marlborough College and its immediate curtilage as a place of historic and public interest', and 'to educate the public about the archaeological and historical significance and merits of the Mound including organised access by prior appointment.'

These objectives were described in more detail in a strategy paper in 2003, which set out the agenda for the Trust's activities. It began with a statement of what was known about the Mound at that point, which makes interesting reading in the light of subsequent events.

> We know for certain that the Mound formed the motte of a twelfth century castle, which was an important government centre in the west of England in the late twelfth century, but seems to have declined in status in the thirteenth century. It was then part of a major landscape garden created by Lord Hertford in the early eighteenth century.
>
> It may also be a prehistoric mound of a similar type to Silbury Hill, but this must for the moment be no more than a conjecture.
>
> Each aspect of the Mound makes it a monument of national importance, but the multiple nature of its archaeological forms creates its own set of problems.

The strategy proposed for the Trust was then divided into three headings: conservation, restoration and exploration. All of these activities are still ongoing, and what follows is a brief survey of progress to date.

Conservation

Throughout the work on the Mound, there has always been an underlying concern about the stability of its structure, in the light of instances where interventions or natural occurrences have led to substantial damage to similar sites. The subsidence at Silbury Hill in 2000 as the result of earlier excavations and the collapse of part of Oxford castle motte in 2007 were very much in mind. One of the first projects was the installation of stability monitors, which fortunately have shown that the Marlborough Mound is not inherently in danger.

The particular concern at Marlborough was the tree cover and the state of the vegetation. Removal of the trees was a priority from the start, but the potential consequences were erosion and destruction of the surface vegetation. A comprehensive survey in 1999 found a total of seventy-eight trees, quite apart from shrubs and bushes. At the time it seemed that some yew trees might date from the seventeenth century, while the group of limes on the summit were thought to be from the eighteenth century. They are now considered to have replaced earlier elm trees from that period. Besides these were many self-sown trees, notably sycamores. Several of the trees were in a dangerous condition, and in all cases the steep slope of the Mound made tree work difficult and expensive. Tree work has been an ongoing process, and the total cost has been a major item, amounting to £190,000 over fifteen years, with the bulk of the work taking place between 2016 and 2019.

The resulting change in the appearance of the Mound has been dramatic, from an obliterating canopy of foliage to a handful of historic trees. Drawings were prepared at an early stage of the Mound entirely stripped of trees (Fig. 5.2), but the present thinking is that this might be too radical an approach.

The second major conservation process has been the establishment of a foliage covering which will protect against erosion by rainfall, a potential problem on the steep sides, and which is easily maintained. In the last few years, this work has been undertaken very successfully by the College's estates team, who have also managed the replanting of the thorn hedge bordering the spiral path. Much of the original planting had failed because the contractors responsible could not provide on-site maintenance, and the transfer to the estates team has solved this problem.

The spiral path which leads to the summit was badly neglected, and had been eroded in a number of places, particularly on the north-west face. Access to the top at the start of the work was provided by a hideous concrete staircase near the grotto, and this was removed as soon as it was feasible to do so. The work on the path began with excavations to establish the original width of the path, and to analyse its structure. The actual reconstruction of the path began in 2011. In several places, the outer edge of the path had to be reinforced and rebuilt, and progress was slow: in the event, it took eight years to reach the top, at a total cost of £110,000.

Restoration

In a sense, the spiral path was an exercise in restoration as well as conservation. The removal of the water tank and laundry chimney added at the top of the Mound was perhaps demolition rather than restoration, but in a sense restored the area to its early nineteenth-century aspect. The removal

Fig. 5.2 The Mound with all trees removed: architect's drawing.

of the tangle of apparently industrial equipment and wild overgrowth (Fig. 5.3) that disfigured it in 2005 has been as dramatic a change as the removal of the trees, though more or less invisible from below. The chimney flue which goes from top to bottom of the Mound has a concrete outer lining and it was not practical to remove it. Equally, the water tank rested on a massive concrete platform with an access space below, and the latter have to be left in place because of the difficulty of breaking them up and the danger that the operation might destabilise the top of the Mound. The future use of this potentially exciting space (Fig. 5.4) is very much under consideration, though there are limitations because of the relative fragility of the spiral path if there are large numbers of visitors.

There are also two structures on the Mound which needed restoration – the belvedere and the grotto. The belvedere, near to the summit, is a small brick arbour which overlooks the town. The original form of this is unknown, and the decision was taken to build a skeleton image of it in painted steel, while restoring and repairing the seats and floor which have survived. This

Fig. 5.3 The Mound in 2005.

was one of the first tasks which was completed (Fig. 4.1). The grotto at the foot of the Mound was restored between 1980 and 1990 by Diana Reynell, as described in Brian Dix's essay above. However, the roof and the façade were in urgent need of attention; in particular, a large yew tree was growing into the left-hand corner of the grotto. This was removed in 2009, and a major reconstruction of the roof followed over the next two years. The grotto façade was restored on the basis of Baskerfield's drawing of *c*. 1792, which was interpreted as showing a crenellated front. The windows shown in the drawing could be interpreted as openings, but have been restored as blind windows. The interior of the grotto is being surveyed at the time of writing, and some work is undoubtedly needed. This will represent the last stage of the planned conservation and restoration work on the Mound.

Exploration and Presentation

Archaeological exploration was always high on the Trust's agenda, as the reports printed in Appendix E show. By and large – and especially in terms of the top of the Mound and the medieval buildings which were once there

Fig. 5.4 The Mound in 2020.

– the rewards have been meagre, but one single discovery more than compensated for this. The dating of the Mound to within a century or two of Silbury Hill has been hugely exciting and important. It is possible that it might have been achieved without the Trust's work, as the initiative came from English Heritage, which wanted a comparative date because of its research at Silbury. The work done by the Trust, and indeed the simple fact of its existence, made the operation of obtaining cores from the Mound a great deal easier.

Further archaeological work, it is hoped, will continue in the area of the lower bailey, as the Trust has determined that its remit can include the investigation of the context of the Mound, and particularly of what little remains of Marlborough castle. Hopefully, excavation and geophysical surveys will provide at least confirmation of the outline of the castle wall. This process will also contribute to the Trust's aim of bringing the Mound and its history into the College's educational remit. Awareness of the Mound and its implications is already an established topic for first year students and, in the future, there is a proposal for an annual 'Mound day' to open it – within the restrictions imposed by the site and the College's requirements – to a wider audience. This will replace the series of lectures which has now run successfully for fifteen years, in which specialists (including all the contributors to this book) have looked at aspects of the Mound's history. These lectures, and extensive research at the National Archives commissioned by the Trust, have been fundamental to the present volume, which in a sense marks the end of the first stage of the renewal of the Mound, so long neglected and at last seeing the light of day in more senses than one.

Appendix A

Inquisition into the State of Marlborough Castle, 11 September 1327[1]

Inquisition taken at the castle of Marlborough on the Friday next after the feast of the Nativity of the Blessed Virgin Mary in the abovesaid year, before the aforesaid Adam,[2] concerning the defects of the same castle, supervision having been assigned as above, by the oath of Richard de Bray, Nicholas Heved, Geoffrey Aldewyn, John Child, John de Stanbourn, Laurence Broun, Adam le Pich, Nicholas Gramory, Walter le Bowyar, Roger le Taillour, Walter Bythewatre and John le Dyer, who say that there is a certain old bridge outside the castle gate there which ought to be rebuilt, and an outer bridge towards the town from the castle there which ought to be mended, which bridges can be rebuilt and repaired for £40 by estimation beyond [the cost of] the timber. Item, defects in the walls towards the said bridges there can be mended for 60s by estimation. Item the main gate of the said castle there, with the portcullis and chain for the same gate, may be made for 5 marks, beyond the timber, by estimation. Item defects in the chambers above the same gate there may be mended for 100s beyond the timber by estimation. Item, the great hall in the said castle, with the pantry and butlery and the adjoining chambers, and with two chambers next to the same hall, can be repaired in all their defects, both in their roofs and their walls, the carpentry and the stonework, beyond the timber, for £50 by estimation. Item, the great kitchen, with the larder, saucery and the rampart walks ('alura') towards the hall, which have the same defects as above, may be repaired for 10 marks beyond the timber by estimation. Item, the chambers of the tower next to the hall, having the same defects as above, may be repaired for 60s beyond the timber by estimation. Item, the high chamber, with other adjoining chambers

---

[1] E 101/476/4 (extract) – Only the final membrane of what was presumably once a much larger roll now survives here, beginning with the latter part of an inquisition into the state of the castle of Devizes, and continuing with inquests into Marlborough and Gloucester castles. Considerably more of this document is now clearly missing, since the delivery note on the dorse refers to it comprising 'three pieces', and a note at the head of the dorse of the membrane gives a sum total for repairs to the castle of St Briavels, which presumably preceded it on the dorse.

[2] Presumably mentioned in full in the now-missing section of the roll, but almost certainly Adam de Herewynton, chancellor of the exchequer, as per the instructions issued on 16 July.

and the rampart walks ('alura'), having the same defects as above, may be repaired for £20 beyond the timber by estimation. Item the great chapel there, with the rampart walks adjoining it, having damage to the roof, which has been punctured, and other small defects, may be repaired for 60s beyond the timber by estimation. Item the king's wardrobe there, for the king's gowns, with the chambers and the chamber called the brothers' chamber there, which are ruinous, may be repaired for £10 beyond the timber by estimation. Item the house of the almoner, with the granary there, may be repaired for 10 marks beyond the timber by estimation. Item the bakery with the chambers towards the gate, which are ruinous, may be repaired for 100s beyond the timber by estimation. Item, the damage to the castle walls there, inside and out, both in rebuilding parts that have been battered down and in repairing the rampart walks and various parts of the said walls there that have been destroyed, may be built and repaired for £100 by estimation. They say further that the large tower of the said castle there, upon the motte, half of which has been destroyed for a long time, and a certain other smaller tower there, with the walls of the said motte, which towers are ruinous, having defects in their roofs, brickwork and carpentry, together with one house which the constable once inhabited there, with one pit ('puteum') flooded with water and other things noted as pertaining to the said towers, house and well, may be repaired for £300 beyond the timber by estimation. Item, they say that the aforesaid damage occurred during the time of King Edward, grandfather of the present king, during the keeping of Nicholas de Sperscht, and during the time of King Edward, father of the present king, during the keeping of Master Eustace de Hacche and William de Rameshulle.

Sum of money by which the defects to the castle of Marlborough may be repaired – £555 13s 4d.

[on dorse]
Adam de Herwynton, chancellor of the Exchequer, delivered these inquisitions, containing three pieces, here from the Exchequer on the fifth day of February at the beginning of the second year of the reign of King Edward, the third after the Conquest [5 February 1328].

Appendix B

Castellum Merlebergensis[1]
By H. C. Brentnall, F.S.A.

Hardly a vestige of Marlborough Castle, the medieval stronghold, remains – above ground. What may still be concealed under the trees of the Wilderness is another matter; something in the way of foundations has already been revealed by our Archaeological Section in one of its periodic revivals, but that discovery, made during the War, told us nothing definite, and the attitude of successive Bursars to the resulting hole has been pardonably lacking in cordiality. When some of the larger trees fall, as they are likely to do soon, we may learn more. In the meantime some digging in the Mound suggests that at least the dimensions of the Keep may be recovered, though there again successive alterations make it difficult to reach certain conclusions.

If some familiar, like Mr Bligh Bond's Brother Johannes, would impart the information we stand in need of, the task of reconstructing the Castle – at least for the mind's eye – might be simpler. But Marlborough, for all its Arthurian associations, has been less fortunate than Glastonbury. If the thing could be done, there are a number of men who might be invited to testify. Long contact with their activities, as heralded in Letters Patent, enjoined in Letters Close, acknowledged on the Liberate Rolls or recorded in various Ministers' Accounts, has made them almost friends. Alexander Barentin, the King's butler, might tell us much about the wine-cellars; William the balestier, who had charge of the King's artillery, could explain a great deal that must for ever remain obscure in the domestic and military arrangements of the High Tower; and Simon Horn, sent down in 1222 to remodel the farm-management of the Barton, stayed long enough in these parts to see the greater part of the remodeling of the Castle as well. But if any man of the thirteenth century might be induced to revisit the glimpses of the moon, my choice would be a certain Keeper of the King's wardrobe. It is true he went on to higher things, but he was here in those brave but anxious middle years of his century, and, if he could tell us little else, he might at least reveal something of the personality of a man who could rise to positions of dignity and honour though his name was – Peter Chacepork.

---

[1] Reprinted from *Report of the Marlborough College Natural History Society*, 82 (1933), 60–104.

But Peter and Simon, William and Alexander are not likely to communicate the lineaments of our vanished Castle. It would be pleasant to hear, in the romantic diction of Brother Johannes, of summer afternoons with the timber-wains in the Forest and the girls who picked the flints for Master Blouwe's walls, or of the tuns of wine from Gascony so regularly delivered by the right loyal and trusty men of Bristol and Southampton; of the swans and peacocks, the dates and almonds and ginger that our third Henry was wont to lay in 'against the coming of Christmas,' the buck from Savernake and the fat bream from the King's great stew out Poulton way. And if they interspersed their recitals, *more Johannico*, with a figure here and there – the height of the Great Tower or the length of St Nicholas's Chapel – we should be grateful. As it is, we must rely on other documents less complete by far than we could wish and largely devoid of the picturesque, but recommended, perhaps, by merits not commonly allowed to 'automatic' writing.

Certain of these documents have been mentioned already, the Patent, Close and Liberate Rolls. It fortunately happens that most of these, so far as they concern us, have been calendared and indexed and may be consulted in any of our greater libraries. But for royal castles, such as Marlborough was, there is another and often more valuable source of information in the Pipe Rolls, and the transcription of these, which is proceeding at the expense of the Pipe Roll Society (an unofficial organisation), advances more slowly. At the present rate of progress it will be sixty years at least before all those which particularly interest us have been printed. To obtain many of the facts, therefore, on which this reconstruction of the Castle is based I have had to resort to the original rolls, a lengthy and, were it not for the hope of extracting fresh details from each new roll examined, a tedious occupation. And the same description applies to the searching of miscellaneous documents, Ministers' Accounts and others, which sometimes yield points of interest, but more frequently do not.

Perhaps it should be explained that the Rolls of Letters Patent record appointments and commissions and other writs originally sent open, as the name implies, with the great seal attached, that all whom it concerned might read and obey. The Rolls of Letters Close similarly record the writs sent folded to individuals for their particular behest. The subjects so dealt with are very various. To take local instances only, they might contain an order to put the Castle forthwith in a state of defence by reason of a landing of the French at Winchelsea, or a mere minute to the effect that Richard the Ostricher, by reason of his age, had retired from the keeping of the King's goshawks. The Liberate Rolls are records of payments made, so called because the majority of the writs begin with the imperative of the verb *liberare*, to deliver. Others opened with the word *allocate*, allow, or *computate*, reckon, the recipient and the sum and, more valuable for our purpose than either, the consideration always following.

The institution of these records and others, enrolled upon still surviving parchments, is one of the advantages we owe to that disguised blessing, the reign of John. The series begins with the first year of that King and continues, so far at least as the Close and Patent Rolls are concerned, to this day.

The Pipe Rolls, most formidable of documents, began earlier but ended a hundred years ago. When exactly they began nobody knows. There is an isolated roll of the year 1129–30, but the consecutive series starts in 1155. The roll for 1212–13 and those for the period from Easter 1215 to Michaelmas 1217 are missing, which may be unfortunate for us since they fall within the years of most interest in the history of the Castle.

'Pipe Roll' is more or less a nick-name for what is strictly a Great Roll of the Exchequer, and no more likely explanation of the term is forthcoming than that, when stacked together, they resemble a collection of drain-pipes. Each consists of about a dozen composite sheets of parchment, some ten inches wide and about four feet long, and represents the financial statements of the Sheriffs of the different counties returned for audit to the King's Exchequer each Easter. For the most part the information to be derived from the Sheriff's accounts is little to our purpose, since Marlborough Castle was not often in the hands of the Sheriff of Wiltshire. But the returns often include what are known as 'foreign accounts,' and among these the statements of the Constable of the Castle have often proved invaluable. Their appearance among the hundred Pipe Rolls which, in one shape or another, I have consulted is a little capricious. Frequently they are missing altogether; sometimes they are inserted in vacant spaces at the ends of other counties. For instance, in Pipe Roll 57 (13 John), at the end of the last membrane of the Wiltshire roll we read: *Require residuum huius comitatus subter Linc. quia non erat hic locus.* Three rolls further on one of the most interesting of the Marlborough accounts rewards the patient searcher.

The facts extracted from these and other documents will appear in the sequel. For the moment we must turn to consider such purely local evidence as we possess. It does not amount to very much, but what there is of it dominates our whole enquiry.

The three capital facts are the Mound, the Wilderness and the Bathing Place. The first of these is traditionally the site of the Castle Keep. Descriptions of Marlborough from the days of Leland onwards, that is, from the sixteenth to the end of the eighteenth century, record the existence, and gradual disappearance, of the remains of a great donjon tower upon the Mound.

Bailey and moat

The area that we call, with some justification, the Wilderness is shown in the plans of the Castle Inn as the 'Bally,' i.e. Bailey. Its limits have not altered since, and we have no grounds for supposing that they had altered before that date. They are shown in Stukeley's plan of 1723 (?) with perfect clearness, and we can only suppose that they were also the limits of the base-court, or bailey, of the original Castle. That conclusion accords in an interesting way with the evidence of the geological map, which shows, so far as the one-inch scale admits of precision, the belt of valley gravel giving place to alluvium on the southern edge of the Wilderness. It is further reinforced by the position of the Bathing Place, traditionally preserving the line of the moat, and by what we know of other water-courses that once surrounded the same area.

This matter of the moat is obviously crucial, and we will deal with it at once. It is not altogether easy, but admits, I think, of an acceptable solution.

We have no modern references to the moat earlier than the eighteenth century. Very early in it we have the account of the visit of Celia Fiennes, a lady who unfortunately had small use for dates. We know, however, that C House, the Seymour 'Castle,' was about half-built, and we infer that the visit occurred soon after the coronation of Queen Anne in 1702. The passage from Celia Fiennes's Diary has been quoted elsewhere, but part must be repeated here:

> The only Curious thing is out of ye bowling-green. You go many stepps down into a grass-walke ... this leads to the foote of the mount, and that you ascend from ye Left hand by an Easye ascent.... The Low Grounds are watered with ditches, and this mount is Encompass'd about with such a Cannal which Emptys itself into a ffish pond, then it Empts itself into the river. There is a house built over the ffish pond to keep the ffish in. At the ffoote of the mount as I began out of a Green walke on the Left hand to ascend it, so On the Right hand Leads to another such a walke quite round by ye Cannall to the other side of ye bowling-green.

The passage begins clearly enough. We can follow her to the summit of the Mound; but what did she see in the way of what she would have called 'water-works'? Did the 'Cannal' run *all* round the Mount at its actual 'ffoote,' or did it enclose a wider area to the south? On this point she is vague. And again: 'Emptys itself into a ffish pond, then it Empts itself into the river.' The suggestion is of two falls; where were they? Lady Hertford, writing of gardens in 1737 or 1738, says: 'My Lord Hertford has made an alteration in ours this summer.... He has widened the channel of the water that surrounds it to about thirty feet; and at two angles has formed cascades, which though they do not fall from any considerable height have still a very good effect.... The uppermost cascade passes betwixt two artificial rocks.... The lower one, where the stream falls into the main river, has the ruins of an arch built over it.' These cascades must have been opposite either end of the Terrace: they seem to correspond to the features described by Celia Fiennes some thirty years earlier, and they may be located, though they are not shown, on Stukeley's ground-plan here reproduced. This plan is precisely dated 6 July 1723, yet it shows the Terrace itself, which was not in existence before 1740! (Careless, perhaps, but explicable.) It will be seen that Stukeley does not allow a complete moat round the Mound, yet in another view of his, reproduced in the *History of Marlborough College*, there is a distinct hint of the off-take of the missing section in the latitude of the present carpenter's shop, and we must remember that Celia Fiennes was writing a generation earlier. But whether or not the channel existed in the eighteenth century, we shall have no difficulty in proving its presence in the thirteenth.

More puzzling still is Celia Fiennes's last sentence: '… So on the Right hand Leads to another such a walke *quite round by ye Cannall to the other side of ye bowling-green.*' She had left the bowling-green, it will be remembered, at its west side to descend the 'stepps.' Now, therefore, the 'walke,' following 'ye Cannall,' appears *on the east*. Stukeley's plan must again be called in evidence. He was clearly much struck by a feature which since his day has been wholly obliterated, a broad ditch making an angle in what is now the lower part of the Master's garden. He shows it in three separate views: the present Plan, the sketch to be found in the new edition of *The Marlborough Country*, and the town-plan at page 5 of the *Borough Guide*. He omits it wholly from the view reproduced in the *History* of the College. In the two *plans* its longer limb seems to coincide with the boundary of Preshute parish, and therefore with the original limits of the royal manor of the Barton; in the *sketch* it seems, surely by a freak of the pencil, to extend nearly as far as the present Pewsey Road. It will be seen in the Plan here reproduced to be evidently dry, yet it is crossed by a bridge which carried the old Pewsey Road towards the pack-trail up Granham hill. Nowhere does Stukeley suggest that in his day it contained water, but that is not to say that it did not, for some part at least of its course, hold water when Celia Fiennes perhaps walked along it.

Stukeley was convinced that he had found a Roman camp. He drew the present Plan to show its dimensions. He was, of course, quite mistaken, as his kinsman Roger Gale explained. By the date of his fourth view, the one reproduced in the *History of Marlborough College*, it had evidently been filled in to make the new garden there shown for the first time. But it must have been there once, for though he might misinterpret a mere unevenness in the ground into a Roman *fossa*, he would not have invented the bridge which crosses it.

We are confronted, therefore, with the existence of a ditch of unknown age to which we cannot refuse a medieval date. Part of its course, where it runs through the kitchen garden, is still traceable in the levels. Below the Common Room summer-house its presence is still betrayed after much rain by a tendency to flooding, though the raising of what was once a water-meadow, by tipping over it the spoil from the foundations of Field House twenty-five years ago, has effectually obscured a part of its length, and the various terrace-levels in the garden of the Master's Lodge have done whatever remained to be done towards the blanketing of the eastern limb. One thing is obvious; it can never have carried water round northwards to join the moat again below the Mound, since the natural levels are all against it. It would seem that the curious course of the old 'Road over Kennet R.' in Stukeley's plan is partly to be accounted for by an effort to avoid the ditch, though it must remain obscure why it ever entered the ditched area to leave it again by a bridge and turn back eastward, as he shows it.

The inclusion of this southern extension within the wet ditch can hardly have any military significance. The large re-entrant involved, whatever protection it might seem to afford against the menagerie of medieval siege-operations, the rat, the cat, the sow or the ram, would be offset by the sacrifice of the principle of conservation of man-power and its concentration on the shortest inner line of defence. Such a trace could be paralleled in no castle that I ever heard of. But we have a possible explanation in an inquisition recorded on the Patent Roll of 1382, which was to be made into the cost of the alteration of the course of a stream that used to rim round the Castle. It must be remembered that the Castle had by this date ceased to be a fortress. Though there is mention in the same document of repairs, there is no suggestion of any extension of the fortifications to conform to a new line, and we must suppose that the change in the course of the stream was merely intended to include the 'king's garden' within the ditch, along with the mill which appears to have stood on the site of the present summer-house and to have accounted for the fall which Lord Hertford converted into so elegant a cascade.

If this argument be accepted, we may reduce the enceinte of the medieval Castle to the area of the Mound and the 'Bally.' The persistence of the arm of the moat which ran below the present Terrace would be highly awkward to accommodate with any eastward extension of the enceinte, but it may be noted that, apart from the probabilities of the case, our only documentary evidence for the shorter original moat running along the south-east side of the Bailey depends upon the interpretation we have placed on the *alteration* of the course of the stream in 1382. We must suppose it to have joined the north-east arm about half-way down the garden, and the joint streams to have been held up below that point by the sluices mentioned in 1232. What width must we allow for the moat? It is a matter, perhaps, of no great importance, but we must allow enough water to provide a sufficient obstacle. Stukeley tells us that in his day the ditch was 'still twenty foot broad in some part.' We may, I think, assume that this represents a reduction by collapse of the banks and silting from an original width of some fifty feet. But we need not suppose that the channel between the Mound and the Bailey was necessarily as broad, since in fact, if not in theory, it was not an external line of defence, and I have accordingly reduced it here in the reconstruction to thirty feet, which seems to me as much as the foundations already unearthed in the Wilderness will conveniently permit.

Mound

I confess that the Mound presents more difficulties than the Bailey, a fact which, in view of its uncompromising bulk and the traces of fortification still apparent upon it, may seem unreasonable. The Bailey in the Wilderness has suffered much. It has been the rubbish dump of the College for ninety years, and through much of that period the only one. I am told that the spare material discarded when the Eleven was levelled found a resting-place there. The Mound has lent itself to no such treatment, but it has necessarily endured more from the weather, to say nothing of its spiral path, its grottoes, its earlier pond and summer-house, its later tank and chimney. It is difficult at this date to say what its dimensions may have been in the thirteenth-century, how much must be added to its height for weathering or deducted from its circumference for 'spread.' The latter, indeed, is the more serious problem, since it involves other measurements in the general ground-plan of the Castle.

I have had two opportunities, in 1912 and again this year, of examining surface excavations made at the base of the Mound, and on both occasions it was obvious that the layer of vegetable mould covering the chalk thickens gradually towards the bottom and then passes from a deposit of about two feet to a shallow but extensive spread of hardly more than six inches under the dry walling which encircles it. Were it not for that walling it would obviously be more extensive, but it seems likely that walling of some sort has been in position at least since the moat was filled in. It is, moreover, impossible to suppose that means were not taken to prevent the Mound from sliding into the moat when that was in existence. We have evidence for this in the Pipe Roll of 13 John (1211), where there is a record of money spent in putting a 'girth' (*cingula*) 'about the motte' (*circa motam*). The mention in close contiguity of the construction of a lime-kiln suggests that this was no mere camp-shedding but a stone revetment. On the whole, then, we should be justified in making only a slight deduction from the present circumference of the Mound in the attempt to restore its medieval proportions.

One very striking feature in the ground-plan to which the course of the moat restricts us is the extraordinary disproportion between the areas covered by the Mound and Bailey respectively – disproportion in the sense that they are so nearly of equal size. The examination of the plans of many castles of similar age and type reveals none in which the motte occupies so inordinate a place in the scheme, though there are many in which the bailey is smaller. The ground-plan cries out for a second bailey, and hitherto I had always supposed that one existed, and that the area of the College Court roughly represented it. For what other purpose was the great road to the West diverted but to accommodate such an outer bailey? How came the western end of St Peter's parish to be called the Bailey Ward of Marlborough town, if it did not, at the least, abut upon such a bailey? – for it is separated by a hundred yards from the base-court with which we are here concerned. What did the editor of

Camden's *Britannia* mean when he said, in 1610, that 'some few reliques of the walls remain within the compasse of a dry ditch'? A dry ditch cannot refer to water-courses that we know were still running. But it is not impossible that he is speaking of the wall behind the Common Room bicycle shed, which may well have bordered the continuation of Stukeley's 'Roman' ditch; and thus he may help to explain the statement of Celia Fiennes in the next century about the path that ran round by the canal to the other side of the bowling-green. Later references tend to confirm this view. The short stretch of wall referred to has been ascribed to Elizabeth's reign but it could scarcely in that case be mistaken as early as 1610 for medieval fortification. Indeed one would hardly so explain it now, for it is in its visible parts too slight for such an origin. But may it not actually be part of the wall of the King's garden and so bear some relation to the changes of 1382? It lies on the very borders of the royal manor and the parish of Preshute.

But the diversion of the Bath Road and the name of the Bailey Ward remain unexplained. It can only be said that, so far as my investigations have gone, no reference to an outer bailey has anywhere appeared, and it seems clear that none existed at any rate as early as 1300. The specification in the Liberate Roll of 1227 of the *tower and bailey* of the Castle holds good for the rest of the century.

Ground plan

The reconstructed ground-plan reproduced at the beginning of this paper may be taken then to cover all the Castle that existed in the time of its hey-day. But it is necessary at once to make it clear that the details I have shown vary widely in their degrees of probability. For the north-east curtain of the Bailey, for instance, I have nothing to go upon beyond the obvious necessity for its existence within the line of the moat. I have drawn it straight because so far as we know the moat in that section was straight, and I have placed the stables against it because they there seemed handy for the main gate and because, though I know they existed, I can find no other place for them. I might add further at this point that all the flights of steps I have shown leading to the rampart walk or to the upper floors of various buildings are flights of fancy. I would include in that description the covered steps leading up to the Great Tower if I did not think that I had found, since I drew them, some evidence for their existence more or less in that part of the Mound. That such steps were necessary in various parts of the Castle is obvious, but my authorities do not mention them. Purists may object that I should at least have distinguished, by some graphic device or other, between the buildings for which I can quote chapter and verse and the products of my untrammelled imagination. But I would ask those purists to reflect that under the conditions of this enquiry I cannot claim that any feature I show owes nothing to the imagination. If they will read the extracts in the Appendix, on which alone this reconstruction is based, they will see that it must be so.

I do not want to labour the point, but the *Report of the Marlborough College Natural History Society* is by way of being a scientific publication, and I am reporting not observation but deduction. It is open to anyone to study the originals and then to guess again. I only claim that my deductions seem to fit the facts. Of definite measurements I have two only; the width of the Queen's (upper?) chamber, and the length and breadth of the pentice on the west of the Great Hall. But we know also within a few feet the area of the Bailey that contained the great majority of the buildings mentioned, and within that area of some two acres they and the ramparts that protected them must be accommodated.

Curtain, towers and turrets

For the curtain-wall I have allowed a thickness of ten feet. This is quite a usual thickness, and I have borrowed it from the average width of the curtain at Old Sarum as revealed by the excavations of 1911. The extra ground required for the flanking turrets I have borrowed from the moat. In most castles of the motte-and-bailey type the curtain seems to have been regularly carried up the motte to the keep in the form of wing-walls, but the presence of a wet ditch between the motte and the bailey seemed to make this unnecessary and improbable. We are told, moreover, that the gate of the Tower was furnished with a drawbridge and even a barbican, facts which point pretty definitely in the same direction. The curtain therefore appears, but in a slighter form, along the 'moat of the Tower.' The flanking turrets seem naturally to be required at the more pronounced bends in the boundary of the Wilderness. Four only are mentioned, and we could do with more. There is, for instance, the corner of the Bailey near the shallow end of the Bathing Place, which is not specifi-cally mentioned in any document I have come across. I have therefore shown at that point only a rectangular bastion, because the four turrets seemed to lie elsewhere. But I am not entirely happy about the turret at the south-east corner. I have placed there the 'turret *near* the King's hall,' built in 1227. It is to be distinguished from that *'behind* the King's hall,' since the latter was repaired in the same year, but its proximity to the Hall on the scale of conti-guity suggested by the confined area of the Bailey is not too obvious, unless I am wrong in squaring off the eastern corner. Much depends on the point of view in all these determinations, and I have assumed it, not, I think, unwar-rantably, to be some central position such as the open court on the south side of the Chapel. But if the apparent course of the moat through the Common Room garden had not seemed to forbid it, I should have preferred to round off the eastern angle by carrying the curtain-wall across it. This would have brought the turret in question nearer to the Hall, but would surely have necessitated another flanking turret at the resulting angle between it and the Great Gate, for which I can find no authority.

There was no necessary uniformity in the turrets. The one that stood *behind* the Hall was built in three storeys, the one behind the Queen's chamber, we are told, was corbelled, as were probably the others. The King's tower (*turris*, not *turella*), which stood presumably behind his chamber and may have been pierced, as I have shown it, to accommodate the postern, was obviously of more important dimensions than the others. When it was first built I cannot say, but there are entries referring to the year 1241 or 1242 which recall a much later episode in local history when the Memorial Hall was being erected on very similar foundations. The tower split *per defectum fundamenti* and had to be rebuilt. The *mora* or water-logged valley of the Kennet seems always to have been treacherous ground. Six years later came an order to the Constable of the Castle to amend the battlements that have fallen and 'prop up' (so the official translation, but I would like to read 'buttress') the walls and bridges. This second disaster is surely to be read in connection with the former. If the *turris Regis* is rightly placed at the deep end of the Bathing Place and associated with the Postern, the 'bridges' would be the two halves of the bridge that spanned the moat, and the insecurity of the foundations in that corner was causing some collapse of the curtain in its neighbourhood.

It must be assumed that the stone curtain-wall of the enceinte dated from the twelfth century, since we find a note of its repair in 1197. (It may have been knocked about in Hubert Walter's brief siege three years before.) It should be said here that the evidence points to the use of flint or rubble-cored walls faced with ashlar. There is an order for free-stone as early as 1175 and for 400 'quarrels,' i.e. squared blocks, in the same year. The sole remaining fragment of Ludgershall Castle, whose history is closely linked with Marlborough's, shows the flint core only, and local tradition seems to indicate a similar survival here. The excavations at Old Sarum also revealed mainly flint cores in the various walls and buildings, but enough remained to show that they had been originally faced with ashlar. Thousands of tons of free-stone must have been stolen from Marlborough Castle between the reigns of Edward III and Edward VI – one wonders what became of it all.

Wood, however, still played an important part in the defences. In 1225 a 'bretasche,' or wooden tower, was constructed behind the Queen's closet, perhaps on the site of what was afterwards (1238) referred to as 'the turret behind the Queen's chamber,' which was presumably of stone. In 1234 the *hurdicium*, 'horde,' behind the King's great chamber was completed and another 'towards the south,' the exact position of which is difficult to locate. These 'hordes' were the wooden galleries built out along the upper part of the curtain and flanking towers for the purpose of commanding the foot of the wall. They were usually temporary structures fitted in position in times of danger only.

The walls and towers of the Castle, however, were gradually being provided with battlements, which we may assume to have occupied the outer three feet of the parapet leaving an ample rampart-walk behind. The battlements of the Tower and Bailey were under repair in 1227 and at many later dates, though the scheme appears only to have been completed in 1250, when the wall between the King's chamber and the Great Tower was crenellated. This, as I have assumed, was the south-west section and faced the water-meadows. It would therefore be the last direction from which an enemy would attempt an assault, a fact which made it an appropriate situation for the postern gate as it made that part of the Castle the safest for the private apartments of the King and Queen.

Great Gate

The Great Gate would naturally face the town and, as naturally, lie convenient to the western road which passed to the north of the Mound. It must have opened out of the Bailey and not off the Motte, yet not too far from the Motte, if it was to lead to tolerably firm footing for man and beast above the soggy river-flats. When Celia Fiennes went down those many 'stepps,' she approached, though she omits to mention it, the bridge which Stukeley shows and also the unknown artist of 1772, of whose sketch of the Castle Inn the Bursar has a copy. S. H. Grimm in 1788 (*History of Marlborough College*, p. 77) shows us the same bridge end on, and I believe we cross it at the parapet level whenever we visit the Mound. It seems very probable that the bridge which has stood for over two hundred years crosses the buried moat just where the *pons vertens* crossed it in 1238, and that the gatehouse (of which I have found no mention) lay behind it, and the barbican with its upper chamber (built in 1234) in front.

Bridges and barbicans

Three bridges and three barbicans are mentioned. I imagine the second bridge, the 'bridge towards the dovecot,' repaired in 1234 and again in 1249, to be the postern bridge behind the King's chamber. That too had a barbican. How it stood up in that treacherous corner of the morass we do not learn, but it had to be rebuilt in 1249. The dove-cot itself had apparently to be rebuilt in 1242 and was standing in 1251, for it paid tithe in that year. Of its actual position we only know that it was near the Castle and in the parish of Preshute. I hope I have placed it on a fairly dry spot.

The third bridge and barbican communicated with the Great Tower on the Motte. I have placed them just east of the Grotto, largely because a range of buildings, the only connected series mentioned, allowed no room for it further west. The barbican was built in 1211. Normally, of course, an external defence, it is here internal so far as the Bailey is concerned, the intention being to garrison it only when there was danger of the Bailey being lost and in the event of the withdrawal of the defenders to the Great Tower. In view of this fact I have perhaps been imprudent in showing a flight of steps beside it leading to the rampart walk along the inner moat. This might in time of crisis prove an embarrassment – I am not sure. Behind the drawbridge (*pons torneicius* on this occasion, 1241) there was a gate-house (*turella*).

I have referred already to the steps up the Mount and need not apologise for them again. They were defended at the foot by a gate-house and at the top by a fore-building, which carried for the first ten years of its existence, at least, a thatched roof! In 1259 this was replaced by the wooden shingles from the King's kitchen, which can hardly have been much safer, but may have looked less inappropriate. There is some evidence that the Great Tower which crowned the Motte, upon the ruins of which Leland gazed in 1541, was the work of Henry III, for there is mention of a kitchen in the 'new tower' in 1249. In 1250 the 'round tower' is finished, and in the same year the name 'great tower' occurs for the first time, though in 1259 the term 'high tower' seems to be replacing it. At the same time the old tower was still in commission as late as 1249, for repairs were executed on the 'castle and tower' which the new tower should not yet have required.

The old palisade of the earliest wooden keep seems to have survived till after 1211, in which year it was repaired. It presumably stood round the platform on the top of the Motte and may still have been protecting a square wooden tower within till John's reign was over. The first definite suggestion of stone-work on the Mound itself comes in 1226 when 'the walls and battlements of the tower' are already under repair. But what the relation of this tower may have been to the palisade of 1211 or the new tower of 1250 we can hardly hope to learn.

Buildings in Interior

This completes the circuit of the enceinte and we may now enter the Castle by the Great Gate. It must have been provided with one portcullis if not more, but we are told nothing of its defences beyond the drawbridge.

Almonry

In front of us rises the tower of the inner barbican; immediately to the left of the gate-house is the Almonry rebuilt in 1241 and placed (by me) on this site as most convenient for its purpose. It will be seen that there is little room for buildings against the curtain between the Great Gate and that of the Tower, if space is to be left for the movement of horse or footmen. The stables for the former are ranged beneath the rampart walk beyond the Almonry. They were rebuilt in 1259 and beyond them, in a separate block, lie the Queen's stables erected eleven years earlier.

Kitchen

From our position in the fore-court within the Gate we get an admirable view of the Great Hall and the Chapel of St Nicholas, shut off from us, however, by a wooden fence some eight feet high, which runs from the chancel of the Chapel to the King's kitchen, a one-storeyed building reminiscent, perhaps, of the Abbot's kitchen at Glastonbury and surmounted by a lead-covered louvre in the middle of its stone roof for the escape of the smoke.

Hall

Our way to the Hall lies to the left past the kitchen and into a small courtyard surrounded on three sides by various offices. The Hall itself runs out some ninety feet from the Castle wall on the south. It is a lofty building with a porch in the middle of the east wall facing us and a covered way running round by the north to the door of the kitchen. Above the covered way are two large windows one on each side of the doorway. The roof, like all the roofs in this castle, is high pitched and covered with shingles. Its north and south gables are finished with bargeboards (? – *winbargias* in the Latin). Entering the door we find ourselves in a vast chamber with a wooden screen covering the south end and a fireplace in the wall opposite us. Long tables run up the centre to a dais at the north end. Over the King's place in the centre of the transverse table on the dais is a large rose-window. There are other tables on the dais and a door at this end of each of the side walls. The door on the east communicates with a small withdrawing room between the hall and the kitchen; that on the west opens into a large covered cloister built in 1244 at the expense of the old west windows of the hall. This cloister runs all down the length of the hall. It is eighty feet long by twenty-four broad and has two glazed windows looking westward into a small court. In the long back wall there is a fireplace and at the far end under the Hall-turret a garde-robe chamber.

King's quarters: King's tower (wardrobe), King's great chamber

Facing us across an open court lies the covered approach to the King's tower and the postern, which has an upper storey serving as the King's wardrobe. This building is largely inferential: behind it rises something more authentic, the King's Great Chamber. It is approached by a flight of steps, for the ground floor possibly served the purpose of a treasury or strong-room. The steps are roofed over and a covered passage way open at the sides gives access to the Hall pentice in one direction and St Nicholas's Chapel in the other. Such covered passages are a prominent feature in this Castle. That at least one wing of the present passage stood out in the open is shown by an order to 'crest' its roof in 1259.

The dimensions of the King's chamber are uncertain, but they lay presumably somewhere between those of the hall and the Queen's chamber, about each of which we have more definite information. The King's chamber was first built in 1175, but its steps were open to the sky till 1225, in which year the covered way or 'tresance' to the Hall was built, the great covered pentice being added twenty years later. Of its interior decoration we know little, except that it had two large glass windows at the west end and was whitewashed. But the sources from which this account was drawn rarely descend to details, and we may supply them from our general knowledge of the architecture of the period. We may be sure that all Henry III's additions were Early English, and that he was a connoisseur in building is an established fact. But his own apartments, designed evidently at an earlier date, would retain many Norman features.

Queen's apartments: chamber, buttery, wardrobe, chapel

A two-storeyed alley, running probably along the curtain-wall, gave access from the King's quarters to the Queen's. I have supposed that all these apartments lay against the Castle wall, for that was the normal position. The projection of the Great Hall is exceptional, but seems to be required by the presence of the long westward-facing pentice. I have placed the Queen's chamber beyond the King's, partly because that seems their proper relation to the Great Hall, and partly because I saw no other way of disentangling the various tresances, alleys, oriols and porticos to which ground space had to be allotted. At the south end of the Queen's chamber comes, in my view, the Buttery built in 1234 for Isabella, the King's sister. This lady, then twenty years of age, would seem to have lived down here a good deal, for the Constable accounts for numerous sums expended on her maintenance. She was one of those 'unpopular, haughty and troublesome' children of John and Isabella of whom Agnes Strickland tells us, but next year she was married to the German Emperor Frederick II. Her brother, King Henry, did not marry till 1236, and it was doubtless for Queen Eleanor of Provence that the improvements mentioned in 1241 were effected in this Buttery (then called the 'store-room').

With the Queen's chamber we reach, for the moment, firmer ground, for we do know that it measured twenty-four feet in width between the walls. It was necessarily the upper of the two storeys of which the building consisted, and it had a 'great window with a pillar,' probably of (Purbeck?) marble like one of the Hall windows, in each of its four walls. There was a fireplace on each floor and a doorway opened probably into the ground-floor room. For that reason I have supplied a 'vice' or winding turret stair at the north-west corner, though it might have stood elsewhere.

The Queen's closet (the 'small wardrobe' of 1259) was possibly south of her Chamber and over the Buttery.

Another 'tresance' led from the Queen's chamber to her private chapel, which I have shown tucked away in the west angle of the Bailey. I am aware that this arrangement is arbitrary, and it is open to anybody to alter it, if he will leave room for the chambers which certainly ran along the wall of the Tower moat. The Queen's chapel was probably of no great size and dimly lighted. The only window we hear of is a glass one 'before the entrance,' which implies some such ante-chapel gallery as I have shown. Internally we know that it contained 'a crucifix with Mary and John, and the Virgin Mary with her child,' from which we may perhaps infer that it was dedicated to St Mary.

I have used the Queen's tresance as a means of communication also with the chamber of the *domicilla* Alpeys, for whom the King showed his solicitude in 1244. Nothing more, however, is known of her, though it may be supposed that she held some post about the Queen's person. This I have allowed for by putting her next the new wardrobe (W. 2 in plan) built in 1241 with an 'oriol' communicating, as I assume, with the Queen's tresance.

New wardrobe; priests' chamber, old wardrobe, other chambers

And here we come to what seems to be a connected succession of buildings against the curtain 'behind' the Chapel of St Nicholas. An order of 1249 gives us this series following evidently close upon the new wardrobe, which itself was 'by' (1244) or 'behind' (1241) St Nicholas's. The series connects with a lodging for the chaplains built in 1245 and runs in this order according to the Liberate Roll of 1249: the 'old wardrobe' (W.1 in plan), an unallocated chamber, a second chamber extended by another 'oriol' towards the 'priests' chamber,' one or more of which were to be supplied with garde-robe accommodation 'over the moat of the tower' – clear evidence, if such were still needed, for the existence of a water channel between the Motte and the Bailey. None of these buildings need be of any great size, but the row of them forces, as before explained, the Tower barbican rather further to the east than one might have supposed natural.

This block of buildings I have connected with the Great Chapel by a barrier. There were in the Castle 'Old' and 'New lists' which at first I had imagined to refer to a tourneying course. But it was soon clear, as the various buildings obstructing the limited area of the Bailey took shape, that Prince Edward must have indulged his known love of jousting elsewhere. To take part in a tournament was 'to ride the barriere,' and 'lists' in this sense refers only to the barrier that kept the opposing horsemen on 'the up and the down line,' as it were, without risk of an end-on collision. Moreover, the *liceas* of one entry become the *jorull* [?*jarolia*] of another and the reference is to a mere fence erected, as I suppose, to secure greater privacy for the royal quarters. The new barriers of July 1250 were to run from the Chapel to the Kitchen, the old ones, repaired six months earlier, may possibly have run as I have shown them.

Chapel of St Nicholas

The last building we visit in the base-court is the King's Great Chapel of St Nicholas. If we enter it by way of the King's tresance we pass under the bell-turret of 1250, for which 'two sweet-toned bells of moderate size' were ordered in 1252. Among the few valuables still remaining in the Castle in 1390 after its great despoiling we read of 'two bells in the chapel of the said Castle worth £10.' May we infer from this rather considerable value that at least they were still 'sweet-toned'?

There is no means of discovering when St Nicholas's was built, and I have not found anything especially appropriate in the dedication, though it appears that the castles of Ludgershall and Old Sarum had chapels to the same saint. Its windows were first glazed in 1225, and it was enlarged (with the aid of three hundred stones from Devizes) in 1229 by the addition of a chancel. In 1232 a glass window was inserted in the west front, if we may identify this chapel with 'the King's,' as I assume. It contained two, or perhaps three, altars at this date, with wainscoting behind them and one or more crucifixes standing apparently in front of pictures on the altars, but we are not told what the latter represented. The chancel (and presumably the rest of the chapel) was roofed with shingles.

Buildings on Motte

Our tour of the Bailey completed, we cross the drawbridge to the gate of the Tower with a certain discouragement due doubtless in part to weariness of sight-seeing and in part to the steps that we have to climb, but chiefly to uncertainty as to what we shall see on top. I fear we shall reach the fore-building only to be told that visitors are not admitted. There is, of course, good reason to conceal the details of the main defences from prying eyes, but the silence of the records is nevertheless remarkable in view of the comparative wealth of information available about the base-court. It is only in Henry's reign that details accumulate, and Henry's interests were lavished on domestic and ecclesiastical ornament. The quarters of the Constable and the garrison and the technicalities of defence were left perhaps to the successive Constables to arrange, and the details are covered by the record of moneys spent on the *operaciones castri*. In John's time it was different, and we hear more of the lodgings of the *balistarii*, the men who worked the great catapults, their wages and allowances, than of embellishments. In Henry's reign we have evidence that the garrison was maintained and, on occasion, strengthened, but it is only the Chapel of St Leonard that moves the record to particulars.

Chapel of St Leonard

The Pipe Roll entry that mentions this chapel was written just seven hundred years ago, but in the interval it appears to have passed unnoticed – at least by anyone with local interests. It seems justifiable to suppose that St Leonard's was the garrison chapel. There was undoubtedly a chapel in the Tower, as is shown on the Liberate Roll of 1246, and equally certainly it was neither the King's nor the Queen's. St Leonard's particular activities are concerned, I find, with prisoners and captives, and it would be good for the Constable and his garrison to meditate their possible fate. There was a chapel with the same dedication at Ludgershall. But there is some difficulty in finding a suitable site for the chapel on the Mound. The Pipe Roll tells us that it had three permanent (*estantivis*) windows, which means, we gather from other entries, that they were of glass and did not open. Such windows are not easy to accommodate in the presumed thickness of the Tower walls. A not unusual situation for the chapel of a keep was over the fore-building, but we are particularly told that this fore-building was thatched, which seems unsuitable for a chapel. I have accordingly placed it on the second storey above and behind the forebuilding, where its three windows can face south. We are further told that its walls were painted, and that it was furnished with stalls, benches, grilles, prie-dieus and a picture in front of the altar. We may perhaps imagine that this represented the conversion of St Leonard after the battle of Tolbiac (if that is the right man).

We descend the steps of the Tower with greater alacrity than we went up. Our visit to the Castle has been a lengthy one; but it has never been made before. I do not feel sure that we saw everything, even in the Bailey. There must have been more accommodation than we found there for the numerous retinue that attended on the King and Queen when the standard of St George floated above the Great Tower, for distinguished visitors, such as the King of Scotland, or the King's own ministers and their suites. But I have confined myself to the mention of buildings for which I had authority. Whether they occupy anything like their right positions the spade may some day decide. I offer this tentative reconstruction only for what it is worth as a first attempt, in the hope that others may hereafter improve upon it.

Appendix C

Constables of Marlborough Castle

	Appointed	Died or replaced
John fitz Gilbert, 'the Marshal', *marshal of England*		deprived 1158
Alan de Neville, *justice of the Forests*	1158	d. *c.* 1178
Walter de Dunstanville mentioned	1182	1189
John, *brother of Richard I*	1189	deprived 1193
John the Marshal, *son of John fitz Gilbert**	1193	d. 1194
Alan de Neville, *justice of the Forests, grandson of Hugh de Neville*		
William Marshal senior, *son of John fitz Gilbert*	1217	d. 1221
William Marshal junior, *son of William Marshal senior*	1221	deprived 1223
Knights Hospitaller, *king's administrators and bankers*	1223	
Robert Lupus [RLP 426]	1224	
Robert de Meisi* 1224 ?	1228	
John de Eston*	1229	deprived 1232
Peter de Rivaux, *treasurer of Henry III's household**	1232	deprived 1233
Roger de Wascelin*	1233	1233
Robert de Mucegros*	1234	1254
Reynold de Acle*	1254	1254
Henry de la Mare*	1254	1255
Stephen Fromund*	1255	1255
Hugh Garget*	1255	
Robert Walerand	1261, 1263	1262, 1264
Roger lord Clifford	1262, 1264	1262, 1263
Robert de Lisle	1264	1267
Henry Esturmy	1264	
Roger de Cheyney*	1271	

	Appointed	Died or replaced
Nicholas de Sperscht tempus Edward I		
Queen Eleanor	1272	1291
John de Bradeham [TNA DD\ WHb/1954]	1291	
Aymery de St Amand	1294	1294
appointed so that wife may dwell there during his service in Gascony		
Joan, daughter of Edward I	1297	1297
Queen Margaret	1299	1318
Eustace de Hacche		tempus Edward II
Queen Isabella	1308–27	deprived 1321 and 1324; restored 1327
Hugh Despenser the Elder	1307–8, 1321; plundered 1321; restored 1321	forfeited 1326
Oliver de Ingham		1321
William Ramshill	1325; deprived 1329; restored 1330	?1341
John Esturmy	1329	deprived 1330
Robert Russell	1341	1347
Thomas Hungerford	in office 1359	
Joan, Queen Mother	1377	1385
Nicholas de Tamworth	1370	1376
Roger Beauchamp	1376	d. 1380
Roger Power	1380	1382
John de Roches	1382	1386
William Hasthorpe	1386	1393
Sir William Scrope	1393	1399

* See Stevenson, 'The castles of Marlborough and Ludgershall'. All other names are mentioned in the text, except where a reference is given.

Appendix D

Marlborough Castle:
Archaeological Findings for the Medieval Period

Richard Barber

Excavations

The account of the medieval castle in Chapter 3 contains very little about its archaeology. The simple reason for this is that there have been relatively few excavations overall, and only one exploratory dig at the top of the mound. Most of the archaeological material is the result of excavations for other purposes, and the relatively few finds are mostly chance discoveries. What follows is a chronological summary of the recorded results of archaeological excavations and of geophysical surveys. There is more information as to the intended purpose of digs and surveys in the actual reports. The discussions and conclusions of the reports have been omitted, as the evidence from these operations is already reflected in the main body of this book.

In 1724, William Stukeley, in his *Itinerarium Curiosam*, is the first to offer a brief note on any found objects from the site, which he regarded as that of a Roman *castrum* called Cunetio. He saw a large copper coin of the emperor Titus, and was sure that the boundary of the earl of Hertford's garden was one angle of the *castrum* 'left very manifestly, the rampart and the ditch entire'. He marked the plan of the Roman fort on one of his illustrations and wrote: 'I suppose it to have been 500 Roman feet square.'[1] The ditch and rampart were in fact those of the medieval castle; the site of Cunetio was discovered at Mildenhall in the nineteenth century.

The first reports of finds relate to building work on the site of the castle. In 1892, work near the laundry close to the mound did not produce anything medieval; nor did work in 1912 when a chimney was cut up the side of the mound for a water pump engine at the foot. In 1915, an excavation of the castle foundations started

> at a point about 60 feet due South of the Mound. On the second day they struck a flint foundation running approximately East and West; this was followed westwards and signs of a wall turning to the South were found.

[1] See p. 117 above.

In the Winter Term, the operations were continued by following up the foundation eastwards, and by digging a trench towards the Mound between it and the original excavation. The flint foundations soon came to an abrupt termination, but the excavation was continued some distance further in this direction, and also along the southward turn at the west end of the trench.

No continuation of the foundation was revealed by the east trench, but on October 17th a large cooking pot was found, bedded in gravel, to the north of the main line of the trench. Though much cracked, it was almost complete, but broke up when the gravel was removed. This pot is 9 inches high and 12 inches in diameter; a photo of it in its restored condition is reproduced in this Report.

A large number of minor finds were recorded, including bones, sherds of red pottery with black interior, fragments of plaster with red marks, and stone roof tiling, of which some pieces were pierced.[2]

The cooking pot is in fact the only substantial artefact connected with the castle that has been found; it has since disappeared. Similarly, accurate notes and a map of excavations added to the College museum in 1922 cannot now be found.[3]

H. C. Brentnall wrote a number of articles relating to the Mound from 1912 to 1938 in *The Report of the Marlborough College Natural History Society* and *Wiltshire Archaeological and Natural History Society Magazine*. His first contribution is the only substantial archaeological item among them, and follows on from the brief 1915 report.

I believe, however, that actual excavation anywhere upon the site was never undertaken by members of the School until the summer of 1915 when the Mitre Society of O.3, under the auspices of Mr. J. R. Taylor, then Bursar, opened an area in the Wilderness beside the path leading to the Bathing-place and was fortunate enough to strike the foundations of a medieval building. An account of the operations and their results will be found in the 64th N.H.S. Report. Inspired by their example the Archaeological Section obtained in the Summer Term of this year the Bursar's permission to make further excavations, and two areas were attacked. One party devoted itself to opening up the foundations disclosed in 1915, while another ran a trench E.S.E. of the same spot on the other side of the path for some 50 feet in the hope of lighting upon further foundations. The first party, again directed and actively assisted by Mr. Taylor, succeeded in exposing the greater part of the flint work discovered in 1915. ... Little, however, was added to our knowledge by the term's operations. A layer of yellowish earth was exposed to the S.E. of the flint footings on a slightly higher level, some 3 feet below the surface, which suggested a decayed floor or packing of oolite rubble; but

---

[2] J. C. A., 'Notes on an Excavation in the Wilderness', *RMCNHS*, 64 (1915), 22.
[3] Brentnall, '*Castellum Merlebergae*', 38.

its condition was too rotten to allow of any conclusions being drawn as to its purpose. On top of this a loose flint wall, 2 feet wide and rising about 6 inches above the platform, was traceable for several feet in a S.W. direction, till it made a S.E. turn and lost itself among the roots of a large tree. This flint work lay some 6 feet from the footings originally discovered and suggested in the portion exposed no obvious relations to them. Since the fact is not recorded in connection with the work of 1915, it should here be added that the footings unearthed in that year are 4½ feet wide and rise to an average height of about a foot from a depth of about 4½ feet below the surface of the ground. As the whole of the original area has not yet been fully recovered it is not possible to record the length of the footings so far traced. A few sherds of medieval pottery, fragments of coloured plaster and lumps of lime silicate (slag from the royal lime-kilns) such as were discovered on the former occasion and possibly relics of the same find, were practically all of interest that this year's digging yielded.

The south eastern trench proved almost entirely barren, unless a pronounced accumulation of flint about 12 feet from its northern end, where it abutted on the path, represented the remains of a wall running N.E. and S.W. These vestiges were followed a short distance in side cuttings which yielded nothing striking enough to warrant further investigation. The section of the ground, however, exposed in the main trench was not without interest. It revealed some four feet of accumulated chalk rubble and light coloured earth overlying a dark band of mould from four to six inches in thickness. Beneath this the solid chalk was struck, of a consistency which suggested the presence of the same chalk rock which occurs, for instance, four feet below the lawn in front of Sick House. It seems probable that the dark band of soil represents the level of the original mould or of medieval occupation, and the hard chalk beneath it the bed on which the foundations of ancient buildings in the Wilderness were presumably laid. It corresponds in depth from the surface to the stratum on which the flint footings of the earlier excavation lie on the other side of the footpath, and it indicates how far we must go down in any further attempts we make to recover the ground plan of the Castle Bailey.[4]

In 1932, Brentnall noted the discovery of fragments of a medieval mullioned window under the Bath Road. In the substantial article on the castle as a whole in 1933, reprinted in Appendix B, he summarised the overall state of our archaeological knowledge bluntly, saying that 'Hardly a vestige of Marlborough Castle, the medieval stronghold, remains – above ground.' The main body of the article is a detailed attempt to reconstruct the layout of the castle, and to create a suggested plan, which was printed with the article. This is discussed below, in relation to the recent geophysical surveys.

---

[4]   Brentnall, '*Castellum Merlebergae*', 37.

Brentnall's article entitled 'The Curtain Wall of Marlborough Castle', which appeared in the 1937 report, centred on the discovery in the previous year[5] of the foundations of that wall during the construction of new classrooms, Leaf Block, which spanned the outer line of the castle:

> The building operations, so far as they concern us here, necessitated four trenches running east and west and one running north and south. (These directions are only roughly accurate.) Towards the west end of each of the four first mentioned the picks soon struck a mass of flint rubble, below which there appeared closely packed sarsen boulders ranging from one to two feet in diameter. The removal of this material left in each of the eight faces of the trenches a clear section of the foundations of a massive wall.
>
> The rubble began about 2 ft. 3 in. below the surface, and the sarsens lay on a bottom some 3 ft. lower. The requirements of the modern builders, owing perhaps to the raising of the ground-level, did not necessitate as deep a trench as the earlier work, and the bottom of the sarsen footings was not reached. This is to be regretted, but the extreme depth can later be established in another section of the wall.
>
> Comparison of the different sections in the sides of the trenches revealed the foundations of a wall varying in width from 7 ft. 6 in. to 9 ft. But the interior or western face was easier to determine than the outer. The lucky intervention of Whit Monday at a time when one of the middle trenches was only partially excavated made it possible to uncover a length of the interior face still showing some half-dozen courses of dressed and well-laid flints resting on the sarsen footings. But in no other place did we establish the actual line of the inner face of the wall, and nothing approaching a definite limit could be discovered on the exterior or eastern face. It can only be said that the average width of the material exposed was about 8 ft. or a few inches more.
>
> It was remarkable that, so far as we could observe, very few fallen stones from the upper courses of the wall and no accumulation of the flint rubble with which it was presumably filled were visible in the trenches. This would seem to indicate a deliberate destruction of the wall at some period and the removal of the material for some other purpose.
>
> In the southern sections exposed the axis of the wall ran on a bearing of 348°, or 12° west of true north. But about thirty feet north of the south wall of the class-rooms as since erected – somewhere, that is, about the middle of the western part of the central passage of the building – it changed direction slightly. The bearing of the axis became 341°, a variation of seven degrees from the original line. Complete accuracy is not claimed for these measurements owing to the difficulty of establishing the wall-face, but it is unlikely that they are seriously incorrect.

---

[5] There is a brief report in *RMCNHS* (1936), 19.

In two survey articles in *Wiltshire Archaeological and Natural History Magazine* in 1936 and 1938, Brentnall notes the apparent survival of part of the keep at the top of the mound. However, the details are very vague: in 1936 he records: 'What little remains above ground (if the elevation justifies that expression) is to be seen on the summit of the motte, where a buttress of the keep was laid bare some years ago.' Two years later he claims that 'Even to-day the periphery of the keep is traceable, and a few years ago we unearthed at least one of its buttresses. The diameter of the Keep appears to have been 120 feet, but successive "improvements" have ruined the evidence both inside and out.'

Joanne Best, in her 1995 dissertation, mentions Brentnall's note, and prints a photograph in this context which claims to show 'the remains of a wall just below the summit of the Mound, on the north-west slope'. Best's work is currently only available in a photocopied version, and the photograph is very poorly reproduced.[6] Despite a careful search, it has not been possible to identify these remains.

The last excavations reported by the Marlborough College Natural History Society were in 1955–56, when there was considerable activity.[7] P. E. C. Hayman reported as follows:

> In the Summer Term, 1955, a trench was dug under the direction of R. H. L. Disney straight down to a depth of just under five feet on the little plateau below the spiral footpath at the western edge of the Mound. Below the topsoil was a layer which almost certainly consisted of the soil thrown down when the spiral footpath was cut in the 17th century: the presence of 'dried peas' instead of an old turf-line supported this view. Beneath the 'dried peas' was a layer of soil which contained medieval refuse (fragments of building materials, bones, shells, etc.) and Norman pottery – the accumulated deposit of the period from the building of the castle to the cutting of the spiral. Below this was a thin layer of flint. The lowest layer above the natural was of packed chalk and soil. This mixed layer also yielded Norman pottery. If, as seems probable, this lowest layer was part of the main body of the Mound, then the Mound may be taken to be Norman; but there are two important weaknesses in this argument. First, this layer being so near to the edge may well represent a Norman enlargement of an earlier mound, and secondly, it may be questioned whether the dating evidence in this layer at its thinnest can be held to be adequately sealed. No charcoal was found.

> During the Summer Term, 1956, a second trench (begun in the previous Summer holidays by A. W. Witheridge, assisted by A. Gunston of Bath, with

---

6 Best, 'The Marlborough Mound', photograph 3.
7 A personal note: the editor remembers taking part in excavations in 1957 or 1958, led by P. E. C. Hayman, to the north-west of the mound, between the physics laboratories and the rose garden, which uncovered what may have been modern foundations. No record of these has been found either in the College archives or his papers; Caroline Montagu, his daughter, kindly checked the latter.

whom he had previously been working at Snail Down, and the Rev. P. E. C. Hayman) was cut into the Mound, after breaking through the retaining wall, some six feet south of the boiler house, as near as possible to the site where charcoal was found in 1910. D. A. Hewat and R. H. L. Disney were in charge. A similar section was obtained. Norman pottery was found in both the flint and rubble surface and in the layer of medieval accumulation below. The layer above the natural proved to be somewhat complex. At the outer end of the trench this layer was of very mixed and ill-defined consistency but was generally similar to that found in the 1955 excavations and considered then to be probably the main body of the Mound. As the trench was cut deeper into the Mound, this layer, which followed the contours of the Mound, was seen to be made up of four interlocking but fairly clearly defined bands: (i) packed chalk and soil, (ii) silty soil, (iii) tightly packed chalk rubble with occasional pieces of chalk rock and (iv), at the lowest level, another band of river earth containing irregular and scattered deposits of charcoal and a few burnt flints. Charcoal in small pieces was also sparsely scattered throughout the bands of this multiple layer. At the outer end of the trench the two bands of silty soil merged into each other and into the chalk bands, and throughout the trench the lower charcoal-bearing band merged into the natural below without any clear line of demarcation. The bands seemed to be contemporary: their surfaces overlapped and interlocked each other and neither continuous turflines nor 'dried peas'[8] were found. … The trench was cut into the Mound as far as was practicable without using timbering …

The western moat

Although the excavations and finds now to be described are not in themselves of any great importance, they provide an excuse for a wider discussion on the subject of the lie of the moat on the western side of the Mound and for drawing attention to what is already known on the subject.

During the Autumn Term, 1956, the contractor's workmen, preparing the site west of the Mound for the new Physics Laboratories, reported that, while driving a pile, they had encountered an obstruction some five feet down. This proved to be composed of roughly dressed Sarsen stones, apparently fallen from a piece of masonry, the top of which lay just below the surface immediately to their west. It seemed likely at the time that here was a part of the Castle and … when it became obvious that the masonry was in fact part of a wall running north and south on the same general line as the moat, approximately 32 feet from the retaining wall at the foot of the Mound, the excavations were limited to following it in each direction and, in order to get a complete cross-section, to digging a trench at right-angles to it.

---

[8] The flint and rubble deposits may be the slipped accumulation of a now invisible layer of 'dried peas'.

The wall, 40 inches wide at the top, was stoutly constructed of Sarsen blocks, with some freestone, set in sandy yellow mortar. It petered out almost immediately to the south of the point where the pile had ultimately been driven beside it and appeared to have been robbed. To the north it continued until it passed under the remaining laboratories. The side facing the Mound was flat and regular and went down sheer for about six feet before spreading into (what seemed to be) irregular foundations. The west side came out, about one foot six inches down, in a narrow step and then sloped back inwards to the same conjectural foundations: only above the step was this face flat and regular. Water level was at a depth of four foot and it was therefore impossible to reach the actual bottom of the foundations. The top of the wall had been levelled with limestone tiles, no doubt from the Castle, and, near the laboratories, with small Sarsens set in greyish mortar. This levelled surface had for a considerable distance been used as a footing for foundations, which in some places were concrete and in others brick. The bricks were of no great age and were similar to many found locally.

On the side facing west, the wall was backed with clay. Local workmen stated that this clay was similar to that obtained in the Devizes-Lavington area and regularly used in the district for puddling. In the clay, about seven inches below the top of the step, was found the only piece of evidence closely dateable – the bowl of a clay pipe by Thomas Hunt of Bristol, c. 1650. There was no trace of any deposit between the clay and the stonework. On either side of the wall was rubble, which, on the west side above the clay, contained a high proportion of broken building materials. Below the rubble on the east side was moat-silt in which were found traces of domestic refuse, bones, mussel shells and also reed stalks.

The Marlborough Mound Trust commissioned a GPR survey of the top of the mount by Wessex Archaeology in 2017, which identified two anomalies that were considered likely to be archaeological. This was followed up by an exploratory excavation in 2020, with the following result:

Excavation comprised of a 2 m square hand excavated test pit that was stepped in at 1 m below ground. A further central 1 m square was excavated by hand to an additional depth of 0.5 m, with a sondage and hand augering in the north-east corner taking the total depth of excavation down to 2.60 m from ground level, the top of a circular (or ring) high bank material.

The evaluation has proven that although the very centre at the top of the mound has been heavily truncated, up to at least a depth of 2 m by construction of the central water tank in the early part of the 20th century, where the circle (or ring) of high bank material encircles the Mound, there is an element of in-situ and surviving buried ground and topsoil.

A portion of a deliberately backfilled foundation trench was discovered, which is at the correct depth and on the same alignment for it to be inferred to as relating to the northern anomaly located by the GPR survey. The evaluation has proven there to be a strong potential for further archaeology to remain buried beneath this, and that a layer of redeposited material above (and immediately below the buried ground surface and topsoil) is likely deliberate made ground; perhaps landscaping in the Later Medieval to Post Medieval period.

The lowest deposit encountered appears to be comprised of shallow and alternating layers of flinty gravel and silty sand. It is likely these deposits are a component of original Mound construction material. Given the depth and consistency of the deposit it is possible that the alternating layers reflect a single phase of later Neolithic Mound building activity.[9]

It seems unlikely that further excavations at the top of the mound can be justified, given the extent of the disturbances created when the large water tank and other structures were placed there, and from an earlier period, the reshaping of the top when the spiral path was installed.

---

[9] Wessex Archaeology, 'Marlborough Mound Phase 4 Investigations', iii.

Excavations of the bailey wall

A. J. Roberts

In 2019, excavations were carried out at the site of the 1936 trench which had uncovered a section of the medieval wall adjoining Leaf Block. These were conducted under the supervision of A. J. Roberts of Archeoscan by students working with Matt Blossom. The initial trench revealed that the site of the 1936 dig had been wrongly recorded on the map which had been drawn up at the time. Two sarsen stones which may have come from the outer wall of the bailey were found. A further trench was then opened to the east over the recalculated projected line of the wall. At a depth of approximately 0.5m a heavily mortared surface was uncovered. This had a number of larger sarsen boulders and flint nodules embedded in it. The wall foundation had a width of 2.6m. To the eastern side a line of sarsen boulders were tightly mortared together to form a distinct edge to the feature. A small sondage on the eastern side has revealed a further line of sarsens at a depth of -1.979m (below site datum). To the west, and by inference to the inside, there is a distinct edge to the wall. In parts there is a distinct line of mortared and dressed stonework. The wall has a slight curvature, more obvious on the eastern edge.

A main feature of the wall is a distinct rectangular cut into the line of the wall (Fig. D.1). Measuring 2.5m in length, it cuts halfway into the width of the wall. The base of the feature is uneven and the edges are not dressed, suggesting that perhaps dressed stone, or some other structure, may have been removed from the void. The absence of large sarsens in the void is significant. It suggests that the cut is contemporary. It is possible that this is the base of an internal structure such as a garderobe or chimney.

To the west of the cut is a rammed chalk floor. Cut into this is a circular pit-like feature containing fill. This deposit is a dark brown clayey fill that contains a number of animal bones, oyster shells and fragments of stone roof tile. The bottom of the fill has not yet been reached due to the restrictions of the trench, but a dressed wall stone was present in the northern section. The feature started to take a more circular form the deeper it went. The rammed chalk floor runs under the main wall foundation, thus pre-dating it or at least contemporary with it. The floor forms the western edge of the rectangular cut in the floor. The fills of the cut are overlain by another fill. The first of these is a darker black fill that contains a very high number of oyster shells and some animal bone suggestive of a midden. This may be significant at the bottom of the rectangular cut. The second fill is a gravelly mix of degraded mortar and flint nodules probably from the degradation of the mortar in the wall foundation. What is notable is that there are no large rounded sarsens within the loose dark fill. If the tree has destroyed the foundation (that does contain large sarsen stones) then it could be expected that they would still be within the fill. Their absence may lend weight to the fact that the rectangular cut on the inside of the wall was there before the tree exploited the space.

To the west of the main wall foundation are a number of different fills that have been disturbed to varying degrees. The lowest deposit reached to date is a fine gravel consistent with fill that appears elsewhere in the trench. A coarser gravel layer sits above this and blends wi th a dark clay with flints layer. Above these layers is a sequence of burning layers consistent with dumping and making up the ground levels in more recent times. Bounded by the wall foundation to the west and by a regular line of gravel to the north, it could be that this level dates to the landscaping period of Lady Hertford's garden landscaping in the seventeenth century. The finds from this area include some twelfth- to fourteenth-century pottery illustrating the very disturbed nature of the deposits around the wall.

The gravel fill that butts against the mortar of the wall foundation is similar to that on the eastern side of the wall. The fill seems to be a mix of degraded wall foundation/mortar probably arising when the castle wall was robbed/levelled at the end of its useful life. It is from the eastern fill that a few fragments of pottery dating from the twelfth and thirteenth centuries were recovered. There is also a fill of gravel 2m wide that projects at ninety degrees for the wall foundation. It is perhaps no coincidence that it is located on the outside of the wall at the point where the rectangular cut on the inside of the wall is located. It is also at this point that the wall takes a small turn to the west. It is conceivable that this gravel is structural.

The gravel fills are either side of the main wall foundation, a heavily mortared structure containing flint nodules and large rounded sarsen boulders. There is little doubt that these are the remains of the foundation of a monumental structure. The linear, slightly curved, aspect of the structure strongly suggests that it is the foundation of the wall of the medieval castle. The eastern edge of the structure is more defined with a line of sarsen boulders mortared together and on a very solid bed of mortar and flint nodules. The distance between the two outer edges of the wall foundation is approximately 2.6m (8ft 6in) and it is aligned on a bearing of 152 degrees. This is very similar to the description of the wall remains noted in 1936 during the construction of Leaf Block and reported by H. C. Brentnall.[10] He wrote:

> ... soon struck a mass of flint rubble, below which there appeared closely packed sarsen boulders ranging in diameter from one to two feet in diameter. Comparisons of the different sections in the sides of the trenches revealed the foundations of a wall varying in width from 7ft 6in to 9ft. But the interior western face was easier to determine than the outer ... the interior face still showing some half-dozen courses of dressed and well-laid flints resting on the sarsen footings ...

[10] See p. 162 above.

Fig. D.1 Images of the wall foundation constructed of mortared sarsen boulders and flint nodules.

Title
Marlborough Castle
Conjectured
Plan

2022

Conjectured plan
of castle
after Brentnall

Observed line of
Bailey Wall

Conjectured wall

Ground Penetrating
Radar Anomaly

N
W E
S

Scale:
Drawn By:
A.J.ROBERTS

archeoscan@hotmail.com
www.archeoscan.com
(07901 745140)
© A.J.ROBERTS

Pond

Leaf Block

1936

2022

Heywood

Modern Langl

Mount

Motte

Henry Hony

Kempson
Centre

Ellis Theatre

CCF

Innovation

Range

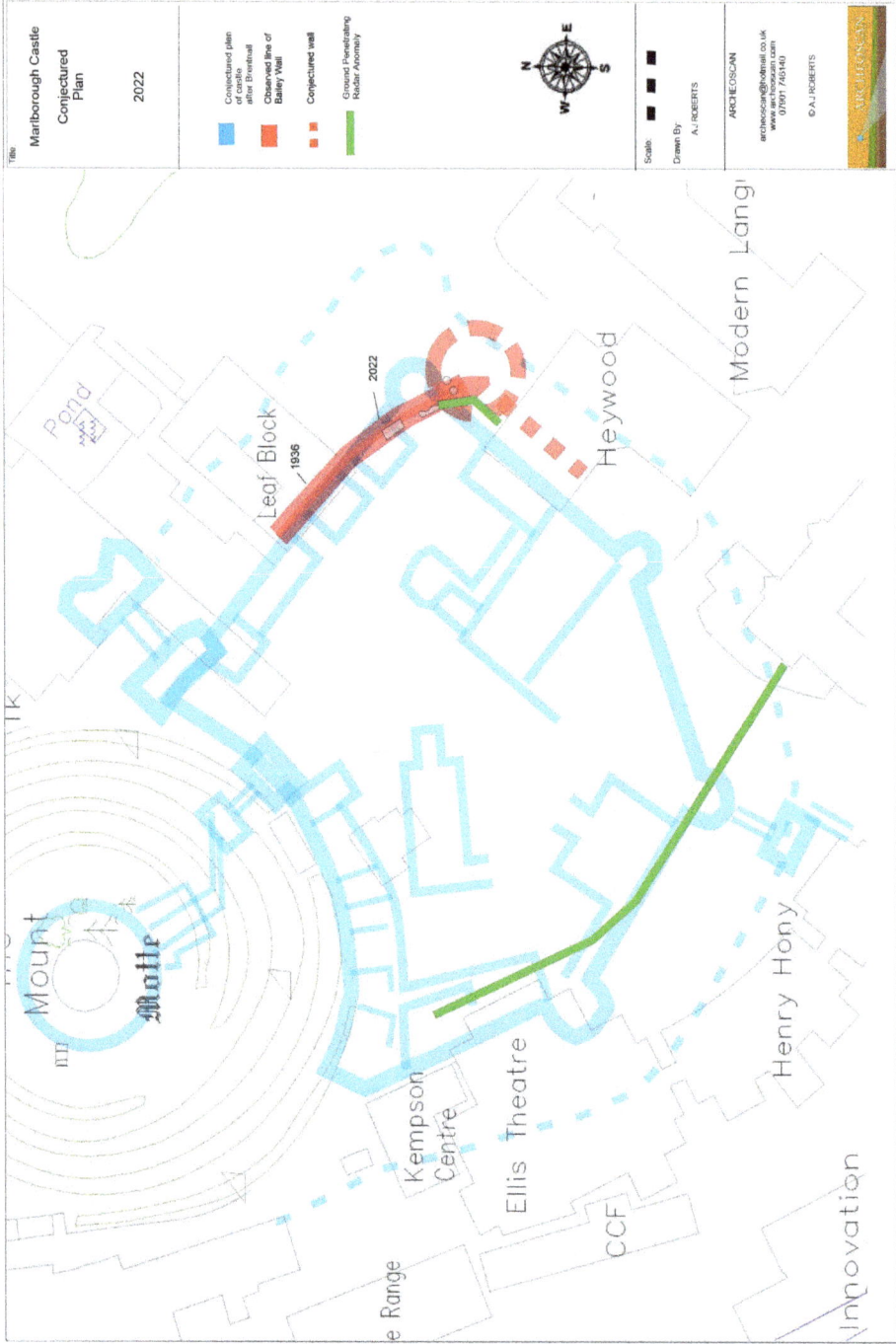

Fig. D.2 Geophysical results mapped on H. C. Brentnall's plan from RMCNHS, 48 (1938) (March 2022).

Fig. D.3 The bailey wall as excavated by March 2022.

The excavations on the bailey wall have continued during 2021 and 2022. The footpath to the south of the previous excavations was removed, enabling the exploration of the area close to the conjectured south-eastern tower of the castle bailey. A further length of the bailey wall footings was exposed. Like that seen in the earlier excavation, it was constructed of flint nodules tightly mortared. Fewer sarsen stones were evident in the newly exposed section of wall footings as it approached the corner tower. The footings continued to have an average width of 2.6m, although the western (inside) edge of the new portion was damaged in parts, possibly by the action of tree roots. The indentation into the footings was similar to that noted on the northern section, and therefore could possibly have been contemporary with the castle, the dressed stone having been removed. Under the remaining mortar and flint nodule course was a footing of flint nodules without mortar that was, presumably, to provide an initial foundation on which the mortared courses were laid.

To the south, the wall footings transitioned to a wider spread of flat mortar that extended beyond the limits of the excavation. This has been interpreted as the possible base of the south-east corner tower. It is also no coincidence that this area coincides with the local contours of the landscape as the ground surface falls away to the east and south, suggestive of possible structures underground at this point. As the wall foundation approaches the tower, the mortar changes slightly in composition and there are fewer flint nodules visible on the mortar surface. It is tentatively speculated that the tower may have been constructed at a different time to the bailey wall. It may also be witness to a different team of builders. Within the internal dimensions of the visible part of the tower, two pits had been cut into the mortar floor. Two metres in diameter, they contained different fills. The easterly pit had been used as a rubbish pit and was full of refuse dating to the eighteenth century. Some fragments of pottery bore the partial wording 'castle' and may date from the time that Lady Hertford's main residence was used as the Castle Inn. The second, complete, pit had a more uniform fill suggesting a quick backfill, but contained no definitive dating material. On balance, it is probable that these pits are contemporary with the building and possibly contained vessels of some description.

There was no evidence of a moat immediately against the foundations of the wall, suggesting that this was further to the east. On the eastern side a mortared surface extended in parts from the wall to the extent of the excavations; however, this was a very limited space. One section of the footings to the west (inside) had a well-dressed face and was associated with a flat mortared surface. This could be a glimpse of an internal room on the inside of the castle wall. Also, on the western side of the wall several irregular mortared, chalk and flint nodule surfaces were encountered, suggestive of internal structures. However, this space was extremely limited, and it was difficult to interpret with confidence the form or function of these deposits.

The combined exposure of the excavations has revealed a portion of the bailey wall footings in the south-east corner of the castle. The wall clearly has a slight curvature to the east and does not have a straight form here as suggested by Brentnall. There is evidence that a tower stood in the south-east corner, but the physical limits of the excavation prevent an accurate assessment of its overall diameter.

Bibliography

Abbreviations

RMCNHS   Report of the Marlborough College Natural History Society
WANHSM   Wiltshire Archaeological and Natural History Society Magazine
Other abbreviations are listed alphabetically below.

Allen, M., *Mints and Money in Medieval England* (Cambridge, 2012).
Annales Monastici, ed. H. R. Luard (Rolls Series 36, London, 1865).
Anon., 'Additions to museum and library', *WANHSM*, 50 (1943), 203–4.
Arnold-Forster, Frances, *Studies in Church Dedication* (London, 1899).
Astill, Grenville G, *Historic Towns in Berkshire: An Archaeological Appraisal* (Reading, 1978).
Aston, M. and C. Lewis (eds), *The Medieval Landscape of Wessex* (Oxford, 1994).
Atkinson, R. J. C., 'Silbury Hill', in R. Sutcliffe (ed.), *Chronicle: Essays from Ten Years of Television Archaeology* (London, 1978), pp. 159–73.
Aubrey, John, *Monumenta Britannica, Or a Miscellany of British Antiquities; Part 3 and Index*, ed. John Fowles (Sherborne, 1982).
Baker, J. and S. Brookes, *Beyond the Burghal Hidage: Anglo-Saxon Civil Defence in the Viking Age* (Leiden, 2013).
Barber, M., H. Winton, C. Stoertz, E. Carpenter and L. Martin, '"The brood of Silbury?": A remote look at some other sizeable Wessex mounds', in J. Leary, T. Darvill and D. Field (eds), *Round Mounds and Monumentality in the British Neolithic and Beyond* (Oxford, 2010).
Barber, Richard, *Magnificence: Princely Splendour in the Middle Ages* (Woodbridge, 2020).
Barker, D., T. Sly, S. Chaussee and E. Richley, 'Report on the Geophysical Survey at Old Sarum, Wiltshire March-April 2014', The Old Sarum Landscapes Project Research Report No. 1 (Unpublished Report: Archaeological Prospection Services of Southampton, 2014).
Barratt, Nick, 'The Revenues of John and Philip Augustus Revisited', in S. D. Church (ed.), *King John: New Interpretations* (Woodbridge, 1999), pp. 75–99.
Bartlett, Robert, *England under the Norman and Angevin Kings 1075–1225* (Oxford, 2000).
Bayliss, A., C. Cartwright, G. Cook, S. Griffiths, R. Madgwick, P. Marshall and P. Reimer, '"Rings of fire" and Grooved Ware settlement at West

Kennet, Wiltshire', in P. Bickle, V. Cummings, D. Hofmann and J. Pollard (eds), *The Neolithic of Europe* (Oxford, 2017), pp. 249–78.

Beckles Willson, Anthony, 'Alexander Pope and the Grotto at Crux Easton' (Unpublished research note, The Twickenham Museum Archive, February 2009).

——, *Alexander Pope's Grotto in Twickenham*, 2nd edn (Twickenham, 2014).

Best, Joanne, 'The Marlborough Mound: An Archaeological Study' (Unpublished dissertation, University of Bristol, 1995).

——, 'Appendix: The Marlborough Mound', in A. Whittle, *Sacred Mound, Holy Rings: Silbury Hill and the West Kennet Palisade Enclosures: A Later Neolithic Complex in North Wiltshire* (Oxford, 1997), pp. 169–70.

Bettey, J. H., *Wessex from AD 1000* (London and New York, 1986).

Bingley, W. (ed.), *Correspondence Between Frances, Countess of Hartford (afterwards Duchess of Somerset) and Henrietta Louisa, Countess of Pomfret, Between the Years 1738 and 1741*, 3 vols (London, 1805).

Blair, J., *Building Anglo-Saxon England* (Princeton and Oxford, 2018).

Blunt, Wilfrid, *In for a Penny: A Prospect of Kew Gardens* (London, 1978).

Bond, J., 'Forests, chases, warrens and parks', in M. Aston and C. Lewis (eds), *The Medieval Landscape of Wessex* (Oxford, 1994).

Bradbury, J., *Stephen and Matilda: The Civil War of 1139–53* (Stroud, 1996).

Bradley, R., *The Good Stones: A New Investigation of the Clava Cairns* (Edinburgh, 2000).

——, *The Prehistory of Britain and Ireland*, 2nd edn (Cambridge, 2019).

Bradley, R. and C. Nimura (eds), *The Use and Reuse of Stone Circles* (Oxford, 2016).

Brady, K., A. Simmonds and C. Champness, 'Neolithic pits and Middle Iron Age settlement at Salisbury Road, Marlborough', *WANHSM*, 113 (2020), 35–55.

Bray, William (ed.), *The Diary of John Evelyn*, 2 vols (New York and London, 1901).

Brentnall, H. C., 'The Mound', *RMCNHS*, 61 (1912), 23–9.

——, 'The Marlborough Castle Mound', *WANHSM*, 38 (1914), 112.

——, 'Castellum Merlebergae', *RMCNHS*, 71 (1922), 37–46.

——, 'Castellum Merlebergensis', *RMCNHS*, 82 (1933), 60–104 (Appendix B above).

——, 'Marlborough Castle', *WANSHM*, 47 (1935), 543.

——, 'The curtain wall of Marlborough Castle', *RMCNHS*, 85 (1937), 42–7.

——, 'Marlborough Castle', *WANSHM*, 48 (1938), 133–43.

Brett, Simon, *Marlborough College: A Short History and Guide* (Brentwood, 1979).

Brooke, J. W., 'Notes on the finding of Neolithic flints', *RMCNHS for 1889* (1890), 104–5.

——, 'Notes on Neolithic flints', *RMCNHS for 1890* (1891), 103.

Brophy, K., '"… a place where they tried their criminals": Neolithic round mounds in Perth and Kinross', in J. Leary, T. Darvill and D. Field (eds), *Round Mounds and Monumentality in the British Neolithic and Beyond* (Neolithic Studies Group Seminar Papers 10, Oxford, 2010), pp. 10–27.

Brophy, K. and G. Noble, 'Henging, mounding and blocking: the Forteviot henge group', in A. Gibson (ed.), *Enclosing the Neolithic: Recent Studies in Britain and Europe* (Oxford, 2012), pp. 21–35.

Brown, A. E. and C. C. Taylor, 'The Gardens at Lyveden, Northamptonshire', *Archaeological Journal*, 129 (1972), 154–60.

Brown, Jane, *My Darling Heriott: Henrietta Luxborough, Poetic Gardener and Irrepressible Exile* (London, 2006).

Brown, Richard, 'The Archaeology of the Upper Ward Quadrangle and the Evidence for the Round Table Building', in Julian Munby *et al.*, *Edward III's Round Table at Windsor* (Woodbridge, 2007), pp. 60–9.

Brown, R. and A. Hardy, *Trade and Prosperity, War and Poverty: An Archaeological and Historical Investigation into Southampton's French Quarter* (Oxford, 2011).

Brown, R. Allen, *The Memoranda Roll for the Tenth Year of King John*, Pipe Roll Society 69 [NS 31] (London, 1957).

——, 'Royal Castle Building in England 1154–1216', *English Historical Review*, lxx (1955), 353–98.

Brownell, Morris R., *Alexander Pope and the Arts of Georgian England* (Oxford, 1978).

Brunon, Hervé and Monique Mosser, *L'imaginaire des Grottes dans les Jardins Européens* (Paris, 2014).

Calendarium Rotulorum Patentium, ed. S. Ayscough and J. Caley (London, 1802).

Cannon, Henry Lewin (ed.), *The Great Roll of the Pipe for the twenty-sixth year of the reign of King Henry the Third A.D. 1241–2* (New Haven, 1918).

Card, N., M. Edmonds and A. Mitchell, *The Ness of Brodgar: as it stands* (Kirkwall, 2020).

Carlyon-Britton, P., 'Bedwin and Marlborough and the moneyer Cilda', *The Numismatic Chronicle and Journal of the Numismatic Society*, Fourth Series, Vol. 2 (1902), 20–5.

Carpenter, David, *Henry III: The Rise to Power and the Personal Rule* (London, 2020).

——, 'The Household Rolls of King Henry III of England (1216–72)', *Historical Research*, 80:20 (2007), 22–46.

Cathcart King, D. J., 'The field archaeology of mottes in England and Wales: Eine kurze Übersicht', in *Chateau Gaillard: Études de Castellologie médiévale. V: Actes du colloque international tenu à Hindsgavl (Danemark) 1–6 September 1970* (Caen, 1972), pp. 102–12.

——, *Castellarium Anglicanum: An Index and Bibliography of Castles in England, Wales and the Islands*, 2 vols (London, reprinted 1983).

Cathcart King, D. J. and L. Alcock, 'Ringworks of England and Wales', *Chateau Gaillard*, III (1969), 90–127.

CCR Henry III: *Calendar of the Close Rolls preserved in the Public Record Office: Henry III, 1227–1272* (London, 1902–75).

CCR Edward I: *Calendar of the Close Rolls preserved in the Public Record Office: Edward I, 1272–1307* (London, 1900–8).

CCR Edward II: *Calendar of the Close Rolls preserved in the Public Record Office: Edward II, 1307–1327* (London, 1892–8).

Challenger, Sheila B., 'Accounts for Works on the Royal Mills and Castle at Marlborough in 1237–8 and 1238–9', in N. J. Williams (ed.), *Collectanea*, Wiltshire Archaeological and Natural History Society, Records Branch XII (1956), pp. 40–2.

Chandler, John, *John Leland's Itinerary: Travels in Tudor England* (Stroud, 1993).

Chaucer, Geoffrey, *Complete Works*, ed. F. N. Robinson, 2nd edn (Oxford, 1957).

Christelow, S. M., 'A Moveable Feast? Itineration and the Centralization of Government under Henry I', *Albion*, 28 (1996), 187–228.

Christie, N. and O. H. Creighton, with H. Hamerow and M. Edgeworth (eds), *Transforming Townscapes: From Burh to Borough: The Archaeology of Wallingford, AD 800–1400* (Leeds, 2013).

Church, S. D., 'Some Aspects of the Royal Itinerary in the Twelfth Century', in *Thirteenth Century England XI* (Woodbridge, 2007), pp. 31–45.

CIM: *Calendar of Inquisitions Miscellaneous (Chancery) preserved in the Public Record Office* (London, 1916–69).

CLR: *Calendar of the Liberate Rolls preserved in the Public Record Office: Henry III, 1232–1272* (London, 1916–64).

Clark, J. G. D., 'Notes on the flint implements on Granham Hill and around Pantawick', *RMCNHS*, 72 (1924), 84–9.

Clarke, B. and E. Elton, 'The lost chapel of Bicknoll, Broad Town, North Wiltshire: final report on excavations at Bicknoll Cottage, 2015', *WANHM*, 109 (2016), 126–42.

Cleal, R. and R. Montague, 'Neolithic and Early Bronze Age', in AAHRG, *Archaeological Research Agenda for the Avebury World Heritage Site* (Salisbury, 2001), pp. 8–19.

Cleal, R. and J. Pollard, 'Neolithic and Early Bronze Age', in M. Leivers and A. B. Powell (eds), *A Research Framework for the Stonehenge, Avebury and Associated Sites World Heritage Site: Avebury Resource Assessment* (Salisbury, 2016), pp. 81–97.

CMR: *Calendar of the Memoranda Rolls preserved in the Public Record Office, 1326–1327* (London, 1969).

Cole, Henry, *Documents Illustrative of English History in the Thirteenth and Fourteenth Centuries* (London, 1844).

CPR: *Calendar of the Patent Rolls preserved in the Public Record Office: Henry III, 1216–1272* (London, 1901–13).

CPR: *Calendar of the Patent Rolls preserved in the Public Record Office: Edward I, 1272–1307* (London, 1898–1901).

CPR: *Calendar of the Patent Rolls preserved in the Public Record Office: Edward II, 1307–1327* (London, 1894–1904).

CPR: *Calendar of the Patent Rolls preserved in the Public Record Office: Edward III, 1327–1377* (London, 1891–1916).

CPR: *Calendar of the Patent Rolls preserved in the Public Record Office: Richard I, 1377–1399* (London, 1895–1909).

Creighton, Oliver H., *Castles and Landscapes: Power, Community and Fortification in Medieval England* (London: 2005).

——, *Designs upon the Land: Elite Landscapes of the Middle Ages* (Woodbridge, 2009).

——, '1066 and the Landscape', in D. Bates (ed.), *1066 in Perspective* (Leeds, 2018), pp. 213–37.

——, 'Early castles in the medieval landscape of Wiltshire', *WANHM*, 93 (2000), 105–19.

Creighton, O. H. and D. Wright, *The Anarchy: War and Status in 12th-Century Landscapes of Conflict* (Liverpool, 2016).

Creighton, O. H. and S. J. Rippon, 'Conquest, colonisation and the countryside: archaeology and the mid-11th- to mid-12th-century rural landscape', in C. Dyer and D. M. Hadley (eds), *The Archaeology of the 11th Century* (London, 2017), pp. 57–87.

Crouch, David, 'Earl Gilbert Marshal and his mortal enemies', *Historical Research*, 87 (2014), 393–403.

——, *William Marshal* (London, 1990).

Cunliffe, B.W. (ed.), *Excavation at Portchester Castle: Vol. II, Saxon* (London, 1976).

Daniell, C., *From Norman Conquest to Magna Carta: England 1066–1215* (London and New York, 2003).

Darvill, T., P. Marshall, M. Parker Pearson and G. Wainwright, 'Stonehenge remodelled', *Antiquity*, 86 (2012), 1021–40.

Davidson, B. K., 'Castle Neroche: an abandoned Norman Fortress in south Somerset', *Proceedings of Somerset Archaeology and Natural History*, 116 (1972), 16–58.

Defoe, Daniel, *A Tour Through the Whole Island of Great Britain*, ed. P. N. Furbank and W. R. Owens (New Haven and London, 1991).

Dix, Brian, 'Experiencing the past: the archaeology of some Renaissance gardens', *Renaissance Studies*, 25:1 (2011), 151–82.

Dix, Brian, Iain Soden and Tora Hylton, 'Kirby Hall and its Gardens: Excavations in 1987–1994', *Archaeological Journal*, 152 (1995), 291–380.

Dixon Hunt, John and Peter Willis (eds), *The Genius of the Place: The English Landscape Garden 1620–1820*, rev. edn (Cambridge, MA, and London, 1988).

Dixon-Smith, Sally Angharad, 'Feeding the Poor to Commemorate the Dead: The Pro Anima Almsgiving of Henry III of England' (Ph.D. thesis, University College London, 2002), 32–3.

Dodd, A. (ed.), *Oxford Before the University: The Late Saxon and Norman Archaeology of the Thames Crossing, the Defences and the Town* (Oxford, 2003).

Drage, C., 'Urban castles', in J. Schofield and R. Leech (eds), *Urban Archaeology in Britain* (London, 1987), pp. 117–32.

Duck, Stephen, 'A Description of a Journey to Marlborough, Bath, Portsmouth, &c. To the Right Honourable the Lord Viscount Palmerston', *Poems on Several Occasions* (London, 1736), pp. 205–36.

Dyer, C. and D. Hadley (eds), *The Archaeology of the 11th Century: Continuities and Transformations* (London, 2017).

EHD: English Historical Documents 1042–1189, ed. D. C. Douglas and G. W. Greenaway (London, 1953).

Ellis, P. (ed.), *Ludgershall Castle, Wiltshire: A Report on the Excavations by Peter Addyman, 1964–1972* (Devizes, 2000).

Eve, A. S., 'On recent excavations at Marlborough College', *RMCNHS*, 41 (1892), 65–9.

Evelyn, John, *The Diary of John Evelyn*, ed. William Bray, 2 vols (New York and London, 1901).

——, *Elysium Britannicum, or The Royal Gardens*, ed. John E. Ingram (Philadelphia, 2001).

Everson, Paul, *Lewes Priory, Sussex: The post-Dissolution mansion and gardens of Lords Place*, English Heritage Archaeological Investigation Report Series AI/7/2005.

Feluś, Kate, *The Secret Life of the Georgian Garden: Beautiful Objects & Agreeable Retreats* (London and New York, 2016).

Fernández Flores, Á., L. García Sanjuán and M. Díaz-Zorita Bonilla (eds), *Montelirio: un gran monumento megalítico de la Edad del Cobre* (Sevilla, 2016).

Field, D., G. Brown and A. Crockett, 'The Marlborough Mound revisited', *WANSHM*, 94 (2001), 195–204.

Fiennes, Celia, *The Journeys of Celia Fiennes*, ed. Christopher Morris (London, 1947).

Foedera, Conventiones, Litterae et cujuscumque generis Acta Publica, ed. T. Rymer, new edn (Record Commission, London, 1816–32).

Fradley, M., 'Scars on the townscape: urban castles in Saxo-Norman England', in Hadley and Dyer (eds), *The Archaeology of the 11th Century*.

Garland, N. and K. Marsden, 'A summary report of Excavations at St Mary's Primary School, Marlborough, Wiltshire', *WANSHM*, 112 (2019), 27–36.

Geoffrey of Monmouth, *The History of the Kings of Britain*, ed. Michael D. Reeve, trans. Neil Wright (Woodbridge, 2007).

Gesta Stephani, ed. and trans. K. R. Potter, with introduction and notes by R. H. C. Davis (Oxford, 1976).

Gibson, A., *The Walton Basin Project: Excavation and Survey in a Prehistoric Landscape 1993–7* (York, 1999).

——, 'Excavation and survey at Dyffryn Lane henge complex, Powys, and a reconsideration of the dating of henge', *Proceedings of the Prehistoric Society*, 76 (2010), 213–48.

Gibson, A. (ed.), *Enclosing the Neolithic: Recent Studies in Britain and Europe* (Oxford, 2012).

Gibson, A., M. Allen, P. Bradley, W. Carruthers, D. Challinor, C. French, D. Hamilton, I. Mainland, M. McCarthy, A. Ogden, R. Scaife, S. Sheridan and C. Walmsley, 'Report on the Excavation at the Duggleby Howe Causewayed Enclosure, North Yorkshire, May-July 2009', *Archaeological Journal*, 168 (2011), 1–63.

Gibson, A., A. Bayliss, H. Heard, I. Mainland, A. R. Ogden, C. Bronk Ramsey, G. Cook, J. van der Plicht and P. Marshall, 'Recent research at Duggleby Howe, North Yorkshire', *Archaeological Journal*, 166 (2009), 39–78.

Gibson, Donald (ed.), *A Parson in the Vale of the White Horse: George Woodward's Letters from East Hendred, 1753–1761* (Gloucester, 1982).

Gillings, M., B. Chan, R. Cleal, S. Eve and J. Pollard, 'Pebbles in the pond: huge posts and some very odd rocks at West Kennet', *British Archaeology*, 183 (2022), 36–40.

Goddard, E. H., 'The mount at Great Somerford', *WANHM*, 45 (1930).

Goldring, Elisabeth, Faith Eales, Elizabeth Clarke and Jayne Elisabeth Archer (eds), *John Nichols's The Progresses and Public Processions of Queen Elizabeth I: A New Edition of the Early Modern Sources*, 5 vols (Oxford, 2014).

Goodall, John, *The English Castle 1066–1650* (London, 2011).

Greaney, S., Z. Hazell, A. Barclay, C. Bronk Ramsey, E. Dunbar, I. Hadjas, P. Reimer, J. Pollard, N. Sharples and P. Marshall, 'Tempo of a Mega-henge: A New Chronology for Mount Pleasant, Dorchester, Dorset', *Proceedings of the Prehistoric Society*, 86 (2020), 199–236.

Hale, D., A. Platell and A. Millard, 'A Late Neolithic palisaded enclosure at Marne Barracks, Catterick, North Yorkshire', *Proceedings of the Prehistoric Society*, 75 (2009), 265–304.

Harfield, C. G., 'A hand-list of castles recorded in the Domesday Book', *The English Historical Review*, 106 (1991), 371–92.

Harrison, E., 'Neolithic activity in Ducks Meadow, Marlborough', *WANSHM*, 94 (2001), 219–23.

Harvey, John, *Mediaeval Gardens* (London, 1981).

Haslam, J., 'Excavations at Cricklade, Wiltshire, 1975', Internet Archaeology, 14 (2003), http://dx.doi.org/10.11141/ia.14.1

——, 'The early development of late Saxon Christchurch, Dorset, and the Burghal Hidage', *Medieval Archaeology*, 53 (2005), 95–118.

Hawkes, John, 'Archaeological assessment of a proposed development at Marlborough College, Wiltshire' (Unpublished client report, AC Archaeology document 8596/1/0, November 1996).

Hayman, P. E. C., 'The mound', *RMCNHS*, 97 (1956), 13–20.

Hayman, P. E. C. and E. G. H. Kempson, 'The early history of the houses built on the site of Marlborough Castle', *RMCNHS*, 99 (1958–9), 34–56.

Healy, F., 'Scientific dating', in M. Leivers and A. B. Powell (eds), *A Research Framework for the Stonehenge, Avebury and Associated Sites World Heritage Site: Avebury Resource Assessment* (Salisbury, 2016), pp. 40–58.

Heaton, M. and B. Moffat, 'A possible outer bailey ditch to Marlborough Castle: excavations at Marlborough College pool', *WANSHM*, 95 (2002), 100–6.

Heiser, R. R., 'Castles, constables, and politics in late twelfth-century English governance', *Albion*, 32 (2000).

Henderson, Paula, 'A Shared Passion: The Cecils and their Gardens', in Pauline Croft (ed.), *Patronage, Culture and Power: The Early Cecils* (New Haven and London, 2002), pp. 99–120.

——, *The Tudor House and Garden: Architecture and Landscape in the Sixteenth and Early Seventeenth Centuries* (London, 2005).

Henry of Huntingdon, *The History of the English People 1000–1154*, ed. and trans. D. Greenway (Oxford, 1996).

Hensey, R., *First Light: The Origins of Newgrange* (Oxford, 2015).

Higgott, T., 'Is Newbury's medieval castle at Hamstead Marshall?', *Transactions of the Newbury District Field Club*, 14:2/3 (1998).

Higham, R. A., 'Shell-Keeps Revisited: The Bailey on the Motte?', http:// http://www.gatehouse-gazetteer.info/csg/Shell%20Keeps-Essay-low-resRev23b.pdf

Higham, R. A. and C. G. Henderson, 'Danes Castle, Exeter: excavations 1992–3', *Proceedings of the Devon Archaeological Society*, 69 (2011), 125–56.

Higham, R. A. and P. A. Barker, *Timber Castles* (London, 1992).

Hinton, J. D., 'The archaeology of eighth- to eleventh-century Wessex', in M. Aston and C. Lewis (eds), *The Medieval Landscape of Wessex* (Oxford, 1994).

Hislop, M., *Castle Builders: Approaches to Castle Design and Construction in the Middle Ages* (Barnsley, 2016).

Histoire des ducs de Normandie et des rois d'Angleterre, ed. Francisque Michel (Paris, 1840).

The History of William the Marshal, trans. Nigel Bryant (Woodbridge, 2016).

HKW: The History of the King's Works, ed. H. M. Colvin (London, 1963).

Hoare, R. C., *The Ancient History of Wiltshire, Vol. 2* (London, 1821).

Holdsworth, P., 'Saxon Southampton', in J. Haslam (ed.), *Anglo-Saxon Towns in Southern England* (Chichester, 1984).

Holley, R., *Castle Hill Calne, Wiltshire: Archaeological Evaluation and Post Excavation Assessment* (Devizes, 2011).

Howell, Margaret, 'The Children of Henry III and Eleanor of Provence', in Peter R. Coss and Simon D. Lloyd (eds), *Thirteenth Century England IV: Proceedings of the Newcastle Upon Tyne Conference 1991* (Woodbridge, 1992), pp. 57–72.

Hughes, M., 'Hampshire castles and the landscape: 1066–1216', *Landscape History*, 2 (1989), 26–59.

Jackson, Hazelle, *Shell Houses and Grottoes* (Princes Risborough, 2001).

Jacques, David, *Gardens of Court and Country: English Design 1630–1730* (New Haven and London, 2016).

Jacques, David and Arend van der Horst, *The Gardens of William and Mary* (London, 1988).

Jamieson, E., 'The siting of medieval castles and the influence of ancient places', *Medieval Archaeology*, 63:2 (2019), 338–74.

John of Worcester, *The Chronicle of John of Worcester*, ed. R. R. Darlington and P. McGurk, Oxford Medieval Texts (Oxford, 1995).

Jolliffe, J. E. A., 'The Chamber and the Castle Treasures under King John', in R. W. Hunt, W. A. Pantin and R. W. Southern (eds), *Studies in Medieval History presented to Frederick Maurice Powicke* (Oxford, 1948), pp. 117–41.

Jones, Barbara, *Follies and Grottoes*, 2nd edn (London, 1974).

Kanter, J. E., 'Peripatetic and sedentary kingship: the itineraries of the thirteenth-century English kings' (Doctoral thesis, King's College, London).

——, 'Peripatetic and Sedentary Kingship: The Itineraries of John and Henry III', in Janet Burton *et al.* (eds), *Thirteenth Century England XIII: Proceedings of the Paris Conference 2009* (Woodbridge, 2011), pp. 11–26.

Keefe, T. K., 'Place-date distribution of royal charters and the historical geography of patronage strategies at the court of King Henry II Plantagenet', *Haskins Society Journal*, 2 (1990), 179–88.

Keene, D. (ed.), *Survey of Medieval Winchester, Parts 1 and 2* (Oxford, 1985), II, 573–5.

Keevill, Graham D. and Neil Linford, 'Landscape with gardens: aerial, topographical and geophysical survey at Hamstead Marshall, Berkshire', in Paul Pattison (ed.), *There by Design: Field Archaeology in Parks and Gardens* (Swindon and Oxford, 1998), pp. 19–32.

Kempson, E. G. H., 'Material for the later history of Marlborough Castle and its successors', *RMCNHS*, 98 (1957), 29–53.

Kinnes, I., *Round Barrows and Ring Ditches in the British Neolithic* (London, 1979).

Laban G. and K. Stewart, 'Evidence for a Stephanic siege castle at the Lister Wilder Site, The Street, Crowmarsh Gifford', *Oxoniensia*, 78 (2013), 189–211.

Lacaille, A. D., 'Wiltshire palaeoliths', *The British Museum Quarterly*, 35:1/4 (1971), 69–87.

Lamont, Richard D. A., 'The significance of Lady Hertford's grotto at Marlborough within the context of developments between poetry, painting and gardening in the 1720s' (Essay for MSt degree in Literature and Arts, University of Oxford, September 2013).

Landon, Lionel, *The Itinerary of King Richard I* (Pipe Roll Society 51 [NS 13], 1935).

Landsberg, Sylvia, The *Medieval Garden* (London, n.d., *c.* 1995).

Lazzaro, Claudia, *The Italian Renaissance Garden: from the conventions of planting, design, and ornament to the grand gardens of sixteenth-century Central Italy* (New Haven and London, 1990).

Leach, P. and P. Ellis, 'Manor Farm, Castle Cary. Excavation and Recording 1999. An Interim Report (Project No. 608)' (Unpublished report, Birmingham Archaeology, 1999).

Leary, J., 'Silbury Hill: A Monument in Motion', in J. Leary, T. Darvill and D. Field (eds), *Round Mounds and Monumentality in the British Neolithic and Beyond* (Oxford, 2010), pp. 139–52.

Leary, J., M. Canti, D. Field, P. Fowler, P. Marshall and G. Campbell, 'The Marlborough Mound, Wiltshire: A further Neolithic monumental mound by the River Kennet', *Proceedings of the Prehistoric Society*, 79 (2013), 1–27.

Leary J. and D. Field, *The Story of Silbury Hill* (Swindon, 2010).

——, 'Journeys and juxtapositions: Marden henge and the view from the Vale', in A. Gibson (ed.), *Enclosing the Neolithic: Recent Studies in Britain and Europe* (Oxford, 2013).

Leary, J., D. Field and G. Campbell, *Silbury Hill: The Largest Prehistoric Mound in Europe* (Swindon, 2013).

Leary, J. and P. Marshall, 'The Giants of Wessex: the chronology of the three largest mounds in Wiltshire, UK', *Antiquity*, 86:334 (2012).

Leary, J., Elaine Jamieson and Phil Stastney, 'Normal for Normans? Exploring the large round mounds of England', *Current Archaeology*, 337 (April 2018), 18–24.

Leatherdale, J. D., 'Survey of the Preshute watermeadows', *RMCNHS*, 99 (1958), 17–23.

Leivers, M., 'The Army Basing Programme, Stonehenge and the emergence of the sacred landscape of Wessex', *Internet Archaeology*, 56, https://doi.org/10.11141/ia.56.2. (2021).

Maddicott, John, 'The Oath of Marlborough, 1209: Fear, Government and Popular Allegiance in the Reign of King John', *English Historical Review*, 126 (2011), 281–318.

Margary, I. D., *Roman Roads in Britain*, 3rd edn (London, 1973).

Marshall, S., *Exploring Avebury: the essential guide* (Stroud, 2016).

Martin, Edward, *Great Bricett Manor and Priory: Lords, Saints and Canons in a Suffolk Landscape* (Ipswich, 2021).

Maurice, G. K., 'The Passing of a River', *Blackwoods Magazine* (January 1947), 24–32; reprinted ('with minor amendments') in E. G. H. Kempson and G.

W. Murray (eds), *Marlborough Town and Countryside* (Andoversford, 1978), p. 46.

McOmish, D., D. Field and G. Brown, *The Field Archaeology of Salisbury Plain Training Area* (Swindon, 2002).

Miller, Naomi, *Heavenly Caves: reflections on the garden grotto* (London, 1982).

Mills, B. J. and W. H. Walker (eds), *Memory Work: archaeologies of material practices* (Santa Fe, NM, 2008).

Moray, Robert, 'Observations from Avebury, Selbern Hill, a mound in Lord Seemer's Garden at Marleborough – Read to the Royal Society on 19 October 1664', The Royal Society, MS Cl.P/7i/10.

Mortimer, J. R., *Forty Years' Researches in British and Saxon Burial Mounds of East Yorkshire* (London, Hull and York, 1905).

Mowl, Timothy, 'Nine rural sisters and their presiding magician – the Cruxeaston grotto, Hampshire', *Garden History*, 43:2 (2015), 284–6.

Munby, J., A. Norton, D. Poore and A. Dodd, *Excavations at Oxford Castle 1999–2009* (Oxford, 2019).

Munby, J. and D. Renn, 'Description of the castle buildings', in B. Cunliffe and J. Munby (eds), *Excavation at Portchester Castle: Vol. IV, Medieval, the Inner Bailey* (London, 1985), pp. 72–3.

Neckam, Alexander, *De Naturis Rerum … with … De Laudibus Divinæ Sapientiæ*, ed. Thomas Wright (Rolls Series 34, London, 1863).

Newman, P., 'Castle Neroche, Staple Fitzpaine, Somerset; An Earthwork Survey' (Unpublished English Heritage Archaeological Investigation Report Series AI/12/2003, 2003).

Noel, M. J., 'Geophysical Surveys of the Wilderness, Marlborough College, Wiltshire' (Unpublished client report by GeoQuest Associates, September 2001).

O'Leary, T. J., 'Excavations at Upper Borough Walls, Bath, 1980', *Medieval Archaeology*, 25 (1981), 1–30.

Ormrod, W. Mark, *Edward III* (London, 2011).

Parfitt, K. and S. Needham, *Ceremonial Living in the Third Millennium BC: Excavations at Ringlemere Site M1, Kent, 2002–2006* (London, 2020).

Paris, Matthew, *Chronica Majora*, ed. H. R. Luard (Rolls Series 57, London, 1872–84).

Pearson and Insall: Nicholas Pearson Associates and Donald Insall Associates, *Marlborough Mound Conservation Management Plan* (Client report for Marlborough Mound Trust, Tiverton and Bath, March 2006).

Phillips, Seymour, *Edward II* (London, 2010).

Piggott, Stuart, *William Stukeley: An eighteenth-century antiquary* (London, 1985).

Powicke, F. M., *King Henry III and the Lord Edward* (Oxford, 1947).

PR: Pipe Roll Society, London. Titles are cited by title or regnal year, volume number and year of publication.

Pryor, S., *A Few Well-Positioned Castles: The Norman Art of War* (Stroud, 2006).

Pugh, Ralph B., *Imprisonment in Medieval England* (Cambridge, 1968).

Ralph de Diceto, *Ymagines Historiarum* in *The Historical Works of Master Ralph de Diceto*, ed. W. Stubbs (Rolls Series 68, London, 1876).

RCh: Rotuli Chartarum in Turri Londinensi Asservati, ed. T. D. Hardy (Record Commission, London, 1837).

Renn, D., *Norman Castles in Britain* (London, 1968).

Richard fitzNigel, *Dialogus de Scaccario*, ed. and trans. Emilie Amt, Oxford Medieval Texts (Oxford, 2007).

Richards, C. (ed.), *Building The Great Stone Circles of the North* (Oxford, 2013).

Richardson, Shaun and Ed Dennison, *Garden and other earthworks south of Wressle Castle, Wressle, East Yorkshire: archaeological survey* (Ed Dennison Archaeological Services Ltd report no. 2014/479.R01, February 2015).

Rippon, S. and B. Croft (eds), 'Post-Conquest medieval', in C. J. Webster (ed.), *The Archaeology of South-West England: South West Archaeological Research Framework, Resource Assessment and Research Agenda* (Taunton, 2007), pp. 205–7.

RLC: Rotuli Litterarium Clausarum in Turri Londinensi Asservati, ed. T. D. Hardy (Record Commission, London, 1833–4).

RLP: Rotuli Litterarium Patentium in Turri Londinensi Asservati, ed. T. D. Hardy (Record Commission, London, 1835).

Robinson, S. and P. Cox, 'Evidence for the Outer Defences of Devizes Castle at the Beeches, Castle Road, Devizes', *WANHM,* 113 (2020), 213–25.

Roger of Howden [Benedict of Peterborough], *Gesta Regis Henrici Secundis*, ed. W. Stubbs (Rolls Series 49, London, 1867), i. 351–2.

Royal Commission on Historical Monuments England, *An Inventory of the Historical Monuments in the County of Northampton; vol. III: Archaeological Sites in North-West Northamptonshire* (London, 1981).

Russell, Josiah C., 'Alexander Neckam in England', *English Historical Review,* 47 (1932), 260–8.

Sabin, D. and K. Donaldson, 'Castle Combe Geophysical Survey for Wiltshire County Council' (Unpublished report: Archaeological Surveys, 2007).

Scarfe, Norman, *Innocent Espionage: The La Rochefoucauld Brothers' Tour of England in 1785* (Woodbridge, 1995).

Scarre, C., *Landscapes of Neolithic Brittany* (Oxford, 2011).

Seabourne, Gwen, 'Eleanor of Brittany and her treatment by King John and Henry III', *Nottingham Medieval Studies,* 51 (2007), 74–110.

Seeber, Karin, '"ye making of ye mount": Oxford New College's Mount Garden revisited', *Garden History,* 40:1 (2012), 3–16.

Shapland, M. G., *Anglo-Saxon Towers of Lordship* (Oxford, 2019).

Shennan, S., F. Healy and I. F. Smith, 'The excavation of a ring-ditch at Tye Field, Lawford, Essex', *Archaeological Journal,* 142 (1982), 150–215.

Sherburn, George (ed.), *The Correspondence of Alexander Pope* (Oxford, 1956).

Shirley, W. W. (ed.), *Royal and other Historical Letters illustrative of the reign of Henry III* (Rolls Series 27, London, 1862–6).

Steane, J. M., 'The Royal Fishponds of Medieval England', in Michael Aston (ed.), *Medieval Fish, Fisheries and Fishponds in England*, BAR British Series 182(i) (Oxford, 1988).

Stevenson, Janet H., 'Preshute', in D. A. Crowley (ed.), *A History of Wiltshire, Volume XII*, Victoria County History (Oxford, 1983), pp. 168–84.

——, 'The castles of Marlborough and Ludgershall in the Middle Ages', *WANHM*, 85 (1992), 70–9.

Strong, Roy, *The Renaissance Garden in England* (London, 1979).

Strutt, K., D. Barker, A. Langlands and T. Sly, 'Report on the Geophysical Survey at Old Sarum, Wiltshire, April and July 2016, and April and July 2017', The Old Sarum Landscapes Project Research Report No. 3 (Unpublished report: Archaeological Prospection Services of Southampton, 2017).

Strutt, K., D. Barker, W. Heard and T. Sly, 'Report on the Geophysical Survey at Old Sarum, Wiltshire, March-July 2015', The Old Sarum Landscapes Project Research Report No. 2 (Unpublished report: Archaeological Prospection Services of Southampton, 2015).

Stukeley, W., *Itinerarium Curiosum or, an Account of the ANTIQUITYS AND REMARKABLE CURIOSOITYS In NATURE or ART, Observ'd in TRAVELS thro' GREAT BRITTAN* (London, 1724; reprinted 1776 [facsimile of 1776 edn Farnborough, 1989]).

Sykes, N. and R. F. Carden, 'Were Fallow Deer Spotted (OE *pohha/*pocca) in Anglo-Saxon England? Reviewing the Evidence for *Dama dama dama* in Early Medieval Europe', *Medieval Archaeology*, 55 (2011), 139–62.

Thacker, Christopher, *The History of Gardens* (Berkeley and Los Angeles, 1979).

Thomas, J., *Dunragit and Droughduil: A Neolithic Ceremonial Complex in Galloway* (Oxford, 2015).

Thorpe, Adam, *On Silbury Hill* (Toller Fratrum, 2014).

Thurley, Simon, *Hampton Court: A Social and Architectural History* (New Haven and London, 2003).

TNA: The National Archives (unprinted documents).

Tobin, Beth Fowkes, *The Duchess's Shells: Natural History Collecting in the Age of Cook's Voyages* (New Haven and London, 2014).

Toulmin-Smith, L. (ed.), *Leland's Itinerary in England and Wales*, 5 vols (London, 1964).

Turner, Rick and Andy Johnson, *Chepstow Castle: Its History and Buildings* (Logaston, 2006).

Turton, A., *Castles in Wessex* (Salisbury, 2010).

Vince, A. G., S. J. Lobb, J. C. Richards and L. Mepham, *Excavations in Newbury 1979–1990*, Wessex Archaeology Report 13 (Salisbury, 1997).

Vincent, Nicholas, 'King Henry III and the Blessed Virgin Mary', in R. N. Swanson (ed.), *The Church and Mary*, Studies in Church History 39 (Woodbridge, 2006), pp. 129–46.

Warren, W. L., *Henry II* (London, 1973).

——, *King John*, 2nd edn (London, 1978).

Waterman, D., *Excavations at Navan Fort 1961–71* (Belfast, 1997).

Watkins, John and Tom Wright (eds), *The Management and Maintenance of Historic Parks, Gardens and Landscapes: The English Heritage Handbook* (London, 2007).

Waylen, James, *A History military and municipal of the town (otherwise called the city) of Marlborough and more generally of the entire Hundred of Selkley* (London, 1854).

Webster, Paul, *King John and Religion*, Studies in the History of Medieval Religion XLIII (Woodbridge, 2015).

Wessex Archaeology, 'Marlborough Mound, Marlborough College, Wiltshire: Spiral Path Fieldwork Report (Report Number 57200.001)' (Unpublished client report, 2005).

Wessex Archaeology, 'Marlborough Mound Phase 4 Investigations', Ref: 079383.03 (Unpublished client report, 2020).

White, P. and A. Cook, *Sherborne Old Castle, Dorset: Archaeological Investigations 1930–90* (London, 2015).

Whittle, A., *Sacred Mound, Holy Rings: Silbury Hill and the West Kennet Palisade Enclosures: A Later Neolithic Complex in North Wiltshire* (Oxford, 1997).

William of Newburgh, *Historia Rerum Anglicarum*, ed. R. Howlett (London, 1884).

——, *The History of English Affairs*, ed. and trans. P. G. Walsh and M. J. Kennedy (Warminster, 1988).

Wiltshire County Archaeology Service, *The Archaeology of Wiltshire's Towns, An Extensive Urban Survey: Marlborough* (Trowbridge, 2004).

Woolgar, C. M., *Household Accounts from Medieval England* (Oxford, n.d. [1992]).

——, *The Great Household* (London, 1999).

Wright, D. and O. H. Creighton (eds), *Castles, Siegeworks and Settlements: Surveying the Archaeology of the Twelfth Century* (Oxford, 2016).

Wright, D. W., O. H. Creighton and M. Fradley, 'The ringwork at Cam's Hill, near Malmesbury: archaeological investigation and landscape assessment', *WAHNM*, 108 (2015), 105–18.

Wright, D. W., O. H. Creighton, S. Trick and M. Fradley, 'Fieldwork in conflict landscapes: surveying the archaeology of "the Anarchy"', *Medieval Archaeology*, 59 (2015), 313–19.

Wymer, J. (ed.), *Gazetteer of Mesolithic Sites in England and Wales* (London, 1997).

Yorke, B., *Wessex in the Early Middle Ages* (London and New York, 1995).

Zega, Andrew and Bernd H. Dams, *Garden Vases* (Paris, 2000)

Notes

1. 'One remarkable earthen-work' :
The Neolithic Origins of the Marlborough Mound

1 Hoare, *Wiltshire*, 15.
2 Best, 'Marlborough Mound'; Field, 'Marlborough Mound revisited'.
3 Eve, 'Recent excavations'; Brentnall, 'The Marlborough Castle Mound'.
4 Brentnall, 'The Mound'; 'The Marlborough Castle Mound'; '*Castellum Merlebergae*'; 'Marlborough Castle'; '*Castellum Merlebergensis*' (Appendix B above); 'The curtain wall'.
5 Brentnall, 'The Marlborough Castle Mound', 112.
6 Brentnall, 'The Marlborough Castle Mound', 112; 'The Mound', 24–5.
7 Eve, 'Recent excavations', 66.
8 Brentnall, 'The Marlborough Castle Mound'.
9 Brentnall, 'The Marlborough Castle Mound', 112.
10 Hayman, 'The mound', 14–15.
11 Best, 'Marlborough Mound'.
12 Field, 'Marlborough Mound revisited'.
13 Field, 'Marlborough Mound revisited', 203.
14 Cleal, 'Neolithic and Early Bronze Age', 18.
15 Brentnall, Appendix B above, p. 141.
16 Margary, *Roman Roads in Britain*, 135; Best, 'Marlborough Mound', 169.
17 Field, 'Marlborough Mound revisited', 203.
18 Stukeley, *Itinerarium Curiosum*.
19 Eve, 'Recent excavations', 66.
20 Brentnall, Appendix B above, p. 141.
21 See pp. 37, 56 above.
22 Toulmin-Smith, *Leland's Itinerary*, 130.
23 See p. 110 above.
24 Field, 'Marlborough Mound revisited', 197–202.
25 Eve, 'Recent excavations', 67.
26 Brentnall, Appendix B above, p. 161.
27 Hayman, 'The mound', 16–20.
28 Eve, 'Recent excavations'; Field, 'Marlborough Mound revisited', 196.
29 Leary, *Silbury Hill*.
30 Leary, 'The Marlborough mound'.
31 Darvill, 'Stonehenge remodelled'.
32 Cleal, 'Neolithic and Early Bronze Age' (2016).
33 Leary and Field, *Silbury Hill*; Leary, 'The Giants of Wessex'.
34 Leary, *Silbury Hill*.
35 Leary, 'The Giants of Wessex'.

36 Leary, 'Silbury Hill: A monument in motion'.
37 Leary, 'Silbury Hill: A monument in motion'.
38 Leary, 'Silbury Hill: A monument in motion'; Leary and Field, *Silbury Hill*.
39 Leary, 'The Marlborough Mound'.
40 Brentnall, *'Castellum Merlebergensis'* (Appendix B above); see also pp. 82–3 above.
41 Leary and Field, *Silbury Hill*; Leary, 'The Marlborough Mound'.
42 Atkinson, 'Silbury Hill'.
43 Stukeley, *Itinerarium Curiosum*, 1776 edition, 64.
44 Stevenson, 'Preshute', 168.
45 Maurice, 'The Passing of a River', 46 [not in *Blackwoods Magazine* version].
46 Leary, 'Silbury Hill: A monument in motion'; Leary and Field, *Silbury Hill*; Marshall, *Exploring Avebury*, 125–6.
47 Leary, 'The Marlborough Mound'.
48 Leatherdale, 'Survey of the Preshute watermeadows'.
49 Maurice, 'The Passing of a River', 46.
50 Heaton, 'Outer bailey ditch to Marlborough Castle'.
51 Wymer, *Gazetteer of Mesolithic Sites*, 340–2.
52 Anon., 'Additions', 203.
53 Brooke, 'Notes on the finding of Neolithic flints'; Brooke, 'Notes on Neolithic flints'.
54 Clark, 'Flint implements'.
55 Brooke, 'Notes on Neolithic Flints'.
56 Wiltshire Heritage Museum, Devizes: acc. no. 1982.110.
57 Clark, 'Flint implements'.
58 Clark, 'Flint implements'; Lacaille, 'Wiltshire palaeoliths'.
59 Harrison, 'Ducks Meadow, Marlborough'; Garland, 'Excavations at St Mary's'.
60 Brady, 'Neolithic pits'.
61 Whittle, *Sacred Mound, Holy Rings*.
62 Bayliss, 'Rings of fire'.
63 Barber, 'The brood of Silbury?'.
64 Greaney, 'Tempo of a mega-henge', 221.
65 Thomas, *Dunragit and Droughduil*; Brophy, '… a place where they tried their criminals', 13.
66 Hale, 'Late Neolithic palisaded enclosure at Marne Barracks', 286.
67 Kinnes, *Round Barrows and Ring Ditches*.
68 Healy, 'Scientific dating', 46.
69 Kinnes, *Round Barrows and Ring Ditches*, 20.
70 McOmish, *Field Archaeology*.
71 Cf. Whittle, *Sacred Mound, Holy Rings*, 149–50.
72 Hensey, *First Light*.
73 Fernández, *Montelirio*.
74 Scarre, *Landscapes of Neolithic Brittany*.
75 Cf. Whittle, *Sacred Mound, Holy Rings*.
76 Leary, 'Silbury Hill: A monument in motion'.
77 Gibson, *Enclosing the Neolithic*.
78 Gibson, 'Dyffryn Lane henge'.
79 Gibson, 'Dyffryn Lane henge', 227.
80 Leivers, 'Army Basing Programme'.

[81] Brophy, 'Henging, mounding and blocking'.
[82] Bradley, *The Good Stones*; Bradley, *Use and Reuse of Stone Circles*.
[83] Waterman, *Navan Fort 1961–71*.
[84] Mortimer, *Forty Years' Researches*; Gibson, 'Recent research at Duggleby Howe'; Gibson, 'Duggleby Howe Causewayed Enclosure'.
[85] Gibson, 'Recent research at Duggleby Howe'.
[86] Kinnes, *Round Barrows and Ring Ditches*.
[87] Gibson, 'Duggleby Howe Causewayed Enclosure', 34.
[88] Gibson, 'Duggleby Howe Causewayed Enclosure'.
[89] Gillings, 'Pebbles in the Pond'.
[90] Gibson, *The Walton Basin Project*.
[91] Parfitt, *Ceremonial Living*.
[92] Shennan, 'A ring-ditch at Lawford, Essex'.
[93] Cf. Mills, *Memory Work*.
[94] Richards, *The Great Stone Circles*, 74.
[95] Card, *The Ness of Brodgar: as it stands*.
[96] Card, *The Ness of Brodgar: as it stands*, 107.
[97] Card, *The Ness of Brodgar: as it stands*, 108.
[98] Card, *The Ness of Brodgar: as it stands*, 94–6.
[99] Whittle, *Sacred Mound, Holy Rings*; Thomas, *Dunragit and Droughduil*, 173; Bradley, *Prehistory of Britain*, 138; Greaney, 'Tempo of a mega-henge', 221.

2. Castles and the Landscape of Norman Wessex, *c.* 1066–1154

[1] William of Newburgh, *Historia rerum anglicarum*, 331.
[2] For key recent studies, see, in particular, J. Blair, *Building Anglo-Saxon England*; Shapland, *Anglo-Saxon Towers of Lordship*; Baker and Brookes, *Beyond the Burghal Hidage*.
[3] See, for example, Bettey, *Wessex from AD 1000*, 13–15. It is notable that the most authoritative academic study of the medieval landscape of Wessex features chapters on topics including the Church, rural settlement, towns and hunting, but not one on castles: see Aston and Lewis, *The Medieval Landscape of Wessex*.
[4] Rippon and Croft, 'Post-Conquest medieval', 205–7.
[5] This paper builds on foundations laid by a number of important county-based studies of castles which have often addressed these aspects. In particular, for Wiltshire, see Creighton, 'Early castles', 105–19; for Hampshire, see Hughes, 'Hampshire castles and the landscape: 1066–1216', 26–59; for a case study of Somerset's Norman castles from a military perspective, see Pryor, *A Few Well-Positioned Castles*, chapter 3.
[6] See for example, *Castles in Wessex*, in which the gazetteer of castles in Wessex comprises a listing of major surviving field monuments.
[7] Yorke, *Wessex in the Early Middle Ages*, 325.
[8] Harfield, 'A hand-list of castles recorded in the Domesday Book', 371–92.
[9] Exeter (48 houses), Oxford (478) and Wareham (73): see Creighton, *Castles and Landscapes*, 140.
[10] Hinton, 'The archaeology of eighth- to eleventh-century Wessex', 42–4.

[11] Creighton, '1066 and the landscape', 213–37.
[12] Creighton, *Castles and Landscapes*, 69, 155, 160–1.
[13] See Dyer and Hadley, *The Archaeology of the 11th Century*; for the landscape of Norman England, see in particular, Creighton and Rippon, 'Conquest, colonisation and the countryside', 57–87.
[14] Keefe, 'Place-date distribution of royal charters', 180–2.
[15] Ellis, *Ludgershall Castle*, 255; see also Stevenson, 'The castles of Marlborough and Ludgershall', 70–9.
[16] Bond, 'Forests, chases, warrens and parks', 151.
[17] See *HKW*, vols I–II.
[18] Heiser, 'Castles, constables', 20–1.
[19] Fradley, 'Scars on the townscape: urban castles', 131–2.
[20] Fradley, 'Scars on the townscape', 131–2.
[21] Drage, 'Urban castles', 117–32.
[22] Keene, *Survey of Medieval Winchester*, ii, 573–5.
[23] Daniell, *From Norman Conquest to Magna Carta*, 117.
[24] Creighton and Wright, *The Anarchy*, 220.
[25] Christie and Creighton, *Transforming Townscapes: From Burh to Borough*.
[26] Christie and Creighton, *Transforming Townscapes*, 148–50.
[27] Christie and Creighton, *Transforming Townscapes*, 296–8.
[28] Munby, *Excavations at Oxford Castle 1999–2009*, chapter 4.
[29] Henry of Huntingdon, *The History of the English People*, 720–1.
[30] Robinson and Cox, 'Evidence for the outer defences'.
[31] Creighton and Wright, *The Anarchy*, 208–13.
[32] White and Cook, *Sherborne Old Castle*, 124–8.
[33] Higham and Barker, *Timber Castles*.
[34] Munby, *Excavations at Oxford Castle 1999–2009*, 128–39.
[35] Hislop, *Castle Builders*, 11.
[36] Ellis, *Ludgershall Castle*.
[37] Ellis, *Ludgershall Castle*, 5.
[38] Ellis, *Ludgershall Castle*, 246.
[39] For listings of early castles, see Renn, *Norman Castles*; Cathcart King, *Castellarium Anglicanum*.
[40] Leary, 'The Marlborough mound', 137–63.
[41] Creighton, 'Early castles', 116. Another clear example of a prospect mound occasionally misidentified as a motte is the mound in the garden of Littleton House, Littleton Panell, Wiltshire (Wiltshire HER No. ST95SE625).
[42] Creighton, 'Early castles', 105–19.
[43] Clarke and Elton, 'The lost chapel of Bicknoll', 126–42.
[44] Cathcart King and Alcock, 'Ringworks of England and Wales', 90–127; for discussion, see Creighton, *Castles and Landscapes*, 46–9.
[45] Heaton and Moffat, 'A possible outer bailey ditch', 100–6.
[46] Wiltshire County Archaeology Service, *The Archaeology of Wiltshire's Towns*, 21.
[47] Creighton, *Castles and Landscapes*, 161.
[48] See Creighton, *Castles and Landscapes*, 193.
[49] Bond, 'Forests, chases, warrens and parks', 141–4.
[50] Sykes and Arden, 'Were fallow deer spotted?', 150.
[51] Jamieson, 'The siting of medieval castles and the influence of ancient places'.

52 Creighton, 'Early castles', 116.
53 See, for example, Cathcart King, *Castellarium Anglicanum*, 500.
54 Creighton, 'Early castles', 112.
55 Jamieson, 'The siting of medieval castles', 354.
56 Strutt, 'The Old Sarum Landscapes Project'; for full reports, see Strutt, *Reports on the Geophysical Survey at Old Sarum*.
57 Ellis, *Ludgershall Castle*, 246.
58 Sabin and Donaldson, 'Castle Combe Geophysical Survey'.
59 Holley, *Castle Hill Calne, Wiltshire*.
60 Cunliffe, *Excavation at Portchester Castle*, ii, 56–60.
61 Baker and Brookes, *Beyond the Burghal Hidage*, 110–12.
62 Munby and Renn, 'Description of the castle buildings', 72–3.
63 Graham and Davies, *Excavations in Trowbridge*, 61–2.
64 Graham and Davies, *Excavations in Trowbridge*, 58–60.
65 *Gesta Stephani*, 43, 92–3, 96–7.
66 Goddard, 'The mount at Great Somerford', 88–9.
67 Leach and Ellis, 'Manor Farm, Castle Cary'. For a summary, see Blair, *Building Anglo-Saxon England*, 393.
68 Davidson, 'Castle Neroche', 16–58; for re-evaluation of the earthworks, see Newman, 'Castle Neroche'.
69 Munby, *Excavations at Oxford Castle*, chapter 3; Blair, *Building Anglo-Saxon England*, 399.
70 Holdsworth, 'Saxon Southampton', 340–1.
71 Brown and Hardy, *Trade and Prosperity*, 6.
72 Creighton and Wright, *Castles, Siegeworks and Settlement*.
73 *Gesta Stephani*, 96–7.
74 *Gesta Stephani* , 220–1.
75 Bradbury, *Stephen and Matilda*, chapter 6.
76 Creighton and Wright, *The Anarchy*, 34–118.
77 Allen, *Mints and Money in Medieval England*, 34.
78 Christie and Creighton, *Transforming Townscapes*, 359.
79 William of Newburgh, *History of the English People*, i, 98–9.
80 Henry of Huntingdon, *The History of the English People*, 740–1.
81 *Gesta Stephani* II, 73: 144–9.
82 Creighton and Wright, *The Anarchy*, 62–74.
83 Haslam, 'Excavations at Cricklade, Wiltshire'.
84 *Gesta Stephani*, 180–2; see also Creighton and Wright, *The Anarchy*, 226.
85 O'Leary, 'Excavations at Upper Borough Walls, Bath', 1–30; Haslam, 'The early development of late Saxon Christchurch', 95–118.
86 Creighton and Wright, *The Anarchy*, 62–74.
87 Christie and Creighton, *Transforming Townscapes*, 202–8.
88 Laban and Stewart, 'Evidence for a Stephanic siege castle', 189–211.
89 Dodd, *Oxford Before the University*.
90 Wright, 'Fieldwork in conflict landscapes', 313–19.
91 Wright and Creighton, *Castles, Siegeworks and Settlements*, 40–9.
92 Higham and Henderson, 'Danes Castle, Exeter', 125–56.
93 Wright, 'The ringwork at Cam's Hill', 105–18; Wright and Creighton, *Castles, Siegeworks and Settlements*, 96–104.

94 Wright and Creighton, *Castles, Siegeworks and Settlements*, 82–94.

95 See p. 22 above. [Leary chapter, Hamstead Marshall]

96 Henry of Huntingdon, *The History of the English People*, 758–9.

97 Vince, *Excavations in Newbury 1979–1990*; for the problematic documentary evidence for a castle at Newbury, see Astill, *Historic Towns in Berkshire*, 51, 56.

98 Higgott, 'Is Newbury's medieval castle at Hamstead Marshall?', 28–9.

3. Marlborough Castle in the Middle Ages

1 Stevenson, 'The castles of Marlborough and Ludgershall', 70.

2 *RC*, 135.

3 Cathcart King, *Chateau Gaillard V*, 103–6.

4 Higham, *Shell Keeps*, 'Conclusions and observations', 48–57.

5 Higham and Barker, *Timber Castles*.

6 The minimal medieval material found on and around the Mound is discussed in Appendix D above.

7 John of Worcester, *Chronicle*, ii, 14–15.

8 Christelow, 'A Moveable Feast?', 212; Church, 'Some Aspects of the Royal Itinerary', 31–45.

9 Christelow, 'A Moveable Feast?', 215.

10 *EHD*, 180.

11 *EHD*, 181.

12 For Henry's itinerary see Christelow, 'A Moveable Feast?', 210–28.

13 *HKW*, ii, 1010.

14 *Annales Monastici*, iv, 22.

15 'Keep' is only used from the sixteenth century onwards; the medieval word was 'donjon', but I have preferred the more familiar word.

16 *Annales Monastici*, ii, 51.

17 *Gesta Stephani*, 169.

18 *Gesta Stephani*, 107.

19 John of Worcester, *Chronicle*, iii, 303.

20 Ralph de Diceto, *Ymagines Historiarum*, 308; this is one of the earliest references to Merlin in English sources. Crouch, *William Marshal*, 19.

21 Geoffrey of Monmouth, *History*, 174.

22 Russell, 'Alexander Neckam in England', 263.

23 Neckam, *De Naturis Rerum*, 461.

24 *PR 22 Henry II, 1175–1176* (25, 1904), 172.

25 *PR 22 Henry II, 1175–1176* (25, 1904), 171, 188.

26 *PR 23 Henry II, 1176–1177* (26, 1905), 98 ('quarrellos': *ODMLBS* s.v. *quarrellus* translates this as crossbow bolts or quarrels, but as it is in the context of building works, it must mean dressed or 'squared' stones). Tiles: *PR 25 Henry II, 1178–1179* (28, 1907), 88, 108.

27 Roger of Howden, *Gesta Regis Henrici*, i, 351–2.

28 Keefe, 'Place-Date Distribution of Royal Charters', 185–6.

29 *Gesta Stephani*, 139. Translation from *HKW*, ii, 1009.

30 Barber, *Magnificence*, 150.

31 *HKW*, ii, 1012–16.
32 *Foedera*, I.i, 30.
33 Landon, *The Itinerary of King Richard I*, 3.
34 *petrary*, a smaller catapult than the mangonel.
35 *PR 6 Richard II, 1194–1195* (43 [NS5], 1928), 175, 211, 212, 251, 256; translation from H. C. Brentnall, '*Castellum Merlebergensis*' (Appendix B above).
36 *PR 6 Richard II, 1194–1195* (43 [NS5], 1928), xv.
37 Unpublished lecture text, courtesy of Jeremy Ashbee.
38 On the de Nevilles see the relevant entries by David Crook in *ODNB* (online: Alan, version 3 January 2008; Hugh, version 26 May 2016).
39 *RLP*, i, 81b, 84b.
40 Carpenter, *Henry III: The Rise to Power*, 4.
41 Maddicott, 'The Oath of Marlborough, 1209'.
42 *PR 1 John, 1199–1200* (48 [NS10], 1933), 174.
43 TNA, Ancient Correspondence, SC1/1/5.
44 *PR 13 John, 1211–1212* (66 [NS28], 1953), 83; *Calendarium Rotulorum Patentium*, 41.
45 Warren, *King John*, 208.
46 Close Roll fragment, 1215, in Brown, *The Memoranda Roll*, 134.
47 *RLP*, 135–7.
48 Kanter, 'Peripatetic and sedentary kingship', 728.
49 *History of William the Marshal* (ll.16015–18), 194.
50 *CPR 1216–1225*, 62.
51 *History of William the Marshal* (ll.16048–50), 194.
52 Kanter, 'Peripatetic and sedentary kingship'.
53 Barber, *Magnificence*, 260.
54 Carpenter, *Henry III: The Rise to Power*, 386–7.
55 Bartlett, *England under the Norman and Angevin Kings*, 144.
56 *Constitutio Domus Regis*, ed. S. D. Church, in Richard fitzNigel, *Dialogus*: marshals 211, bakers 201.
57 *CLR 1245–1251*, 137.
58 *Histoire des ducs de Normandie*, 116–18.
59 For the section which follows see *TNA* E/101/349/7, m.15–16. Jonathan Mackman kindly provided the translation.
60 Woolgar, *Household Accounts*, 16–18, for a detailed analysis of the offices.
61 Vincent, 'King Henry III and the Blessed Virgin Mary', 129.
62 *CCR: Henry III, 1234–1237*, 397; *CLR 1226–1240*, 246.
63 *CCR: Henry III, 1254–1256*, 265, 270, 272, 332; *CCR: Henry III, 1256–1259*, 7.
64 Jolliffe, 'The Chamber and the Castle Treasures'.
65 Richard fitzNigel, *Dialogus de Scaccario*, 9.
66 Jolliffe, 'The Chamber and the Castle Treasures', 125.
67 Barratt, 'The Revenues of John and Philip Augustus', 97.
68 Jolliffe, 'The Chamber and the Castle Treasures', 128.
69 *RLC*, i, 86.
70 Jolliffe, 'The Chamber and the Castle Treasures', 131.
71 *RLP*, i, 134.
72 Jolliffe, 'The Chamber and the Castle Treasures', 139.
73 Writ to 11 abbeys and 5 priories, issued at Runnymede on 23 June, *RLP*, i, 144.
74 *RLP*, i, 145–50.

[75] Carlyon-Britton, 'Bedwin and Marlborough'.

[76] Dixon-Smith, 'Feeding the Poor', 32–3.

[77] *RLC I*, 27; Church, 'Some Aspects of the Royal Itinerary', 41–2.

[78] Dixon-Smith, 'Feeding the Poor', 282.

[79] Dixon-Smith, 'Feeding the Poor', 282.

[80] *CLR 1245–1251*, 285.

[81] *RLC*, i, 560, 565, 581.

[82] *RLC*, i, 530.

[83] For what follows, see Seabourne, 'Eleanor of Brittany'.

[84] *RLC*, i, 546. Crossbowman in 1222–3: TNA, E 372/67 m. 13.

[85] For what follows, see Crouch, 'Earl Gilbert Marshal'.

[86] Paris, *Chronica Majora*, iv, 135–6.

[87] *CLR 1260–1267*, 218.

[88] *CPR Henry III: 1258–1266*, 350.

[89] Powicke, *King Henry III and the Lord Edward*, 503.

[90] Powicke, *King Henry III and the Lord Edward*, 547–9.

[91] Howell, 'The children of Henry III and Eleanor of Provence'. Entries on the Close Rolls (*CCR Henry III: 1254–1256*, 265, 270, 272, 283, 332; *CCR 1256–1259*, 7) and Liberate Rolls (*CLR 1251–1260*, 272, 345) show that she was there from early February, through Lent, and again in July, November and December.

[92] *CCR Henry III: 1254–1266*, 288.

[93] Paris, *Chronica Majora*, v, 632.

[94] Paris, *Chronica Majora*, v, 632.

[95] *HKW*, i, 478.

[96] *CCR Edward I: 1272–1279*, 528, 529.

[97] TNA, SC1, Special Collections: Correspondence. There are twenty-eight letters in all.

[98] *CPR Edward I: 1281–1292*, 218–19.

[99] *CPR Edward I: 1292–1301*, 452.

[100] *CCR Edward I: 1292–1301*, 431; *CCR Edward I: 1302–1307*, 153, 175.

[101] *Foedera*, II.i, 38.

[102] *CPR Edward II: 1317–1321*, 115.

[103] *CPR Edward II: 1317–1321*, 578; Phillips, *Edward II*, 373–7.

[104] *CCR Edward II: 1318–1323*, 544.

[105] *CPR Edward II: 1317–1321*, 578; *CPR Edward II: 1321–1340*, 40, 44.

[106] *CCR Edward II: 1318–1323*, 437.

[107] Ormrod, *Edward III*, 20.

[108] Ormrod, *Edward III*, 529.

[109] TNA, SC6/1055/12, quoted in Bradley, *History of Marlborough*, 42, n. 5.

[110] *CMR*, 87.

[111] *CMR*, 16.

[112] See Appendix A above for the full text.

[113] Eustace de Hacche, constable in 1299, d. *c.* 1315 (*CCR Edward I: 1296–1302*, 286–9, 341; *CCR Edward II: 1313–1318*, 257); William Rameshill, constable in 1325 (*CCR Edward II: 1323–1327*, 593).

[114] *CPR Edward III: 1334–1338*, 206.

[115] *CPR Edward III: 1354–1358*, 106.

[116] TNA, E372/207, rot. 45d.

117 *CPR Edward III: 1367–1370*, 48.

118 TNA, E364/5, rot. G.

119 *CPR Richard I: 1381–1385*, 107, 133, 146.

120 *CPR Richard I: 1381–1385*, 197, 208, 260.

121 *CIM*, v, 127.

122 *CIM*, vii, 119; TNA, C145/281 (9).

123 Stevenson, 'Preshute', 168–9.

124 *PR 13 John: 1210–1211* (66 [NS 28], 1946), 83.

125 TNA, *PR 11 Henry III: 1226–1227*, E372/71, rot. 9.

126 *CCR Henry III: 1227–1231*, 188.

127 TNA, *PR 23 Henry III: 1238–1239*, E372/83, 1238–1239, rot. 9.

128 See p. 81 above.

129 See Appendix B above.

130 Brentnall, 'Marlborough Castle', *WANHM*, 48 (1938), 133–43.

131 *PR 13 John*, 83.

132 This view is supported by Robert Higham (pers. comm.): 'I agree with you that (at Marlborough) a *cingulum* was most likely around the edge of the motte's top rather than its base.'

133 Challenger, 'Accounts for works … at Marlborough', 45.

134 See p. 155 above.

135 Arnold-Forster, *Studies in Church Dedications*, iii, 391–2; for the best account of his cult and its introduction to England see Martin, *Great Bricett Manor and Priory*, 59–67.

136 TNA, *PR 16 Henry III*, E372/76, rot. 5.

137 *PR 16 Henry III*, http://aalt.law.uh.edu/AALT4/H3/E372no76/aE372no76 fronts/IMG_3835.htm

138 Brown, 'The Archaeology of the Upper Ward Quadrangle', 64.

139 See Turner, *Chepstow Castle*, xviii–xix, for a plan analysing the dates of construction.

140 See Appendix D, p. 171 above.

141 TNA, *PR 10 Henry III*, E372/70, rot. 8. I owe the reference to Strood to Jeremy Ashbee.

142 *PR 13 John*, *1211–1212* (66 [NS28], 1953), 83.

143 *PR 6 John*, *1204–1205* (56 [NS18], 1940), 187.

144 TNA, *PR 10 Henry III*, E372/70, rot. 13d.

145 For Henry's piety, his building activities and his court, see Carpenter, *Henry III: The Rise to Power*, 273–348.

146 Carpenter, 'The Household Rolls of King Henry III', 25.

147 Carpenter, 'The Household Rolls of King Henry III', 37.

148 TNA, *PR 18 Henry III*, E372/78, rot. 16.

149 Carpenter, *Henry III: The Rise to Power*, 181.

150 H. M. Colvin, *HKW*, i, 113, gives the following figures for the seven 'residential' castles: Windsor, £15,000; Winchester, £9,665; the Tower of London, £9,683; Nottingham, £2,882; Marlborough, about £2,000; Bristol, £1,759; and Gloucester, £1,661.

151 *RLC*, i, 53b; *CLR 1240–1245*, 80 mentions 'the king's tower … and the round tower' in the same sentence.

152 *CLR 1260–1267*, 504.

[153] *CLR 1267–1272*, 139.

[154] *PR 16 Henry III*: http://aalt.law.uh.edu/AALT4/H3/E372no76/aE372no76
fronts/IMG_3835.htm

[155] *PR 44 Henry III*: http://aalt.law.uh.edu/AALT4/H3/E372no104/aE372no104
fronts/IMG_1898.htm

[156] Carpenter, *Henry III: The Rise to Power*, 182.

[157] TNA, *PR 23 Henry III*, E372/83, rot. 13d.

[158] Challenger, 'Accounts for Works … at Marlborough', 40–2.

[159] *CCR Henry III: 1237–1242*, 320.

[160] Order: *CLR 1240–1245*, 64. Account: Cannon, *The Great Roll of the Pipe*, 176.

[161] *CLR 1240–1245*, 64, 234.

[162] *CLR 1245–1251*, 285.

[163] *PR 31 Henry III: 1246–1247*, http://aalt.law.uh.edu/AALT4/H3/E372no91/
bE372no91dorses/IMG_5696.htm

[164] *HKW*, ii, 1013.

[165] *HKW*, ii, 868.

[166] *PR 42 Henry III: 1257–1258*, http://aalt.law.uh.edu/AALT4/H3/E372no102/
aE372no102fronts/IMG_1525.htm

[167] Challenger, 'Accounts for Works … at Marlborough', 46.

[168] *CLR 1240–1245*, 58.

[169] *CLR 1240–1245*, 306.

[170] Goodall, *The English Castle*, 32.

[171] *CCR Henry III: 1242–1247*, 320.

[172] *CLR 1240–1245*, 234.

[173] *CLR 1245–1251*, 159; *PR 38 Henry III*, TNA E372/98, rot. 11.

[174] *RLC II*, 53b; *RLC II*, 53.

[175] Woolgar, *The Great Household*, 141.

[176] *PR 10 Henry III*, E372/70, rot. 13d.

[177] *PR 44 Henry III*, http://aalt.law.uh.edu/AALT4/H3/E372no104/aE372no104
fronts/IMG_1898.htm

[178] *CLR 1245–1251*, 185.

[179] *CLR Henry III: 1240–1245*, 294.

[180] *CLR Henry III: 1240–1245*, 280; *PR 31 Henry III*, http://aalt.law.uh.edu/
AALT4/H3/E372no91/bE372no91dorses/IMG_5696.htm

[181] *CLR Henry III: 1251–1260*, 161 (door); 409 (transport of wines).

[182] *CLR Henry III: 1251–1260*, 223, 504; *PR 44 Henry III*, http://aalt.law.uh.edu/
AALT4/H3/E372no104/aE372no104fronts/IMG_1898.htm

[183] *PR 33 Henry III*, http://aalt.law.uh.edu/AALT4/H3/E372no93/aE372no93
fronts/IMG_5918.htm

[184] Woolgar, *The Great Household*, 119.

[185] See Appendix D, p. 145 above.

[186] Webster, *King John and Religion*, 128.

[187] *CPR Edward I: 1292–1302*, 77.

[188] Petition: TNA SC 8/77/3817; Joan de Valence's itinerary: Woolgar, *The Great
Household*, 49; writ: *CCR Edward I: 1296–1302*, 58; Phillips, *Aymer de Valence*, 6.

[189] *CPR Edward II: 1324–1327*, 88, 157, 243.

[190] 'Anon.', *Wiltshire Notes and Queries* iv (1902–4), 532. No source is given for this
assertion, however.

[191] Brentnall, 'The Curtain Wall', 3, claims that a tile with a peg hole found near the curtain wall in 1933 should be associated with the entry for purchase of free stone in 1175–6. This entry is more likely to refer to the building of the king's hall, for which seven hundred boards were bought in the same year. See n. 25 above.

[192] *CLR Henry III: 1240–1245*, 64.

[193] *CLR Henry III: 1245–1251*, 185.

[194] Brown, 'Royal Castle Building in England', 371.

[195] *PR 5 John: 1203–1204* (55 [NS17], 1938), 161.

[196] *PR 15 Henry III: 1230–1231*, http://aalt.law.uh.edu/AALT4/H3/E372no75/ aE372no75fronts/IMG_3699.htm

[197] Challenger, 'Accounts for Works … at Marlborough', 47.

[198] Harvey, *Medieval Gardens*, 11.

[199] Shirley, *Royal Letters Henry III*, ii, 67.

[200] Landsberg, *Medieval Gardens*, 120–7.

[201] TNA, Llanthony Cartulary C115, A.4, f.215.

[202] Warren, *Henry II*, 393.

[203] Church, 'Some Aspects of the Royal Itinerary', 38–9; Cole, *Documents Illustrative of English History*, 231–69.

[204] Kanter, 'Peripatetic kingship', 283.

[205] John of Worcester, *Chronicle*, iii, 15.

[206] Pugh, *Imprisonment in Medieval England*, 83–4.

[207] Chaucer, *Works*, 20.

[208] Steane, 'The Royal Fishponds of Medieval England', 39–68.

[209] *RLC*, i, 38.

[210] Shad and lampreys: *CCR Henry III: 1254–1256*, 283; whale: 273.

[211] Steane, 'The Royal Fishponds of Medieval England', 47.

[212] *CCR Henry III: 1234–1237*, 420.

[213] *CLR 1251–1260*, 313.

[214] *Calendar of Fine Rolls, Henry III*, 54/107 (17 December 1269), https:// finerollshenry3.org.uk/content/calendar/roll_067.html#it107_016.

[215] Steane, 'The Royal Fishponds of Medieval England', 39–46, on construction and stocking of ponds.

[216] *CCR Henry III: 1268–1272*, 444.

4. The Mound as a Garden Feature

[1] Stevenson, 'Preshute', 169.

[2] Cf. *CPR 1367–1370*, 48; *1388–1392*, 272.

[3] Toulmin-Smith, *Leland's Itinerary*, iv, 130. Cf. Chandler, *John Leland's Itinerary*, x, xxx.

[4] Harvey, *Medieval Gardens*, 112–14; Creighton, *Designs upon the Land*, 68–70.

[5] Lazzaro, *The Italian Renaissance Garden*, 56–7.

[6] Thurley, *Hampton Court*, 93.

[7] Toulmin-Smith, *Leland's Itinerary*, i, 52–4. Cf. Richardson, *Garden of Wressle Castle*, 9: paragraph 3.9.

8   Henderson, *The Tudor House and Garden*, 127–8.

9   Brown, 'Gardens at Lyveden'. Cf. Dix, 'Experiencing the past', 170–3.

10 Cf. Henderson, 'A Shared Passion'; RCHME, *Northampton*, iii, 106–9 and pls 16–18. See further Henderson, *The Tudor House and Garden*, 225–37 for a gazetteer of surviving examples.

11 Goldring, *Nichols's Progresses*, iii, 572 and fig. 65.

12 Quoted in Thacker, *History of Gardens*, 140.

13 In *Of Gardens* (1625), reprinted in Dixon Hunt, *The Genius of the Place*, 51–6.

14 Henderson, *The Tudor House and Garden*, 108.

15 Dix, 'Kirby Hall', 331–5.

16 Everson, *Lewes Priory, Sussex*, 8–11. Cf. Leary, 'Normal for Normans?', 23.

17 Seeber, '"ye making of ye mount"'.

18 Creighton, *Designs upon the Land*, 209.

19 Aubrey, *Monumenta Britannica*, 682–4. Cf. Keevill, 'Landscape with Gardens', 14–15.

20 Cf. Stevenson, 'Preshute', 169.

21 Entry dated 9 June 1654: cf. Bray, *Diary of John Evelyn*, i, 285.

22 Evelyn, *Elysium Britannicum*, 195.

23 Cf. Fiennes, *Journeys*, 331; Defoe, *A Tour Through Great Britain*, 124.

24 Moray, *Observations*.

25 Hayman and Kempson, 'Houses built on the site of Marlborough Castle'.

26 Wessex Archaeology, *Marlborough Mound*.

27 Cf. Stevenson, 'Preshute', 170.

28 Fiennes, *Journeys*, 330–1.

29 WSRO, T/A: Preshute tithe map and apportionment (Elcot and Manton tithings), 1843–7.

30 Cf. Field, 'Marlborough Mound revisited', 197 and 199–200.

31 Cf. Pearson and Insall, *Marlborough Mound*, 122–3.

32 Stukeley, *Itinerarium Curiosum*, 1724 edn, pl. 1.

33 Hoare, *Wiltshire*, 15.

34 Scarfe, *Innocent Espionage*, 144.

35 British Library, MS Add. 15547 no. 199.

36 Wiltshire Heritage Museum, Devizes: acc. no. 1982.3170. Cf. Pearson and Insall, *Marlborough Mound*, figs 11–12.

37 Pearson and Insall, *Marlborough Mound*, 54.

38 Cf. Watkins and Wright, *Management and Maintenance*, 309–13.

39 Cf. Thorpe, *On Silbury Hill*, 54 and 100.

40 Stevenson, 'Preshute', 169.

41 Piggott, *William Stukeley*, 66.

42 Stukeley, *Itinerarium Curiosum*, 1724 edn, pls 3 and 63; 1776 edn, pl. 11.

43 Cf. Piggott, *William Stukeley*, 162 and 166.

44 Cf. Piggott, *William Stukeley*, 36–7.

45 Stukeley, *Itinerarium Curiosum*, 1776 edn, pl. 11.

46 Stukeley, *Itinerarium Curiosum*, 1724 edn, pls 3, 63 and 62 respectively.

47 Cf. Piggott, *William Stukeley*, 166.

48 Jacques, *Gardens of Court and Country*, 67 and 372.

49 Stukeley, *Itinerarium Curiosum*, pl. 63.

50 Cf. Jacques, *Gardens of Court and Country*, 204–6.

51 WSRO, T/A: Preshute tithe map and apportionment (Elcot and Manton tithings), 1843–7.
52 Fiennes, *Journeys*, 331.
53 Leary, 'The Marlborough Mound', 142.
54 WSRO, PHA 3565.
55 Bingley, *Correspondence*, i, 122–3. Cf. Waylen, *History of Marlborough*, 384.
56 Stukeley, *Itinerarium Curiosum*, 1724 edn, pl. 62.
57 Cf. Feluś, *Secret Life of the Georgian Garden*, 82–108, 126–8.
58 Bingley, *Correspondence*, iii, 356–8; cf. Waylen, *History of Marlborough*, 386.
59 WSRO, PHA 3565.
60 Stukeley, *Itinerarium Curiosum*, 1724 edn, pl. 62.
61 Jacques, *Gardens of Court and Country*, 156–7. Cf. Jacques, *Gardens of William and Mary*, 207–9: Appendix B, for types of trees and shrubs that might be planted.
62 E.g. British Library, Add. 15547 no. 199; Wiltshire Heritage Museum, Devizes: acc. no. 1982.3170. See above and Fig. 4.4.
63 Miller, *Heavenly Caves*; Brunon, *L'imaginaire des Grottes*.
64 Cf. Strong, *Renaissance Garden in England*, 138–47.
65 Jones, *Follies and Grottoes*, 145–75; Jackson, *Shell Houses*.
66 Cf. Dixon Hunt, *The Genius of the Place*, 8–9 and 122–4, which reprints an extract from *The Moralists: A Philosophical Rhapsody* published in 1709.
67 Brownell, *Alexander Pope and the Arts*, 254–71; Beckles Willson, *Alexander Pope's Grotto*.
68 Sherburn, *Correspondence*, iv, 254.
69 *The Spectator*, no. 632, 1714.
70 Cf. Lazzaro, *The Italian Renaissance Garden*, 132.
71 Brown, *My Darling Heriott*, 55–6; Lamont, 'Significance of Lady Hertford's grotto'; Thorpe, *On Silbury Hill*, 95–7.
72 Duck, 'Journey to Marlborough', lines 116–21.
73 Bingley, *Correspondence*, i, 103. Cf. Waylen, *History of Marlborough*, 384.
74 Beckles Willson, 'Pope and the Grotto at Crux Easton'. Cf. Mowl, 'Nine rural sisters'.
75 Cf. Pearson and Insall, *Marlborough Mound*, 160 and 166.
76 Cf. Pearson and Insall, *Marlborough Mound*, appendix 6.
77 Annotation to photograph no. 3 reproduced in Pearson and Insall, *Marlborough Mound*, 168.
78 Cf. Pearson and Insall, *Marlborough Mound*, 167.
79 Cf. Tobin, *The Duchess's Shells*.
80 Cf. Pearson and Insall, *Marlborough Mound*, 163.
81 Cf. Pearson and Insall, *Marlborough Mound*, 169–70.
82 Cf. Pearson and Insall, *Marlborough Mound*, 169.
83 Cf. Pearson and Insall, *Marlborough Mound*, 170.
84 Cf. Zega, *Garden Vases*, 67.
85 Pers. comm., the late Mrs Diana Reynell.
86 Pearson and Insall, *Marlborough Mound*, 170.
87 Brentnall, '*Castellum Merlebergae*'; and '*Castellum Merlebergensis*' (Appendix B above).
88 Archives of the Duke of Northumberland at Alnwick Castle, DNP: MS 127 part B, f178. I owe this reference to Christopher Hunwick, archivist.

89 National Heritage List for England, List Entry Number 1005634.
90 National Heritage List for England, List Entry Number 1273151.
91 National Heritage List for England, List Entry Number 1001239.
92 WSRO, 9/19/246–7. Cf. Brett, *Marlborough College*, 21–4.
93 Cf. Waylen, *History of Marlborough*, 545.
94 Gibson, *Parson in the Vale of the White Horse*, 9 November 1754.
95 Cf. Kempson, 'Later History of Marlborough Castle', 44–5.
96 Pearson and Insall, *Marlborough Mound*, 27–30.
97 Cf. Field, 'Marlborough Mound revisited', 200.
98 Pearson and Insall, *Marlborough Mound*, figs 20–7. Cf. Thorpe, *On Silbury Hill*, 98–9.
99 Ordnance Survey, Wiltshire sheet 29.9 – 1st edition 1883, revised 1899, 1922, 1943; with National Grid survey from 1969 onwards.
100 Noel, *Geophysical surveys*. Cf. Hawkes, *Archaeological Assessment*.
101 Pearson and Insall, *Marlborough Mound*, 116–21.
102 Field, 'Marlborough Mound revisited', 195–6.
103 Leary, 'The Marlborough Mound', 137.
104 Blunt, *In for a Penny*, p. 8 fn.; cf. Thorpe, *On Silbury Hill*, 54 and 99.
105 Pearson and Insall, *Marlborough Mound*, 108.

Contributors

JIM LEARY is Lecturer in Field Archaeology at the University of York, and a specialist on prehistoric mounds; he led major excavations at Silbury Hill in 2007–08, as well as those at Marlborough and the Round Mounds project on the dating of castle mottes.

JOSHUA POLLARD is a Professor in Archaeology at the University of Southampton, and has worked extensively on the neolithic landscape of Stonehenge and Avebury.

OLIVER CREIGHTON is Professor of Archaeology at the University of Exeter. He has published widely on medieval castles and their social and landscape contexts.

BRIAN DIX specialises in the archaeology of historic parks and gardens, working widely throughout Europe as well as at British sites.

Index

References to figures are indicated in *italics*. References to endnotes consist of the page number followed by the letter 'n' followed by the number of the note, e.g. 195n132.